Hume's Sentiments

FOR RACHEL AND
LAURA

Hume's Sentiments

Their Ciceronian and French Context

PETER JONES

the University Press
Edinburgh

© Peter Jones 1982
Edinburgh University Press
22 George Square, Edinburgh

Set in Monotype Plantin 110 series by
Speedspools, Edinburgh
Printed in Great Britain by
Redwood Burn Limited
Trowbridge, Wilts

British Library Cataloguing in Publication Data
Jones, Peter
    Hume's sentiments:
    their Ciceronian and French context.
    1. Hume, David
    I. Title
    192   B1498

ISBN 0 85224 443 6

Contents

Acknowledgments

This book is based on lectures given at the University of Edinburgh and at numerous universities in North America between 1965 and 1976. I am most grateful to a large number of friends for their interest in, and encouragement of, my work during that time, but I wish particularly to thank: Páll Árdal, Lewis Beck, John Bricke, Nicholas Capaldi, Kenneth Merrill, Terence Penelhum, W. H. Walsh. A special vote of thanks is due to Donald Livingston, with whom I have had invaluable discussions over several years. It was he who first suggested that I gather together some of my work into book form, preferably in time for the celebrations in 1976, commemorating the bicentenary of Hume's death. Other duties intervened, however, not least those of organising and taking part in those celebrations, but the University of Edinburgh generously granted me a period of leave in 1978 to complete the book and to begin the preparation of further studies for publication. It is proper also to acknowledge here a debt that might otherwise go unnoticed. My reflections on Hume have been greatly influenced by the work of three scholars, without whose contributions my own topics and conclusions, although differing from theirs, might never have achieved focus: I refer to the books by John Laird (1932), Norman Kemp Smith (1941), and John Passmore (1952). I am additionally grateful to the Editors of *Philosophy*, *Philosophical Quarterly*, and *Philosophical Studies*, and also to Austin Hill Press, and Fordham University Press, for permission to use again passages from essays of mine previously published by them; full details are given in the relevant notes, and in the bibliography. I should add that in those publications I referred to this book under the provisional, but un-informative, title of 'Aspects of Hume'.

Finally, I owe a particular debt to my family who, for so long, have patiently endured talk about Hume, whose space has been invaded by countless ancient volumes, and whose time has been stolen in the pursuit of issues that were hardly of urgent concern to them.

Abbreviations

When page references to Hume's works are given in the text and notes, the following abbreviations are used:

A = *An Abstract of A Treatise of Human Nature*, in *An Inquiry Concerning Human Understanding*, ed. C. W. Hendel, Indianapolis, 1955.

D = *Dialogues Concerning Natural Religion*, ed. N. Kemp Smith, Indianapolis, n.d.

E = *An Inquiry Concerning Human Understanding*, ed. C. W. Hendel, Indianapolis, 1955.

G = *Essays, Moral, Political, and Literary*, ed. T. H. Green & T. H. Grose, London, 1875.

H = *The History of England*, London, 1786.

L = *The Letters of David Hume*, ed. J. Y. T. Greig, Oxford, 1932.

LG = *A Letter from a Gentleman*, ed. E. C. Mossner & J. V. Price, Edinburgh, 1967.

M = *An Inquiry Concerning the Principles of Morals*, ed. C. W. Hendel, Indianapolis, 1957.

N = *The Natural History of Religion*, ed. H. E. Root, London, 1956.

NL = *New Letters of David Hume*, ed. R. Klibansky & E. C. Mossner, Oxford, 1954.

T = *A Treatise of Human Nature*, ed. L. A. Selby-Bigge, Oxford, 1888.

Reference is also made to Hume's *Early Memoranda*, edited by E. C. Mossner in 'Hume's Early Memoranda, 1929-1740: The Complete Text', *Journal of the History of Ideas*, Vol.9, 1948.

A reference to (L.1.349), for example, is to page 349 of Volume 1 of *The Letters of David Hume* as listed above, and a reference to (T.543) is to page 543 of the *Treatise*.

The form of reference to other works varies with the editions used, and explanation is given at the first occurrence if the reference is not to volume and page numbers.

Introduction

This book is intended for readers with a general interest in eighteenth-century thought, as well as for specialist scholars of Hume. Its aims are to make a modest contribution to the history of philosophy, to advance our understanding of some lesser-known aspects of Hume's writings, and to inaugurate a revision of some commonly held interpretations of Hume's views. Above all, however, the book is intended, not as a series of recondite footnotes to well-understood if peripheral issues, but as a prelude to further studies of both an historical and analytical kind: all of the writers mentioned, and all of the philosophical topics touched on, require detailed discussion that I have not attempted. Section or chapter summaries have been provided to help readers through the sometimes dense, and perhaps unfamiliar, material, but an overall statement of what has, and what has not, been ventured may be helpful at this point.

In *A Letter from a Gentleman*, in which he anonymously defends himself against attacks on his *Treatise*, Hume re-affirmed his view that "the Propositions of Morality" are not "the Objects *merely* of Reason", but are to be understood rather as "the Feelings of our internal *Tastes* and *Sentiments*". He adds, referring to himself, that "in this Opinion he concurs with all the antient Moralists, as well as with Mr *Hutchison* Professor of Moral Philosophy in the University of *Glasgow*, who, with others, has revived the antient Philosophy in this Particular" (LG.30). A few pages earlier, Hume cites both Socrates and Cicero as having "carried their Philosophical Doubts to the highest Degree of Scepticism", and he observes that "all the antient Fathers, as well as our first Reformers, are copious in representing the Weakness and Uncertainty of *mere* human Reason" (LG.21). Cicero's influence on Hume's religious views is well known, but his overall influence has not been generally acknowledged. The first chapter therefore contains an account of the major principles and conclusions in Cicero which dominated Hume's thought throughout his life. Students of Hume will recognise that, to avoid saturating the text with cross-references, I have confined my discussion of Cicero to those claims which have precise parallels in Hume; some of these are explored in the second chapter and, more generally, in the final chapter.

Two other features of the first chapter should be mentioned. Hume lived in France, of course, whilst writing the *Treatise*, and he was widely read in French philosophy and literature, as was first noted by Laird.[1] The detailed influence of Malebranche on Hume's thoughts about causation is shown in the first chapter, and the profound debt of the essay 'Of the Standard of Taste' to the Abbé Dubos is established in the third chapter; Hume's familiarity with French speculation about language is indicated in the fourth chapter. Bayle's influence on Hume is well known, and has been discussed by Laird, Kemp Smith, and more recently by Popkin;[2] only occasional reference is made to it in this book, because a separate study is planned. Laird argued that Hume owed more to Hutcheson than to any other British philosopher, and Kemp Smith made that debt the key to his own interpretation. Nothing is ventured here on this issue, although it would certainly be absurd to deny Hume's knowledge of Hutcheson's writings, or the presence of Hutchesonian tenets within Hume's philosophy. What is offered, however, is a brief discussion of Hume's possible knowledge of Newton's work. It is argued that his knowledge was slight, and that his layman's understanding of Newtonian ideas and method, although clearly evident in his own account of both mental and social mechanisms, should not be exaggerated. The main aim of the first chapter, indeed, is to show that important elements of Hume's thought are misrepresented or even overlooked, unless the French connection is underlined, and the Ciceronian dimension acknowledged.

According to William Cullen,[3] Hume maintained on his death bed "that he had not yet finished the great work" of delivering his countrymen "from the Christian Superstition". Religious claims and practices were a constant target of Hume's arguments, and orthodox writers such as Leland clearly recognised the extent of his attacks.[4] Hume accepted most of Bayle's reflections on the respective domains of reason and faith, and in line with their shared allegiance to Cicero, broadened his own discussion to cover the relations between reason and sentiment in life as a whole.[5] Chapters 2 and 3 show Hume's attempt to deal with this issue in two contexts, religion and art, where a person's reactions might be held to be most personal and idiosyncratic. Further study will be needed to show that the interpretation offered applies equally to Hume's account of moral and political judgements.

Chapter 2 begins with a discussion of testimony. All sides in the religious disputes said something about the notion, because all historical claims made use of it; philosophers generally linked the search for reliable criteria for reports about the past, with reflection on the nature and criteria of belief. Hume's views on these issues are briefly compared with those of his predecessors, and the chapter concludes with an outline of his little known claims about the origins and development of religions in the *Essays* of 1741–2, and *The Natural History of Religion*.

Hume's remarks on criticism, art, beauty and language are almost unknown, even to specialists in the field. Chapters 3 and 4 concentrate on these topics. The peculiar interest of Hume's albeit fragmentary comments is that he amplifies his account in the *Treatise* of the causes of human reactions, by assigning certain constructive tasks to the mind; by so doing, he prepares the ground for a notion of appropriate response, and for a notion of criticism as a rational endeavour. In the seventeenth and eighteenth centuries, it was commonplace to complain about the ambiguity of many terms prominent in French philosophical writing, such as *idée, âme, sentiment, expérience, science*; such ambiguity was often mirrored in the equivalent English terms, and it is suggested in Chapter 3, indeed, that the ambiguity of the term 'sentiment' initially leads Hume into muddles about the nature of appropriate response, and then allows him to avoid them. Hume's observations on art and criticism are interesting because they occur at a time before the modern discipline of aesthetics had been clearly identified and separated from other ranges of investigation, and also because they contain the germs of many views developed systematically by later writers. Finally, apart from its French inheritance, Hume's essay on taste, with its concluding twist, shows clearly where his main interest in practical philosophy lies.

By this point of the discussion a reader might well feel that Hume's views, although more learned and in some respects more subtle than expected, are less original, less revolutionary, and thereby less interesting than has often been claimed. One aim of Chapter 5 is to forestall such a verdict, first by re-affirming the Ciceronian dimension of Hume's philosophy, and second by establishing links between that philosophy and the views of modern thinkers such as Wittgenstein. Wittgenstein, we have often been told, not only found Hume's work repellent, but sought to overthrow everything it stood for;[6] the significant parallels between their claims, however, suggests that on these matters Wittgenstein's ignorance was matched only by his arrogance.

A great deal of quotation is woven into the text of this book, but there is no detailed explanation, defence or criticism of the passages cited as likely sources of Hume's views; nor is there discussion of the differences between Hume and his mentors. These are proper tasks for another occasion, along with sustained analysis of how his views on causation, belief, imagination, and the passions, for example, fit into the broad picture here sketched. One further word about that picture should be offered now, however, and it can be broached by way of two related questions: How were his alleged mentors identified? What did Hume expect of his readers, in the way of knowledge and interests? Anyone trying to establish his intellectual debts must begin by taking Hume's explicit acknowledgements seriously. A study of the authors named throughout Hume's works is then easily augmented by a study of the references cited by those authors themselves, by a study of the learned journals of the time, and of the books listed in the surviving or reconstructed catalogues of Locke and Adam Smith, for example.[7] Such studies help us not only to grasp the nature of the context in which Hume thought of himself as writing, and his own synthesis of diverse intellectual traditions and interests, but also to identify the sources which most inspired him. Readers of Hume must decide, as they must for any other writer, what weight to place on the various elements of each text, and which silences are intentional, which are not. Some of Hume's precise expectations of his readers no doubt changed along with changes in his reputation, and his goals; but throughout his life he was writing for a small, educated élite which, because of a common background, could be expected to recognise borrowings and allusions, and to look for certain tenets and assumptions, many of which would carry implications for religion. Unless he specifically complains of ambiguity, Hume merely assumes that the meaning is self-evident of the passages he refers to, along with the point of the reference; frequently, that point is precisely to signal his agreement with the quoted author. The presumed equivalence between what Hume says and what his author says may sometimes surprise us, as may his very occasional textual criticism of other writers. There can be no doubt, however, that he assumes the goal of every writer to be, what I call in this book, textual *transparency*; and that he sometimes uses the device borrowed from traditional rhetoric, and in which I follow him, of merely juxtaposing passages deemed to require no additional comment.

In the *Treatise*, Hume remarks of a certain argument that the "conclusion is just, tho' the principles be erroneous; and I flatter myself, that I can establish the same conclusion on more reasonable principles" (T.550). The picture of Hume that emerges from this book is of a writer who structured his own search for reasonable principles on a prior acceptance of Cicero's conclusions: conclusions not only about morality, politics and religion, but about the nature of man, and even philosophy itself. He may well have assumed a greater consistency in Cicero's thought than some of his eighteenth-century readers did, but he never wavered in his support for those conclusions or in his insistence, which he mentions four or five times, that Cicero's own theoretical support for them was weak. To say that Hume can be seen as a Ciceronian humanist is to say that his intensely moral goal is a philosophy of man, for man; it is to say that no legitimate appeal can be made to the supernatural in explanation of nature, or for help in difficulty; it is to say that a study of the traditions of society, including its language and literature, is a condition of understanding it, and improving it. If only one of Hume's most deeply held views about philosophy could be mentioned, it might be that philosophy could legitimately only be based on, and be justified by reference to, the pre-reflective views of common life. Philosophy could criticise, explain, improve such views, of course, but such efforts must themselves be judged by and against other views of common life; further, such analysis is artificial in the sense that it presupposes the existence of those views, which, moreover, will continue to influence people's lives independently of self-conscious analysis. There is an external world; events do cause other events; moral principles do influence actions; works of art do please people – these, and their like, are incontrovertible facts, Hume holds, around which our lives revolve whatever philosophers may say. The practice of philosophy could be condoned, and even celebrated, where beneficial and practical consequences could be traced to it; it could not be condoned, however, if it claimed for itself special insights, or held out groundless promises or threats which distracted men and women from their daily cares and duties.

It will be urged, quite properly, that Cicero associated man's self-realisation and progress with the right use of reason, and that Hume could align himself consistently with Cicero only by redefining that notion in his own terms. In making such a move, however, Hume merely followed another of his heroes, Bayle. Bayle constantly referred to Cicero, and in the Dictionary article on Ovid commended him for remarking on "la servitude de l'ame sous l'empire des passions", and for referring to "l'esclavage de la raison" to the passions – in the English translation o. 1739, there even occurs the italicised sentence: "reason had become the slave of the passions" (cp. T.415).[8] In another work, which we know Hume studied, Bayle seemed to endorse what Cicero deplored; man, Bayle argued, is not guided by abstract general principles, but by "l'inclination naturelle pour le plaisir, le goût que l'on contracte pour certain objets . . . ou quelque autre disposition qui résulte du fond de notre nature". It followed, he maintained, that "ce ne sont pas les opinions générales de l'esprit, qui nous déterminent, mais les passions présentes du coeur".[9] Hume's own summary of Book I of the *Treatise* declares that the philosophy "is very sceptical and tends to give us a notion of the imperfections and narrow limits of human understanding" (A.193). Three points are then singled out. First, "almost all reasoning is there reduced to experience"; second, belief, including belief in the "*external* existence" of things, is "a peculiar sentiment"; third, "we assent to our faculties and employ our reason only because we cannot help it" (A.194). In *A Letter from a Gentleman*, which, like all of Hume's works before 1748, was published anonymously, we are told that one aim of the *Treatise* was

> to abate the Pride of *mere human Reasoners*, by showing them, that even with regard to Principles which seem the clearest, and which they are necessitated from the strongest Instincts of Nature to embrace, they are not able to attain a full Consistence and absolute Certainty. (LG.19)

The problem is that too many thinkers place "too great a Confidence in

mere human Reason, which they regard as the *Standard* of every Thing";
but reason "is not able fully to satisfy itself with regard to its own Operations, and must in some Measure fall into a Kind of implicite Faith, even
in the most obvious and familiar Principles" (LG.21). Hume wants to
argue that demonstrative reasoning is inert, in the sense that it cannot
influence actions; that the "actuating principle of the human mind is
pleasure or pain" (T.574); that if beliefs can be causes of actions, they
must be at least analogous to those "peculiar sentiments", in being
detectable, and more akin to "*the sensitive, than of the cogitative part of
our natures*" (T.183). To establish the causal efficacy of beliefs Hume
restricts himself, initially, to "merely internal" experience (T.102),
leaving for later discussion the logical grounds of belief. One problem
facing Hume, and one recognised by most of his predecessors from Cicero
to Locke, is whether any inner experience can be an adequate criterion of
knowledge. Hume is anxious to concede nothing to the claims of religious
faith, not least because no impression (with which faith must be associated) points beyond itself to its possible cause or effects; but with his
equal insistence on displacing the traditional authority of deductive
reasoning, careless readers might conclude that he leaves no room for
thought at all. This is the opposite of Hume's intention, however. Both
in the *Treatise* and the later works, he argues that "probable reasoning" is
the guide to life (T.103). He happily asserts that "no truth appears to me
more evident, than that beasts are endow'd with thought and reason as
well as men", but he adds that one must not "suppose such a subtility
and refinement of thought" as can be found only among philosophers
(T.176–7). The very titles[10] of Sections IV and V of the first *Enquiry*
reflect Hume's aim to show that *a priori* reasoning cannot alone establish
any matter of fact, and that factual reasoning is not a product of the understanding; at no stage does Hume suggest that the terms 'reasoning' and
'reasons' be abandoned, or that men's lives should not be influenced by
reasoning and reasons – *properly* understood. But:

> What is commonly, in a popular sense, called reason, and is so much
> recommended in moral discourses, is nothing but a general and a
> calm passion, which takes a comprehensive and a distant view of its
> object, and actuates the will, without exciting any sensible emotion.
> (G.II.161; cp. T.458)

The ancient sceptical arguments rehearsed by Cicero, and relentlessly
pursued by Bayle, convinced Hume that almost all the traditional metaphysical and religious dogmas lacked the certainty, or even the intelligibility, claimed for them; moreover, he wanted to demonstrate the
bewilderment that results from applying sceptical tools too often. It is
worth remarking that Hume never again gives the impression, conveyed
at the end of Book I of the *Treatise*, of half-succumbing to the intoxication
of limitlessly wielding the sceptical tool. Certainly, his decision to set aside

puzzles apparently irresolvable by thought, is a decision based on his view about the proper balance between thought, feeling and action, and further grounded in the fact that basic human responses effectively block un-disciplined indulgence in sceptical reasoning. Here it should be said that Hume's initial attempt to model his method on that of the national hero, Newton, seemed to lose its appeal as time went on; besides, reference to experience was commonplace among Hume's predecessors, and even association of ideas was a notion not original to him – and there was no intention to cast his own account in a mathematical mould. Hume's topic, of course, was man himself, beginning with an explanation of "the principles and operations of our reasoning faculty, and the nature of our ideas" (T.xix). Very clearly he is not concerned to offer an analysis of the mind and its operations in terms of physiology and brain chemistry, and nowhere does Hume reveal any leanings towards the reductionist and materialist views that were starting to appear in the first half of the eighteenth century. He may have felt that such analyses threatened aspects of his humanism; there is no suggestion that his references to thoughts and feelings, to motives and intentions could be properly replaced by references to non-mental phenomena.

Hume held that man's natural resistance to sceptical argument is reinforced by his social nature, and the need to reason and communicate with others; these same needs severely constrain the rule of passion. In the two *Enquiries* it is these points that Hume stresses, and he even uses against unbridled scepticism the very argument he reviled when used to defend religion: its adverse social consequences. *The Natural History of Religion* is partly designed to show that this rather startling concession need not be extended to religion itself. Any future comparative study of the *Treatise* and later works, will need to consider how Hume's mixed motives and goals changed, and fragmented into separate works; it is no accident that both the *Abstract* and the first *Enquiry* concentrate on the discussion of causation, and that this provided the focus for heated debate among scientists in Scotland towards the end of the century. The dramatic claims about scepticism and the domain of the passions, which Hume looked back on as exaggeration, perhaps excited less response because they were taken to be demonstrations of excesses to be avoided, rather than of recommended routes. An exceedingly minor work, by a contemporary of Hume's, shows us the views gaining approval among the educated Moderates by 1760:

> Reason indeed is but a weak principle in Man, in respect of Instinct, and generally is a more unsafe guide – The proper province of Reason is to investigate the causes of things, to shew us what con-sequences will follow from our acting in any particular way, to point out the best means of attaining an end, and in consequence of this, to be a check upon our Instinct, our tempers, our passions and tastes:

but these must still be the immediately impelling principles of action.

A later passage is also of interest to us:

one of the principal misfortunes of a great Understanding, when exerted in a speculative rather than an active sphere, is its tendency to lead the Mind into too deep a sense of its own weakness and limited capacity. It looks into Nature with too piercing an eye, discovers every where difficulties never suspected by a common Understanding, and finds its progress stopt by obstacles that appear insurmountable. This naturally produces a gloomy and forlorn Scepticism, which poisons the chearfulness of the temper, and by the hopeless prospect it gives of improvement, becomes the bane of science and activity. This Sceptical Spirit, when carried into life, renders Men of the best Understandings unfit for business.[11]

By means of selective quotations the writings of any person can be made to fit a slogan; and a variety of slogans and labels has been proposed for Hume. Nothing in this prelude to Humean studies, however, lends support to claims that he is adequately described as a phenomenalist, logical positivist, Newtonian of the moral sciences, aesthetic subjectivist, or Wittgensteinian victim. But to anyone interested in the context and thought of a subtle and complex philosopher that should be no surprise.

ONE

Hume's Beginnings

In this chapter I shall supplement recent work on some aspects of the intellectual background against which Hume's thought may be understood.[1] Every writer, of course, absorbs terminology, views and assumptions from his studies and from his contemporaries, and in the case of a writer as learned as Hume, the scope for such influences is wide. Hume did not align himself completely with any of his predecessors, but there are two writers to whom he owed a special debt. Philosophically, his beginnings are rooted in the scepticism, naturalism and rhetorical method of Cicero, with the scepticism, in particular, underpinned by his reading of Bayle; in addition, he was intrigued by the psycho-physiological speculations of Malebranche, some of which were acknowledged to derive from Descartes's *Traité de l'homme*, a work that Hume seems not to have known. Hume thought that there was too little theoretical support in Cicero, but he admired his attitude and sought to adopt most of his conclusions; Malebranche helped him in his search to support those conclusions, although Hume entirely rejected the roles assigned to God.[2] Evidence of these two debts is available in two letters of 1737 and 1739, respectively, the first of which was addressed to Michael Ramsay:[3]

> I shall submit all my performances to your examination, and to make you enter into them more easily, I desire of you, if you have leisure, to read once over le [*sic*] Recherche de la Verite of Pere Malebranche, the Principles of Human Knowledge by Dr Berkeley, some of the more metaphysical Articles of Bailes Dictionary; such as those on Zeno and Spinoza. Des-Cartes Meditations would also be useful but I don't know if you will find it easily among your acquaintances. These books will make you easily comprehend the metaphysical parts of my reasoning and as to the rest, they have so little dependence on all former systems of philosophy, that your natural good sense will afford you light enough to judge their force and solidity.

That letter referred to the first Book of the *Treatise*; the second letter refers to the manuscript of Book III, and is addressed to Francis Hutcheson, whose influence on Hume is important but has been exaggerated, I believe, by Kemp Smith: "Upon the whole, I desire to take my catalogue of Virtues from *Cicero's Offices*, not from the *Whole Duty of Man*. I had,

indeed, the former Book in my Eye in all my Reasonings" (L.1.34).[4]
Having mentioned Grotius and Pufendorf earlier in the letter, Hume
goes on to discuss Cicero's *De Finibus*. I shall outline those doctrines of
Cicero, Malebranche, and some other writers in what I call *The French
Connection*, which seem to have left an impact on Hume's thought.

It should be noticed that although the *Treatise* and first *Enquiry* are
hardly overburdened with references to other authors, Hume in fact
names his intellectual debts and targets more conspicuously than many
of his predecessors. Locke names fewer writers in his *Essay*, and Descartes
intentionally omitted all references from his *Meditations*; and it was
standard practice in theological disputes not to name opponents, as we
may see in the writings of the Port-Royal apologists, for example, or even
in Butler's *Analogy*. Hume's expectation that his readers would recognise
relevant allusions no doubt mingled with his enthusiasm for the originality
of his ideas, but there are more important reasons behind the omission
of references. Above all, he accepted the view stemming primarily from
Bacon (e.g. *Novum Organum* Aphorisms Book 1, §§84ff.), found in
Hobbes (e.g. the closing paragraphs of *Leviathan*),[5] but taken up with
increasing insistence by Descartes, the writers of the Port-Royal, and
then Malebranche, that one should concentrate on arguments and
evidence, not on authorities.[6] Hume himself refers to what he calls a
principle of authority which "makes us regard their judgment, as a kind
of argument for what they affirm" (T.320), and explicitly states that he
has "all along endeavour'd to establish my system on pure reason, and
have scarce ever cited the judgment even of philosophers or historians on
any article" (T.546).[7] In *A Letter from a Gentleman* he clearly implies
that it is improper to employ authorities "in any Philosophical Reasoning"
(L G.20), a view he re-iterates nearly twenty years later, in 1761, when
he expresses preference for attempts to "establish . . . principles in general
without any reference to a particular book or person" (L.1.349). To defer
to authority smacked of dogma and scholasticism, and everything that
seventeenth- and eighteenth-century rationalists and empiricists alike
sought to displace; to reject appeal to authority was to assert one's
individual competence to reason. It is notable that Hume draws attention
to his intellectual debts in his two anonymous tracts of 1740 and 1745, the
Abstract and the *Letter from a Gentleman*, and that although the references
disappear again from the first *Enquiry*, they prominently adorn the second
Enquiry. Walpole castigated Hume for omitting his sources from the first
volume of his *History*, and Hume subsequently provided full documenta-
tion.[8] The *Abstract*, following up a footnote in the Introduction to the
Treatise, locates that work in the tradition of Locke, Shaftesbury,
Mendeville, Hutcheson and Butler, and claims that it improves on the
accounts of probabilities and inductive reasoning given by Locke, Malebranche and in the Port-Royal *Logic*. Leibniz had indicated a need for

such improvement, as had Butler in the *Analogy*, which was possibly one reason why Hume wished the Bishop to have a copy of the first two books of the *Treatise* (L.1.27). Apart from those named above, the only other modern philosophers named in the *Treatise* are Bacon, Berkeley, Hobbes, Clarke, Malebranche, Bayle and Spinoza – and none of these names appears more than twice. The first *Enquiry* does not name Shaftesbury, Mandeville, Hutcheson or Butler – and of these the second *Enquiry* names only Shaftesbury – but the names of Descartes, Cudworth, Tillotson, Pascal, Arnauld and Nicole appear. The phrase "*the Newtonian* philosophy" appears in the Appendix to the *Treatise* (T.639), and Newton is the subject of the well-known encomium at the end of the *History of England* (Ch.lxxi). Apart from that reference, Newton is named only seven times in Hume's works: once in the *Essays* (G.1.183), once in the anonymous *Letter from a Gentleman* (LG.28), the same passage, revised, re-appearing in the first *Enquiry* (E.84n), once in a flippant letter (L.1.159), once in the second *Enquiry* (M.34), once in the *Natural History* (N.64n), and once in the *Dialogues* (D.136). None of the references provides evidence that Hume had closely studied the original texts, or needed more than a general acquaintance, augmented, perhaps, by commentaries or dependent theological works, such as those by Clarke or Cheyne. But in view of the declaration in the Introduction to the *Treatise*, that he intended "the application of experimental philosophy to moral subjects" (T.xx; cp. A.183, 192), we should consider briefly Hume's position.

Hume and Newton

In connection with Newton, we may usefully distinguish two questions: What did Hume know? and What did Hume need? I believe that the answer to both questions is the same: Less than often has been claimed, and less than Hume himself originally may have thought.

Some historical reminders are in place here.

It is uncertain whether Hume spent the full four years of study as an undergraduate at Edinburgh University. If he studied for only three years, then he could not have studied under the great pupil of Newton, Colin Maclaurin, who took up his chair in 1725, and he may have received little or no instruction in physics. The normal four-year curriculum was as follows:[9] the first year was devoted to Greek grammar, and the rules of rhetoric, with special reference to Cicero and Ramus; the second year was devoted to practical rhetoric and to logic, and the third to Aristotelian ethics and politics, with special attention to natural law. In that third year Grotius and Pufendorf were central authors, as we can see from Maclaurin's own manuscript notes taken when he was a student in Gershom Carmichael's class at Glasgow.[10] Finally, in the fourth year, physics was studied, and the more elementary parts of the Newtonian system; the theories of movement, gravity and light were thought to be too difficult. "Soon"[11] after taking up his post, probably within two or three years, Maclaurin's mathematical classes became so popular that he divided them into four groups, according to proficiency; the third group read a part of the *Principia*, and only the fourth group read all of it with Maclaurin. Alexander 'Jupiter' Carlyle of Inveresk reports that, because he was well prepared, he was able to take three successive years of Maclaurin's mathematical classes between 1736 and 1738.[12]

Apart from textbooks by men such as David Gregory and John Keill, guides to Newton's work were few. English translations of s'Gravesande's commentary were available from 1720 and in 1728 Pemberton published his authorised popularisation, although even his book contained too much mathematics for some readers.[13] Eventually and posthumously, Maclaurin's own masterly commentary appeared in 1748. Voltaire had published *Lettres Philosophiques* on the continent in 1734, following its success in England in the previous year; the four essays in the book on aspects of Newton's work are all heavily indebted to Pemberton. Voltaire declared that while few people in London read Descartes because his works had lost their utility, even fewer read Newton because too much knowledge was required to understand him; nevertheless, everyone talked about them, partly because a translation had appeared of Fontenelle's famous eulogy on Newton, of 1727.[14] From the turn of the century, encyclopaedias begin to carry entries on Newtonian concepts and methods, although only the fifth edition (1736) of John Harris's *Lexicon Technicum* does so. Ephraim Chambers, in his remarkable *Cyclopaedia* of 1727, in which he sought to explain Newton's views to the educated reader, observed that the common expression 'Newtonian Philosophy' could be understood in very different ways, depending on the presumed knowledge of the audience and the required precision by the speaker. Indeed, he distinguishes five main ways in which the phrase is used, ranging from the specific and technical, in writers like s'Gravesande, to the rather general, where it simply covers the methods Newton is understood by the writer to have used, and is synonymous with the phrase 'experimental philosophy'.[15]

From such observations – the fact that Hume nowhere says that he has been engrossed in scientific, as opposed to classical or historical, studies (see L.1.16), the fact that Pemberton, Fontenelle, Voltaire and others saw a need to explain Newton to readers who did not, because they could not, study the original texts – we may surmise that Hume was familiar, at most, with the Prefaces, Definitions and Axioms of *Principia*, together with the General Scholium, the Rules of Reasoning in Book III and Cotes's famous Preface in the second edition. In addition, Hume would have been familiar with parts of the *Opticks*, but especially with the Queries appended to Book III. There is no evidence that Hume was competent to follow the mathematical core of *Principia*, and we may infer that he understood the 'Newtonian method' in one or more of the non-technical senses that became extremely popular in the first half of the eighteenth century. A brief elaboration of these points must suffice in this context.

In the opening sentence of the Preface to the first edition of *Principia* (1686), Newton identifies himself with "the moderns" who reject "substantial forms and occult qualities". Having outlined what he is going to explain by reference to the forces of gravity, he adds:

> I wish we could derive the rest of the phenomena of Nature by the same kind of reasoning from mechanical principles, for I am induced by many reasons to suspect that they may all depend upon certain forces by which the particles of bodies, by some causes hitherto unknown, are either mutually impelled towards one another, and cohere in regular figures, or are repelled and recede from one another.[16]

While Hume pondered on the implications of such a remark, he found himself quite unable to accept the notions of absolute time and absolute space as they occurred in the Scholium to the Definitions,[17] but it is significant that he omitted his own muddled discussion in the *Treatise* from the first *Enquiry*. With a sharper focus on his main aims and theses, such a discussion, even if improved, was irrelevant. Newton's 'Rules of Reasoning in Philosophy', which are given at the beginning of Book III, convinced Hume, however, of the value of a similar set in his own endeavour. Newton's rules, in their brief form, are as follows:

1. We are to admit no more causes of natural things than such as are both true and sufficient to explain their appearances;
2. Therefore to the same natural effects we must, as far as possible, assign the same causes;
3. The qualities of bodies, which admit neither intensification nor remission of degrees, and which are found to belong to all bodies within the reach of our experiments, are to be esteemed the universal qualities of all bodies whatsoever;
4. In experimental philosophy we are to look upon propositions inferred by general induction from phenomena as accurately or very nearly true, notwithstanding any contrary hypotheses that may be imagined, till such time as other phenomena occur, by which they may either be made more accurate, or liable to exceptions.[18]

Hume's general version of these, in the Introduction to the *Treatise*, stresses the need for generality and parsimony in the formulation of principles, and their grounding in experience, together with the avoidance of hypotheses which claim "to discover the ultimate original qualities of human nature" (T.xxi). Hume also develops a more precise set of 'Rules by which to judge of causes and effects', but although there is some overlap, Hume's fundamental assumptions about man and his nature are already driving him apart from Newton, as we shall see throughout this book.[19]

It is well established that in France, Cartesians such as Rohault,[20] Régis and Fontenelle successfully resisted Newtonian views until the 1730s, when Maupertuis and Voltaire undertook explicit defence of Newton against Descartes;[21] Hume himself referred to the situation in an essay of 1742, 'Of the Rise and Progress of the Arts and Sciences' (G.I.183), to which we shall refer again in the next two chapters. Gradually, in Britain particularly, the *Opticks*, in which Newton 'proved' each theorem by 'experiment' was seen to have implications for his earlier, exclusively mathematical work.[22] But two features of Newton's position caused trouble to opponents: his views on hypotheses and on occult qualities. Official and unofficial apologists alike, Pemberton and Maclaurin, John Harris and Ephraim Chambers, all echoed Cotes's insistence in the Preface to the second edition of *Principia*, that "gravity can by no means be called an occult cause of the celestial motions, because it is plain from the phenomena that such a power does really exist. Those rather have recourse to occult causes, who set imaginary vortices of a matter entirely fictitious and imperceptible by our senses, to direct those motions."[23] Newton himself took up the issue in Question 31 of Book III of the *Opticks*, contrasting passive principles such as *vis inertiae* and active principles such as gravity, which "are manifest Qualities, and their Causes only are occult".[24] In the same context, Newton prescribed the proper method of enquiry:

> As in Mathematics, so in Natural Philosophy, the Investigation of difficult Things by the Method of Analysis, ought ever to precede the Method of Composition. This analysis consists in making Experiments and Observations, and in drawing general Conclusions from them by Induction, and Admitting of no Objections against the Conclusions, but such as are taken from Experiments, or other certain Truths. For Hypotheses are not to be regarded in experimental philosophy.... By this way of Analysis we may proceed from Compounds to Ingredients, and from Motions to the Forces producing them; and in general, from Effects to their Causes, and from particular Causes to more general ones, till the Argument end in the most general.[25]

Hume shows himself aware of this method in one of his most Newtonian sections, *Enquiry* VIII (e.g. E.94), and like Newton he both vilified the use of hypotheses and freely employed them himself – a point we shall refer to in the next chapter. Although the criteria for counting senses of terms are obscure, recent scholars have detected as many as nine different senses of 'hypothesis' in Newton's writings.[26] While his early defenders did not reach that conclusion, they realised that for non-mathematical readers they should try to explain the novelty of Newton's procedure.

Reference to Pemberton and Maclaurin will suffice to establish the point.

Both writers begin with a history of philosophy, in order to establish the background against which Newton may be understood, Pemberton emphasising the value of making "practical deductions from natural causes", and Maclaurin declaring that natural philosophy "is chiefly to be valued as it lays a sure foundation for natural religion and moral philosophy".[27] It is intriguing to notice that Hume, in the Introduction to the *Treatise*, specifically argues that "*Mathematics, Natural Philosophy, and Natural Religion*, are in some measure dependent on the science of MAN", and that "the science of man is the only solid foundation for the other sciences" (T.xix, xx). At the outset, therefore, Hume separates himself from Newtonians. Returning to the commentators, we may note that Pemberton declares that it is ridiculous to reject an avowedly incomplete Newtonian account simply because, at the moment, no further advance is possible; moreover, "the common sense of the word miraculous can have no place here, when it implies that it is above the ordinary course of things".[28] Pemberton makes an important observation in connection with scepticism:

The proofs in natural philosophy cannot be so absolutely conclusive, as in mathematics. For the subjects of that science are purely the ideas of our own minds. They may be represented to our senses by mathematical objects, but they are themselves the arbitrary productions of our own thoughts. . . . It is only here required to steer a just course between the conjectural method of proceeding, against which I have so largely spoke; and of demanding so rigorous a proof, as will reduce all philosophy to mere scepticism, and exclude all prospect of making any progress in the knowledge of nature.[29]

Pemberton follows the established practice of praising Bacon for recognising the importance of argument by induction, and on several occasions stresses the need to determine which causes are necessary to produce known effects.[30] Defending Newton's notion of attraction, he observes that what Newton said "was not intended by him as a philosophical explanation of any appearances, but only to point out a power in nature not hitherto distinctly observed, the cause of which, and the manner of its acting, he thought was worthy of a diligent enquiry".[31] Maclaurin's text was not available until 1748, that is, after Hume's first *Enquiry*, but before the second *Enquiry* and the two major works on religion; indeed, we know that Hume quoted from Maclaurin in the *Dialogues*.[32] It may be noted, however, that Maclaurin himself at times clearly alludes to the *Treatise*, although not by name, as well as to Locke and Berkeley.[33] Maclaurin criticises Descartes for basing so much of his argument in the *Principles* on the *first cause* and for deriding "that knowledge of causes which is derived from the contemplation of their effects", and furthermore, for reducing everything to mechanism.[34] This standard theological

view encourages a reader to expect certain other views, and in due course
they appear, first in an outline of what is today called the Argument from
Design, and later in more extensive reflections on natural theology.[35]
Maclaurin regards the sceptical nature of philosophical thought as "fruitless" and "extravagant": "as we are certain of our own existence, and of
that of our ideas, by internal consciousness; so we are satisfied, by the
same consciousness, that there are objects, powers, or causes without us,
and that act upon us". He is not prepared to discuss, however, how
external objects act upon the mind, or how accurately ideas represent
objects.[36] Clarifying several points which continued to worry opponents,
Maclaurin insists that Newton never implied "that a body can act upon
another at a distance, but by the intervention of other bodies", never
claimed to explain how attraction worked, and, furthermore, sometimes
used hypotheses constructively for "reducing facts or observations of a
complicated nature to rules and order".[37] Maclaurin paraphrases the
account of proper method, quoted from the *Opticks* above, adding that
after the most general causes have been reached by the method of analysis,
"we should then descend in a contrary order; and from them, as established principles, explain all the phenomena that are their consequences,
and prove our explications: and this is the *synthesis*".[38] Like Pemberton
before him, Maclaurin notes that in Newton's view "the fabrick of the
universe, and course of nature, could not continue for ever in its present
state, but would require, in process of time, to be re-established or
renewed by the same hand that formed it".[39]

Hume need not have turned to Cotes's Preface to learn of the compatibility of Newton's views with orthodox theology, since two prominent
theologians, against whom Hume subsequently argued continuously, had
already enlisted Newtonianism in the service of religion: Samuel Clarke
(1704) and George Cheyne (1705). Hume may have thought that such
followers went beyond the views of Newton himself, for he sharply distinguishes[40] Newton and "some of his followers" on the hypothesis of an
ethereal fluid to explain universal attraction. Moreover, in the *Natural
History*, he writes:

> Xenophon's conduct, as related by himself, is, at once, an incontest-
> able proof of the general credulity of mankind in those ages, and the
> incoherencies, in all ages, of men's opinions in religious matters. . . .
> It is for the same reason, I maintain, that Newton, Locke, Clarke, &c.
> being *Arians* or *Socinians*, were very sincere in the creed they pro-
> fessed: And I always oppose this argument to some libertines, who
> will needs have it, that it was impossible but that these philosophers
> must have been hypocrites. (N.63n–64n; cp. LG.21)

It is possible that Hume derived the label from Voltaire's seventh *Philosophical Letter*, where Newton, Clarke and Locke are all named as
Arians, or, as the title indicates, as Socinians or Anti-Trinitarians. Even

if Hume wondered about Newton's own theological views, he could not have known about Newton's deep interest in alchemy, the background to which was provided by his early study of the mechanical philosophies of Hobbes, Descartes and Gassendi.[41]

Long ago, Burton (*Life and Correspondence*, 1.94) remarked that Hume's work is surprisingly "free from exploded opinions in the physical sciences", apart from a few references to "animal spirits".[42] But the works are free from such opinions because of Hume's total lack of interest in contemporary science, some of which might have been grist to his mill. The speculative hypotheses which appear in the *Dialogues* are nearly all traceable to essentially literary predecessors such as Fontenelle or Montesquieu, or to the standard works of theologians or free-thinkers. Thus both general claims of the form that "all the changes of which we have ever had experience, are but passages from one state of order to another" (D.174) may be found equally in orthodox Cartesians such as Fontenelle[43] and secular Newtonians such as Diderot (*Lettre sur les aveugles*, 1749); and more particular suggestions, such as the view that comets are the seeds of the universe (D.177) are more likely to come from Hume's admired Fontenelle than from Buffon; whose name appears in the *Letters*, and some volumes of whose *Histoire Naturelle* Hume owned in 1766. But there is no reference to Buffon's exciting speculations on the origins of the universe or of man, no apparent interest in Hutton's revolutionary geological theory which had developed over thirty years from the 1750s – Hutton numbered Black and Smith among his closest friends, as did Hume – no single mention of La Mettrie, whose work, like that of Hobbes a century earlier, everyone read but most were reluctant to name,[44] and no mention of the agricultural experiments of the time.

Aside from his limited capacity to judge such work, there are at least three related reasons for Hume's neglect of it. First, although he disapproved of the theological use of and appendages to Newtonian principles, he could see the general direction of science, along with everyone else, not least his friends among the *Encyclopédistes*: it was a trend to materialism, a view inimical to Hume's Ciceronian humanism, with its irreducible reference to man. Secondly, although he rested much of his 'system' on what it was "natural" to do – as we shall see in the final chapter – and this linked man with other animals, his habitual dualism led him to resist any fully mechanistic account of such "natural" behaviour – of the kind provided by La Mettrie, for example. Thirdly, although he talks of a *science* of human nature, constantly refers to his *system*, and wants to import the *methods* of natural philosophy into moral philosophy, Hume sharply separates his own tasks and conclusions from those of the natural scientist. For example:

> my intention never was to penetrate into the nature of bodies, or explain the secret causes of their operations . . . at present I content

myself with knowing perfectly the manner in which objects affect my senses, and their connections with each other, as far as experience informs me of them. This suffices for the conduct of life; and this also suffices for my philosophy, which pretends only to explain the nature and causes of our perceptions, or impressions and ideas. (T.64)

An *Appendix* insertion at this point declares that problems can be avoided by confining speculation "to *the appearances* of objects to our senses", rather than to their real nature; such modest scepticism is in accord with the best Newtonian method of dealing with phenomena such as the vacuum (T.639). Notoriously, the experiments Hume undertakes in his chosen sphere are thought experiments (e.g. T.6, 333ff.), and he even claims that "there is a much greater complication of circumstances" in moral philosophy than in natural philosophy (T.175). He does not deny that the mental is dependent on the physical – "all our perceptions are dependent on our organs, and the disposition of our nerves and animal spirits" (T.211) – but he dissociates himself from physical enquiry; discussing impressions which "without any introduction make their appearance in the soul", he asserts that "as these depend upon natural and physical causes, the examination of them would lead me too far from my present subject, into the sciences of anatomy and natural philosophy" (T.275). The fact that a single method is effective in different kinds of context does not mean that one kind of context is reducible to the other. Thus he can recommend the use of some of the methods adopted by anatomists in his own "anatomy of the mind" (T.325), even though a physical account of how the structure and texture of my skin absorbs and reflects light leaves unaffected my reasonings about why a cheerful countenance inspires me "with complacency and pleasure" (M.115).

Certainly Hume tried to make use, in a general way, of what he understood of Newtonian method (cp. E.45, 84n); and several Newtonian concepts suggested illuminating analogies in his 'experimental', that is 'experiential', account of the "mental world" (T.12), most notably *attraction*, which Hume converts into associative powers or mechanisms. Conspicuously Newtonian passages occur in the *Treatise* Book II, Part III, and its correlative part in the first *Enquiry*, Section VIII; but his dismissal of arbitrary hypotheses and insistence on grounding claims in experience are not exclusively in the Newtonian tradition. In the *Abstract* Hume declares that those who have banished hypotheses from moral philosophy "have done a more signal service to the world" than Bacon, "the father of experimental physics" (A.184); and although there is praise for the use made of the principle of the association of ideas in the *Treatise*, the core of Book I of that work is properly identified as the discussion of causation. Newton is not mentioned, but the topic, at least, would be taken by many readers as compatible with a Newtonian interest. *A Letter from a Gentle-*

man was intended as a defence against the charge of atheism and scepticism in the *Treatise*, and names are artfully distributed to indicate eminent predecessors who held the views to which Hume's opponents objected. Descartes and Clarke are identified as particular philosophical targets of the *Treatise*, and, although Newton's name appears, there is no hint of Newtonian method or concerns being worthy of comment. In fact, Hume's own philosophical reflections led away from Newton, and we must now look at some of the other influences on his thought.

Malebranche and The French Connection

After leaving University, Hume first turned to a study of the law, and was thought competent enough, twenty years later, to be appointed Judge-Advocate to a military expedition. There is no doubt that during his legal studies he became more familiar with the theories of Grotius and Pufendorf, to whom he refers in a letter to Hutcheson (L.1.33; see also M.123n), and with the orations of his beloved Cicero; in 1742 he writes to Henry Home, later Lord Kames, that a modern lawyer would be reprimanded if he followed Cicero's practices.[45] After his legal studies and extensive philosophical reading on his own, Hume went to France, and eventually settled at La Flèche, the centre of Cartesian and Malebranchian studies. It has been established recently that many of Hume's early memoranda were culled from the journals of the time that summarised learned works, journals such as *Mémoires de Trévoux* and *Histoire des ouvrages des savans*;[46] but it is clear that subsequently, and almost certainly while at La Flèche, if not before, he immersed himself in the works themselves. Of these, the two most important were by Bayle and by Malebranche. It is also likely that at this time Hume became familiar with French theological debate, and with the extensive French discussions on grammar, rhetoric, language and the relative merits of the ancients and moderns, to all of which topics Hume referred periodically throughout the remainder of his life. The French Connection is clearly evident in several of the *Essays* published in 1741–2, which may indicate that some of them were at least drafted in France.

For at least two centuries, Descartes was the man against whom subsequent Western philosophers measured their own tasks, agreements and disagreements, and Hume was no exception. Even without the proof of the letter, quoted above, in which Hume advises reference to the *Meditations* in order to discern his own directions, Hume's metaphysical and theological arguments are conspicuously directed against what he understood of Descartes and his followers; and the *Letter from a Gentleman* identifies the "Cartesian Doctrine, of Secondary Causes" as one target in the *Treatise* (L G.29). Descartes's methods, topics, distinctions and conclusions formed a permanent background for Hume's thought. Our present concern, however, before turning to Malebranche, is to draw attention to the Port-Royal *Logic* of 1662, the importance of which to Hume has been mentioned by a few commentators but insufficiently emphasised.[47] Descartes influenced the work, of course, at almost every point, and unknown to most of their readers, the authors had access to his unpublished papers, although they should not be regarded as uncritical ciphers.[48]

At the outset Arnauld and Nicole assert that in metaphysics nothing is more important than to establish the origin of our ideas.[49] Spiritual ideas must not be confused with corporeal images, of course, but the word *idea* is one of several that are so clear that they admit of no explanation by others that are clearer.[50] Following Descartes, we should take ideas to be "everything which is in our mind when we can say with truth that we conceive a thing, in whatever way it may be conceived", and we should recognise that "we conceive a great number of things without any images".[51] It is held to follow from these tenets that "we can express nothing by our words, when we understand what we say, without having an idea of the thing which we signify by our words. . . . For it would be a contradiction to maintain that I know what I say in pronouncing a word, and that, nevertheless, I conceive nothing in pronouncing it but the sound of the word itself."[52] The authors contend that

> we are not able to express our thoughts to each other, unless they are accompanied with outward signs . . . this custom is so strong, that even when we think alone, things present themselves to our minds only together with the words to which we have been accustomed to have recourse in speaking to others.[53]

We shall revert to these views when discussing Hume's reflections on language in Chapter 4. Arnauld and Nicole agree with Descartes and Pascal that there are two kinds of definition, which must on no account be confused: definitions of names, which are arbitrary and today would be called stipulative; and definitions of things, which may seek to be exact by explaining a thing's nature by reference to its essential attributes, or which may be less exact, when we learn enough about a thing's accidents to enable us to pick it out. These less exact definitions of things are properly called *descriptions*, and it will be recalled that Hume says he can offer only *descriptions* of belief, pride, humility (E.62; T.277, 398).[54] It is emphasised that although it is arbitrary which ideas are joined to which sounds, and that men often have different ideas of the same things, nevertheless men use the same words to express their ideas.[55] It is the task of grammarians to list and explain the ideas which men have agreed to connect with certain sounds, since explanation of how a word is commonly taken requires reflection on usage.[56] One should note that "to signify, in relation to a sound uttered or written, is only to excite an idea connected with that sound in our mind, by acting on our ears or our eyes".[57] But words excite both principal and accessory ideas, as had been pointed out in the Port-Royal *Grammar* of 1660, although, properly speaking, the principal ideas constitute the signification of a word. Different sets of words can express the same principal signification, of course, as in 'You lied', and 'You know the opposite of what you said'.[58]

Arnauld and Nicole explicitly recommend an attitude of critical indifference or disinterestedness in the present kind of enquiry, and deride those who fear that such enquiry endangers religion or the state.[59] Although we can have no knowledge of anything outside us save through the medium of ideas, Gassendi was right in thinking that the question about the origin of ideas resolved itself into the question of whether all ideas are acquired through the senses; since we do not acquire the idea of *being* through the senses, to give but one example, the answer must be 'No'.[60] The authors state that even when the words are taken only in relation to the five bodily senses, there is considerable equivocation over the words *sens* and *sentimens* – a fact which we shall notice in Hume (p.98). Three things commonly take place, they claim, when we use our senses, as, for example, when we see something: certain movements take place in bodily organs such as the eye and the brain; these movements are the occasion of our mind conceiving something, as in the idea of red or orange; thirdly, we form a judgment on what we see, attributing properties to it.[61]

Part IV of the Port-Royal *Logic* is devoted to an elaboration of Cartesian views on method, and in the next chapter we shall refer to the discussion of testimony and miracles, with which Hume was certainly familiar. We have already quoted Newton's insistence, underlined by his disciples, that analysis should precede synthesis, and it is here only necessary to note that in their own discussion of these notions, Arnauld and Nicole conclude by summarising Descartes's four rules from his second *Discours*:

1. Never to accept anything as true which we do not clearly know to be so;
2. To divide each of the difficulties we examine into as many parts as possible, and as may be necessary for resolving it;
3. To conduct our thoughts in order, by commencing with objects the most simple and the most easily known, in order to ascend by degrees to the knowledge of the most complex, supposing even, from the order between them, that they do not naturally precede each other;
4. To make, in relation to everything, enumerations so complete, and surveys so general, that we may be assured of having omitted nothing.[62]

Such longstanding formal models influenced the presentations of even the most ardent anti-Cartesian writers, and it is possible that only his deep literary interests helped Hume to escape from their evident impact on the opening of the *Treatise*, for example, to the polished form of the first *Enquiry*, and the quite different model in the *Dialogues*, a model towards which, as it happens, Descartes had moved in his posthumously published work.

In this context it should be recorded that while Hume was a student, in 1724, there appeared an English translation of a work which aimed to bring the Port-Royal *Logic* up to date, by incorporating insights from Locke and, presumably, from Malebranche, although his name is not mentioned at all. J-P. de Crousaz first published his book in 1712, under the title *La logique, ou système de réflexions qui peuvent contribuer à la netteté et à l'étendue de nos connaissances.* His discussions usually begin by elaborating the doctrines of the Port-Royal, bringing certain matters into sharper focus; the main sections deal with perceptions and ideas, judgment, reasoning, and method. On the topic of ideas, he remarks that philosophers

> fancy that because, when they see, there is always an object of our sight, which is different from the Perception, whereby it is represented and known to us, in the same manner, the Understanding has its Eyes and its Objects.... Is it not more natural, as well as shorter, to conceive that the Thought is self-conscious, and that by such a Consciousness of its way of thinking, it learns to know what a Tree is, and so with other Objects ?[63]

During the course of extensive discussion on the topic of words and language, Crousaz urges that "most words, used by Men, express their Sentiments and Passions rather than their Ideas"; "sacred Words", for example, are spoken "without any Meaning", and are "at most attended with some Sensations".[64] He agrees with Locke that children are taught to speak before they are taught to think, and asserts that in order to think well, it is necessary to speak exactly.[65] Some words "have no meaning", "signify nothing", such as *chance*, whereas others "are not void of sense, but they express only Ideas, without any actual objects answering those words", such as *substance, figure, number*; some words, such as *nothing*, indicate the absence of an idea. "If the Language of Men was exact" it would be sufficient to follow use in order to understand them – the reference is presumably to grammarians such as Vaugelas – but different men use the same word to express different ideas, and the signification of words changes insensibly over a period of time; moreover, since words express both principal and accessory ideas, and it is over the latter that most men differ, etymological investigation is useless in this context.[66] The point of language is communication, "to convey our Thoughts into the Minds of others", and in the interpretation of other people's discourse we should avoid, as far as possible, making an author contradict himself.[67] We need to learn the use prevalent in his time, and discover any personal oddities in his expression:

> constant use sometimes makes a figurative Expression as intelligible and clear as the most simple: custom often has annexed to Words a Sense very different from that you would draw from their Etymology. Often, again, the Knowledge of the Thing it self decides

whether the Sense be literal or figurative; and by Consequence, the Explication of the Thing it self, ought then to go before the Reflections upon the Figure or Metaphor in which it is expressed.[68]

Above all, Crousaz contends, "we must not confound Grammatical Distinctions, that serve only to remove the equivocal Meaning of some Terms, with Logical Distinctions, that keep us from confounding different Species of the same Genus".[69] Remarks such as these lie behind Hume's own reflections on language, and Crousaz's views on custom, on comparison as "the essence of what is called *Relation*", on imagination, the passions, scepticism and natural belief, together with his Ciceronian references, could all have helped Hume to clarify his own position. There is no evidence, however, that Hume read Crousaz's treatise, or his vast folio attacking Sextus and Bayle, entitled *Examen du Pyrrhonisme*.

We cannot be certain how Hume understood Malebranche – he may not have detected, or been interested, for example, in crucial differences in the notion of *idée* in Arnauld and Malebranche[70] – but my purposes will be served by indicating the passages Hume cited, and some central tenets which challenged him in the formulation of his own system. Hume's own 1684 edition of Malebranche, in Edinburgh University Library, has a few undatable pencil marks against passages which seem unlikely to have been especially interesting to Hume; the explicit references to Malebranche in the *Treatise* and *Dialogues* are unmarked in the copy.[71]

Malebranche is piously quoted (in a translation presumably by Hume himself) by Demea in Part 11 of the *Dialogues* (D.142), and he is referred to twice in the first, and once in the second, *Enquiry*.[72] Of these references only one is significant. Hume rejects Malebranche's doctrine, which he says is only "insinuated" by Descartes himself, "of the universal and sole efficacy of the Deity" (E.84n). Hume certainly objected to the roles assigned to God in Malebranche's doctrines, but with his own interest in the logical and epistemological problems of causation, he failed to see the intentionally theological character of Malebranche's endeavour, where negative arguments were meant to lead to the positive conclusion of God, and where this move was not seen as merely saving the argument. One reference in the *Treatise* (T.249) refers to the same point, but earlier Hume embodies a partial translation from his precise reference to "Father *Malebranche*, Book VI. Part ii. chap. 3, and the illustrations upon it" (T.158n); on the next page (T.159) Hume's characterisation of the "Cartesian" position is also a translation from Malebranche Book VI.[73] The "illustrations" referred to are found in *Éclaircissement* XV, 'Touchant l'efficace attribuée aux causes secondes':

Il y a des Philosophes qui assurent que les causes secondes agissent par leur matiére, leur figure & leur mouvement, & ceux-ci ont raison en un sens; d'autres, par une *forme substantielle*. Plusieurs, par les *accidens* ou les *qualitez*; quelques-uns par la *matiere* & la *forme*; ceux-ci, par la *forme* & les *accidens*; ceux-là par certaines *vertus* ou *facultez* distinguées de tout ceci.[74]

Hume had written:

There are some, who maintain, that bodies operate by their substantial form; others, by their accidents or qualities; several, by their matter and form; some, by their form and accidents; others, by certain virtues and faculties distinct from all this. (T.158)

What really excited Hume, of course, were Malebranche's reflections on causation and on the nature of mental activity. In the same Book VI, to which Hume referred above, Malebranche wrote:

Il n'y a donc point de forces, de puissances, de causes veritables dans le monde matériel & sensible; & il n'y faut point admettre de formes, de facultez, & de qualitez réelles pour produire des effets que les corps ne produisent point, & pour partager avec Dieu la force & la puissance qui lui sont essentielles.

After asserting that there is no necessary connection between our willing to move an arm, and the movement of the arm, he adds that "les causes *naturelles* ne sont point de véritables causes":

Cause véritable est une cause entre laquelle & son effet l'esprit apperçoit une liaison nécessaire, c'est ainsi que je l'entens. Or il n'y a que l'être infiniment parfait, entre la volonté duquel & les effets l'esprit apperçoive une liaison nécessaire. Il n'y a donc que Dieu qui soit véritable cause, & qui ait véritablement la puissance de mouvoir les corps.[75]

Éclaircissement XV elaborates this point, in terms which seem to anticipate Hume:

quelque effort d'esprit que je fasse, je ne puis trouver de force, d'efficace, de puissance, que dans la volonté de l'Etre infiniment parfait. . . .

Il est vrai que dans tous les siécles cette puissance a été reconnuë pour réelle & véritable de la plûpart des hommes; mais il est certain que ç'a été sans preuve, je ne dis pas sans preuve démonstrative, je dis sans preuve qui soit capable de faire quelque impression sur un esprit attentif.[76]

Malebranche held that since force and motion are not contained in our notion of bodies, bodies cannot be said to move themselves: "La force mouvante des corps n'est donc point dans les corps qui se remüent, puisque cette force mouvante n'est autre chose que la volonté de Dieu".[77]

Although he rejected the inference, of course, Hume accepted the premise, and also Malebranche's view that, in the absence of detectable necessary connection, mind cannot be said to move bodies, either.

In the *Treatise* (T.164), *Abstract* (A.186) and first *Enquiry* (E.44), Hume uses Malebranche's example of colliding balls to illustrate the

causal relation, an example which occurs several times. The version in
Éclaircissement XV, three pages after the passage cited by Hume in T.158,
reads:

> Quand je vois une boule qui en choque une autre, mes yeux me
> disent, ou semblent me dire, qu'elle est véritablement cause du
> mouvement qu'elle lui imprime; car la véritable cause qui meut les
> corps ne paroît pas à mes yeux. Mais quand j'interroge ma raison, je
> vois évidemment que les corps ne pouvant se remuer eux-mêmes,
> & que leur force mouvante n'étant que la volonté de Dieu qui les
> conserve successivement en différens endroits; ils ne peuvent com-
> muniquer une puissance qu'ils n'ont pas, & qu'ils ne pourroient pas
> même communiquer quand elle seroit en leur disposition.[78]

These clarifications refer to a passage in Book VI which states how bodies
are connected:

> Les corps sont unis ensemble en trois manieres par la *continuité*, par
> la *contiguité*, & par une troisiéme maniére qui n'a point de nom
> particulier, & que j'appellerai du terme géneral d'*union*. . . .
>
> Par ce troisiéme terme, *union*, j'entens encore un je ne sçai quoi
> qui fait que deux verres, ou deux marbres, dont on a usé & poli les
> surfaces en les frottant l'un sur l'autre, s'attachent de telle sorte,
> qu'encore qu'on les puisse tres-facilement separer en les faisant
> glisser, on a pourtant quelque peine à le faire en un autre sens.[79]

In the first *Enquiry* (E.42–3) Hume uses three of Malebranche's
examples within two paragraphs – the smooth pieces of marble, the
billiard balls, and the nutritive power of bread – revealing once again the
seductive power of a striking illustration. It is worth noting that Locke, in
An Examination of P. Malebranche's Opinion of Seeing All Things in God,
concentrates entirely on Book III Part 2, but makes no mention of the
discussion of the causal connection; however, although not the best
qualified to complain, he does object to Malebranche's variable use of the
term *idea*.

Following Descartes and the writers of the Port-Royal, Malebranche
distinguishes between two kinds of perceptions: pure and sensible, the
latter being "des *modifications* de l'esprit"; "par ce mot *idée*, je n'entends
ici autre chose, que ce qui est l'objet immédiat, ou le plus proche de
l'esprit, quand il apperçoit quelque objet, c'est-à-dire ce qui touche &
modifie l'esprit de la perception qu'il a d'un objet".[80] Ideas are of a
spiritual nature, carrying no existence or resemblance implication to
anything else, and they are capable of representing quite different
things.[81] The ideas of sense differ from those of imagination only in
degree of force, which is why those in a fever or violent passion, or while
fasting, think they are sensing what they are really only imagining.[82]
Malebranche holds: "un homme ne peut pas former l'idée d'un objet s'il
ne le connoît auparavant, c'est-à-dire s'il n'en a déjà l'idée, laquelle ne

dépend point de sa volonté".[83] The imagination itself is characterised as
the mind's capacity to make absent things present,[84] and the distinctness
with which one imagines objects depends on the traces made by the
animal spirits in the brain.[85] In all practical sciences, including morality
and politics, that is, in "la science de l'homme",[86] we must judge by
probabilities, which often have a force as convincing as demonstration.[87]
On this last point, of course, Hume, having followed Malebranche in
substance and terminology, thought that the present speculations were
"too concise" (A.184). Malebranche also insisted, however, that we
recognise and acknowledge the ubiquity of natural judgments (*jugement
naturel*), which are essential to the preservation of life, even though they
can sometimes mislead us.[88] He first introduces this point while discussing the errors of sense, and expands it after working through Descartes's
answers, mainly in *La Dioptrique*, to the problem of how sight informs us
of the distance of objects – a problem that intrigued Berkeley. Malebranche concludes:

> Je croi devoir encore avertir que ce n'est point nôtre ame qui forme
> les jugemens de la distance, grandeur, &c. des objets sur les moyens
> que je viens d'expliquer, mais que c'est Dieu en consequence des
> loix de l'union de l'ame & du corps. C'est pour cela que j'ai appellé
> *naturels* ces sortes de jugemens pour marquer qu'ils se sont en nous,
> sans nous, & même malgré nous.[89]

It is a natural judgment that what we sense is outside us, just as it is a
natural judgment that heat is in the fire, or pain is in the hand.[90] Malebranche is tempted to treat such natural judgments as equivalent to
sensations, because, as he says in the first edition, the judgment on these
occasions "est si prompt, & l'ame a pris une si grande habitude de le faire,
qu'elle ne le considere plus que comme une simple sensation".[91] All of
these points were important to Hume, and we shall return to them in the
final chapter, but it must be noted that Malebranche identifies the source
of such natural judgments in God: "Je dis Dieu & non pas la nature: car
ce terme vague de *nature* si fort en usage n'est pas plus propre à exprimer
distinctement ce qu'on pense que l'*endelechie* d'Aristote".[92] Malebranche
is here referring to Cicero, *Tusculan Disputations*, Book i, Ch. x, §22,
and the confusion arising because Aristotle used the term *entelecheia*
(*perfectio*), denying any movement in the soul, but Cicero reported him
as using *endelecheia* (*continuatio*), implying continuous movement,
which, for Malebranche, must be sustained by God. Malebranche remarks that it is a common prejudice, noted by the writers of the Port-
Royal *Logic*, that our sensations are in the object, but such a view is as
absurd as that of substantial forms.[93] In fact, we can never judge by the
senses what things are in themselves,[94] but, as the Port-Royal writers
said,[95] can only judge them in their relations. Here, we discover that
bodies are united in the three ways already mentioned: continuity, con-

tiguity, and union. Because extended substance is passive and there can
be no communication of movement between bodies, we must deny that
there is any necessary connection between them, and conclude, as we
have seen above, that bodies cannot act as true causes.[96]

Although it is certain, Malebranche contends, that not all men have the
same sensations from the same objects,[97] the need men have of each other
goes some way to explaining "la communication contagieuse des imaginations fortes";[98] the natural bonds we have with other men lead us to
imitate them, agree with them, and enter into their passions. "C'est le je
ne sçai quoi qui nous agite, car la raison n'y a point de part",[99] as Bouhours
had maintained in *Entretiens d'Ariste et d'Eugène*.[100]

On the topic of language, Malebranche again follows the line taken by
the writers of the Port-Royal *Grammar* and *Logic*:

> Les définitions doivent expliquer la nature des choses; & les termes
> qui les composent, doivent réveiller dans l'esprit des idées distinctes
> & particulieres. Mais il est impossible de définir de cette sorte les
> qualitez sensibles de chaleur, de froideur, de couleur, de saveur, &c.
> lorsque l'on confond la cause avec l'effet, le mouvement des corps
> avec la sensation qui l'accompagne: parce que les sensations étant
> des modifications de l'ame, lesquelles on ne connoît point par des
> idées claires, mais seulement par sentiment intérieur . . . il est
> impossible d'attacher à des mots des idées que l'on n'a point.[101]

Words are inadequate to represent heat or colour, which is one reason
why, as noted by the Port-Royal writers, one cannot convey knowledge
of colour to a blind man: "on ne peut se faire entendre, quand celui qui
écoute n'a pas les mêmes idées que celui qui parle".[102] It is even possible,
if not probable, that what causes a sensation of blue in one person, may
cause a sensation of green in another.[103] When Locke silently adopted this
point, he changed the colours to blue and marigold (*An Essay Concerning
Human Understanding*, Book II, Ch.xxxii, §15). Malebranche re-affirms
the then standard view that the connection between the idea of a square,
say, and the word 'square' is arbitrary (*volontaire*);[104] this point needs to
be remembered when examining the claims of experimental chemists and
physicists, for their terms are often equivocal: "le mot de vin par exemple,
signifie autant de choses différentes qu'il y a différens terroirs, de
différentes saisons, de différentes manières de faire le vin & de le
garder".[105] It is not clear whether Malebranche here thought he was
illustrating or departing from the Port-Royal distinction between the
principal and accessory ideas expressed by words.

Following Descartes's terminology in the *Principles*, Malebranche says
that

> par ces mots, *pensée, maniére de penser*, ou *modification de l'ame*,
> j'entends généralement toutes les choses, qui ne peuvent être dans
> l'ame sans qu'elle les apperçoive par le sentiment intérieur qu'elle a

d'elle-méme: comme sont ses propres sensations, ses imaginations, ses pures intellections, ou simplement ses conceptions, ses passions mêmes, & ses inclinations naturelles.[106]

The soul cannot exist without such modifications, he contends, and if we felt neither pleasure nor pain we could not know whether the soul was capable of feeling modifications; ultimately, we should understand, however, that "on n'a donc point d'idée claire ni de l'ame ni de ses modifications".[107]

I have mentioned only certain aspects of Malebranche's large scheme; I have not examined their logic or their implications, and I have omitted many central doctrines: his claims about parallelism between brain states and mental phenomena such as ideas and passions, for example,[108] may well have influenced Hume in the formation of his own theory of the passions. Passages such as those I have quoted, however, show that Hume absorbed two major theses into his own system. First, he recognised, as Malebranche pointed out himself,[109] that a major thesis of Book I was that natural judgments are necessary to life: "sans eux on ne peut rendre raison de nos diverses sensations, puisqu'elles les supposent & qu'elles en dépendent nécessairement".[110] Secondly, he accepted Malebranche's account of causal connection as observed by us. In neither case, of course, was Hume willing to follow Malebranche in tracing natural judgments and causal efficacy to God; his own task was to extend those reflections in a non-theological, and thus in the eyes of many, a sceptical, direction, and for that task he was able to derive inspiration from another writer who certainly emphasised the importance of natural judgments: Cicero.

Before turning to Cicero, however, some concluding words on The French Connection are in place. In Chapters 3 and 4 we shall see the considerable influence on Hume's aesthetic thought of J-B. Dubos, who is almost unknown today, and the influence of French grammarians on Hume's thoughts about language. Inevitably, Hume's theological reading brought him into contact with the sometimes bitter debates between French Catholics and Protestant writers. Moreover, the debate on the ancients and moderns, of course, took place largely in France before it moved to England. The profound influence of Bayle on Hume's thought is well known, although there is a place for a detailed study; and Hume knew something of Montaigne and Pascal, although he hardly mentions them.[111] One writer must be mentioned, because his influence has been completely overlooked. Fontenelle, who lived into his hundredth year in 1757, was secretary of the Académie des Sciences from 1697 to 1740; his *éloge* of Newton in 1727 was much admired, and Hume often alluded to *Entretiens sur la pluralité des mondes* and *Histoire des Oracles*, both of 1686 (e.g. G.I.94, 227, 442n; N.34n).[112] Hume also referred to his *Réflexions sur la poétique*, among other works, and it is moreover likely that he was familiar with *De l'origine des Fables*, which was first published in 1724, and the *Dialogues des Morts*. *Entretiens* he admired as an attempt, in dialogue form, to express intellectual matter in a popular but elegant manner, and also for some of its general claims; he was probably not so much interested in the defence of Cartesian physics. One formulation of Fontenelle's view of analogical reasoning should be quoted:[113] "Vous convenez que quand deux choses sont semblables en tout ce qui me paraît, je les puis croire aussi semblables en ce qui ne me paraît point, s'il n'y a rien d'ailleurs qui m'en empêche." Hume possibly derived some of his most speculative examples in the *Dialogues* from Fontenelle, such as the view that a comet "is the seed of the world" (D.177), the comparison between reason and vegetation; and the discussion of the balance between economy and variety in the universe (D.183–5) has one source in Fontenelle, who wrote that nature

> est d'une épargne extraordinaire; tout ce qu'elle pourra faire d'une manière qui lui coûtera un peu moins, quand ce moins ne serait presque rien, soyez sûre qu'elle ne le fera que de cette manière-là. Cette épargne néanmoins s'accorde avec une magnificence surprenante qui brille dans tout ce qu'elle a fait. C'est que la magnificence est dans le dessein, et l'épargne dans l'exécution.[114]

Fontenelle recorded for posterity the tale, originally in Vitruvius (Preface to Book VI of *De Architectura*), of a shipwrecked philosopher who finds footprints in the sand, which Hume remembered when discussing analogical inference (E.152), and which was also used by Montesquieu and Diderot; moreover, Fontenelle suggests that there could be "un sixième sens naturel, qui nous apprendrait beaucoup de choses que nous ignorons", and repeats the familiar view that it would be absurd to say that it was only probable that Alexander lived, in the absence of mathematical proof that he did.[115] Fontenelle's earlier religious speculations were widely cited by Bayle, and the English Deists, and helped to shape Hume's own views. Behind those views, however, whether in Fontenelle or Hume, was a writer to whom Hume owed a major debt, and to whom we now turn.

Hume and Cicero

Every educated reader could discern at the time of its posthumous publication, that Hume's *Dialogues concerning Natural Religion* was modelled on Cicero's *De Natura Deorum*. Most readers, no doubt, could also discern the Ciceronian influence on the earlier *Natural History of Religion*, where it was modestly advertised in footnotes, and in the purely philosophical analyses of theology and religion, where it was not mentioned at all. The debt to Cicero in *Treatise* Book III, to which Hume referred in his 1739 letter to Hutcheson, quoted at the beginning of this chapter, is not acknowledged in the text, although references are given in the re-written version of the second *Enquiry*. The only quotation from Cicero in the *Treatise* occurs in an Appendix footnote to Book I (T.630), which is repeated in the first *Enquiry*. In fact, however, taking his works as a whole, Hume names Cicero more than fifty times, and had studied all his available works; and explicit allusion was often unnecessary since Cicero was the one classical writer familiar to and admired by almost every educated person in France and England in the late seventeenth and early eighteenth centuries.[116]

Hume's interest in Cicero, like that of his contemporaries, centred on the moral, political and religious tenets, on the one hand, and on the rhetorical views, on the other. Cicero's epistemological reflections were generally subordinate to those tenets, and conducted in the light of them, and Hume himself moved towards a similar policy. In Hume's time, orthodox and free-thinker alike felt the challenge of Cicero, and it may be noted that Professor John Pringle devoted his moral philosophy lectures in the University of Edinburgh, in 1740–1, to *De Officiis* and the problems of suicide, immortality, the future state, *decorum, modestia,* and the being and attributes of God (which the note-taker missed).[117] There is no evidence that Hume read Cicero's works as a unified and structured progression from *Academica* to *De Officiis,* as one modern commentator has urged that they should be read, although he does seem to have been fairly clear which views Cicero was merely reporting for discussion, and which were his own.[118]

Because most of Cicero's works are unfamiliar to modern students of Hume, I shall summarise those views which have their most prominent parallels in Hume's work and which may be assumed to be a source of them. Cicero was particularly admired for his synthesis of rhetoric and philosophy, and, apart from his own later attempts at dialogue form, Hume models the structure of the first two books of the *Treatise* on that of *De Officiis,* where the first book is written from the reflexive viewpoint of an individual, and the second analyses his character from the viewpoint of others; it will be remembered that one of the rare critical reviews of Book I complained of the superfluity of first person pronouns. As a preface to the summary and greater subsequent detail, we may list four general theses of Cicero which Hume happily adopted:

1. insistence on the social dimension of man, and recognition of its importance as a necessary condition of stability and coherence in the political realm;
2. recognition that we should seek to live in harmony with Nature, and that *honestum* and *moderatio* ought to form the core of morality;
3. adoption of moderate scepticism only, and rejection of extreme scepticism as incompatible with a practical life, and as indicative of egoism;
4. insistence on the causal principle, together with a rejection of fate, chance, divination; and an attitude of scepticism towards philosophical

theology and most religious practices.

At the beginning of *De Divinatione*, Book II, Cicero lists his philosophical works and their main themes, excluding *De Officiis*, of course, which had not yet been written:

(*a*) *Hortensius*, urging the study of philosophy: (now lost)

(*b*) *Academica*, outlining his own preferred system, and attitude to scepticism:

(*c*) *De Finibus*, examining the distinction between good and evil, on which philosophy itself is founded:

(*d*) *Tusculan Disputations*, setting out the conditions of a happy life, and arguing that virtue alone is sufficient:

(*e*) *De Natura Deorum*, discussing all relevant theological topics, amplified by

(*f*) *De Divinatione* and

(*g*) *De Fato*, both of which argue against divination and fate.

Cicero also draws attention to his discussion of Plato and Aristotle in *De Re Publica*, but (except through quotations in Bayle from Augustine) this work was unknown to Hume, and was only partly rediscovered in 1820; accordingly, we may leave it aside. In line with his declared aim to join together rhetoric and philosophy, Cicero adds to his list of philosophical works *De Oratore*, *Brutus*, and *Orator*; and on his behalf, we must add *De Officiis*.

Three-quarters of *Academica* is extant, one-quarter of which is in final form. It was meant to be Cicero's main epistemological discussion. Varro is made to expound the dogmatic position of Antiochus, to which Cicero himself later replies. It is significant that the Platonic view of man in society is sketched in terms which appealed not only to Cicero, but also to Hume: "they held man to be, as it were, a part of the community comprising the whole human race, and man to be connected to man by the link of common humanity" (*esse coniunctum cum hominibus humana quadam societate: Academica*, I.v.21). Varro is also made to expound Aristotle's notion of underlying substance, and a notion of primary and secondary qualities; and Zeno's view is recorded that

> even the emotions were voluntary and were experienced owing to a judgment of opinion, and he held that the mother of all the emotions was a sort of intemperance and lack of moderation.

Zeno is also said to have argued that sensations are properly understood as a combination of external impression and internal voluntary mental assent (I.x.39–xi.40); furthermore, only those sense presentations are trustworthy that are intrinsically perspicuous – Cicero is here concerned with *enargeia* (see II.vi.17).

Book II of *Academica* is concerned with Antiochus's attack on, and Cicero's defence of, scepticism, and Cicero begins with an observation which he repeats on several occasions, and which undoubtedly interested

Hume: "we hold many doctrines as probable which we can easily act upon but can scarcely advance as certain" (II.iii.8). Antiochus asserts that memory is "the one principal foundation not only of philosophy but of all the conduct of life and all the sciences" (II.vii.22). He even makes the passing suggestion that mind is itself sensation (*etiam ipsa sensus est:* II.x.30), which nevertheless is able to unite some sense perceptions into systems by virtue of their mutual resemblances. Antiochus holds that one who denies the possibility, or even the reliability, of either sense presentations or assent, abolishes all action from life (II.xii.39); and that as soon as a man regains full self-consciousness, which is presumably self-authenticating, he is well able to distinguish between perspicuous and unreal presentations (II.xvi.51).

In his own defence of scepticism, Cicero contends that Antiochus's appeal to self-consciousness is irrelevant to the search for a criterion of veridical experience (II.xxvii.88), and that Epicurus is inconsistent in relying upon his own witness while simultaneously subscribing to the general tenet that if one has been mislead once by the senses, no sense is to be believed (II.xxv.80). Cicero agrees that life would be subverted if nothing were probable, and repeats his view that many sense-percepts must be deemed probable, even though there may be no *differentia* between a true and a false sense-presentation (II.xxxi.99). Action and the withholding of strict assent are quite compatible (II.xxxii.104).

Towards the end of Book II Cicero raises the problem of evil, and quotes (but without approval) the view that the universe has been caused by the purely natural forces of gravitation and motion (*ponderibus et motibus:* II.xxxviii.121). Cicero's own view is that such matters are hidden from us, and that on the human level perhaps the doctors (*empirici*) were right to suspect that uncovering the internal organs changes their character (II.xxxix.122); Hume's parallel anxiety about the mind in the Introduction to the *Treatise* (T.xxiii) may be recalled. Cicero declares, with hesitation, that he does not believe the world to have been built on a divine plan (*Academica*, II.xl.126). He is attracted by the Old Academy's view of the mean in things, and he also argues for the disinterested (*gratuita*) nature of the virtues (II.xliv.135–xlvi.140). As a corollary of these arguments, he urges that if nothing can be comprehended the practice of the arts collapses, art itself being impossible without scientific knowledge, as the example of Zeuxis and Phidias showed (II.xlvii.146). Hume adopted these examples at the opening of the first *Enquiry*.

De Finibus expounds and criticises the ethical systems of the Epicureans, Stoics and Academics, Cicero's own view remaining undetermined although occasionally implied. In dialogue form we are given the Stoic criticism of the Epicurean view, Antiochus's criticism of the Stoic view, and Stoic criticism of Antiochus's view. Cicero declares that man is primarily differentiated from lower animals by reason (*ratio*), which enables him "to discern the causes and effects of things, to draw analogies, combine things separate, connect the future with the present, and survey the entire field of the subsequent course of life" (*De Finibus*, II.xiv.45). Reason has also prompted man to develop social ties, at first within the family, then through friends and fellow-citizens, and finally with all mankind; language, habits and expansible interests all contribute to such development (ibid.). Stoics hold that the Chief Good consists in applying knowledge of natural causes to the conduct of life, and in trying to live in harmony with nature (III.ix.31); the morally good (*honestum*) is to be desired for its own sake (III.xi.36). In the present context, Cicero argues that such a view would be tenable only for creatures consisting solely of pure intellect (IV.xi.28), and that most ethical systems become one-sided when discussing the *summum bonum*, proceeding as if man had no mind, or, on the other hand, was only a mind (IV.xiv.36). In his last work, *De Officiis*, Cicero is much less hesitant, and argues that, properly understood, there can be no conflict between *honestum* and *utile*, goodness and expediency, and furthermore he there adopts the view here canvassed that one constituent in moral goodness is a certain order and moderation (*ordo et moderatio*), which is developed by analogy with beauty in outward forms (*De Finibus:* II.xiv.47; *De Officiis:* I.v.15). In *De Finibus*, Cicero shows some sympathy for the Academic position that all animals have the common end of living according to nature, although their own natures differ; self-preservation and self-development are the earliest instincts of all creatures, later consciously pursued (v.ix.24–6). Self-knowledge requires knowledge of mental and physical powers (v.xvi.44). Man is designed by nature for activity (*ad agendum:* v.xxi.58), and one may view the virtues as implanted by nature, but developed by reason.

In the *Tusculan Disputations* there is considerable discussion of the need to combine the eloquence of rhetoricians and the argument (*rationes*) of philosophers, in order to develop an appropriate philosophical style and secure a wider audience (see e.g. I.iii.6, xlviii.116; II.i.4, iii.8–9; IV.xxxv.55); the point is repeated in *De Officiis* (II.x.35). There are several remarks to the effect that philosophy is a physician of souls, or medicine of the mind – the phrase haunted Hume (G.I.221; *Tusc.* II.iv.11; III.iii.6 *animi medicina*; IV.xxxvii.58), and that the wise man is at peace with himself (IV.xvii.37; cp. III.viii.18). Cicero tends to agree with the Stoics who think that disorders of the soul (*perturbationes*) have their sources in beliefs and judgments within our control (IV.vii.14, xxxi.65; v.xv.43), and also with their view of virtue as an equable and harmonious disposition of the soul (IV.xv.34). After discussing fear of death and endurance of pain, alleviation of distress, and other disorders of the soul, Cicero argues in the final book that virtue is sufficient for the happy life. There also occur in the last book further observations on method. Philosophers should be judged not by isolated utterances, but by consistency (*constantia:* v.x.31). It should be remembered, however, that no one method is suitable to every case (IV.xxvii.59): Aristotle's warning, accepted by everyone in Hume's time. It is further suggested that formal definitions and distinctions are occupations of leisure, whereas a wise man attends to public affairs (v.xxiv.72). While such remarks may have been intended as partial exoneration for his own failure to define his central concepts such as 'nature' or 'virtue', Cicero frequently criticised others for a similar failure: for example, Epicurus's failure to define his notion of pleasure (*De Fin.* II.vi.18, x.30, xxiii.75).

The moral dimension of the *Tusculan Disputations* centres on the need for moderation, a complex notion expressed by several related terms: *moderatio, modestia, mediocritas, clementia, prudentia,* and ultimately *honestum.* The notion, parallel to *eutaxia* and *sophrosyne,* represents the harmony and proportion of virtue, and is crucial not only for an understanding of Cicero, but, as we shall see in Chapter 5, of Hume himself (*Tusc.* I.xxvi.64; II.xix.45; III.x.22; IV.xvi.36; V.xii.36, xxiii.67; *De Fin.* II.xiv.45; V.xxiii.66; *De Offic.* I.iv.14, xxix.102, xl.142; III.iii.13). It is man's duty to ensure that reason, as a master over a slave, rules that part of the soul which ought to obey (II.xxi.48), since pain can be endured only through such self-control. A wise man achieves peace of mind through restraint and consistency, which is the meaning of the proverb that "the frugal man does everything right" (*hominem frugi omnia recte facere: Tusc.* IV.xvi.36–xvii.37): the notion of *frugalitas* itself embodying *moderatio, modestia, temperantia, constantia, continentia.*

There is emphasis on the view that probability should be the guide to life (*Tusc.* I.ix.17; II.ii.5), on the possibility that we have a natural belief in the existence of Gods (I.xvi.36), on the very great influence of habit (II.xvii.40; III.i.2), and on the view that custom cannot conquer nature, for nature is always unconquered (*est enim ea semper invicta:* V.xxvii.78). I shall show in due course that Hume denied the second view, but accepted the remainder. Cicero turned to philosophical composition as a consolation for a series of private tragedies and public disasters that had befallen him. There is no doubt that Hume, like most of his contemporaries, was moved as much by the dignity as by the magnitude of the output, and whenever Hume's reflections turned to sombre topics a Ciceronian reference (e.g. G.I.226n, with reference to the consolations of deafness, *Tusc.* V.xl.116) or allusion was likely: as when, discussing suicide, he remembers Cicero's observations that death may be caused equally by a fly as by a sword (G.II.410, probably alluding to *Tusc.* V.xl.117).

De Natura Deorum is familiar to most readers of Hume, and it will be sufficient as a prelude to discussion in the next chapter, to set out some of the major points that re-appear in Hume's *Dialogues.* Cicero devotes part of Book I and all of Book II to an exposition of Epicurean and Stoic theology; the remainder of Book I, and all of Book III, are devoted to the Academic criticism of these views.

At the outset, it is suggested that the disappearance of piety towards the gods will entail the disappearance of loyalty and social union among men (*De Nat.* I.ii.4), a point often made in Hume's time, and to which he refers, also in an Epicurean context (E.143). Cicero, replying in his own voice, claims that if the doctrines of philosophy have a practical bearing, then he himself has practised in his public and private life the precepts prescribed by reason and theory (I.iii.7). As we have already noted, Hume agreed with Cicero that too often the weight of authority took the place of argument in philosophical discussion (I.v.10).

At the beginning of the dialogues, Cicero states his own epistemological position, which we encountered in *Academica*:

> our position is not that we hold that nothing is true, but that we assert that all true sensations are associated with false ones so closely resembling them, that they contain no infallible mark to guide our judgment and assent. (I.v.12)

The disputants, including Cicero himself, frequently point out that certain properties are inter-dependent, and presuppose in their predication certain kinds of bearers. Thus, if wisdom is predicated of a being, it is necessary to ask what form (*figura*) an intelligent being could conceivably possess (I.x.23–4). Anaxagoras, for example, failed to see that there can be no sentient or continuous activity in an infinite being, and that sentience requires the impact of sensation: "mind, naked and simple, without any material adjunct to serve as an organ of sensation, seems to elude the capacity of our understanding" (ibid. 27). Hume makes a similar point:

> our thought is fluctuating, uncertain, fleeting, successive, and compounded; and were we to remove these circumstances, we absolutely annihilate its essence, and it would, in such a case, be an abuse of terms to apply to it the name of thought or reason. (D.156)

But if there are difficulties over the notion of an incorporeal deity, which Hume takes up (*De Natura Deorum*, I.xii.30; D.159), there are also difficulties about embodied deities and the anthropomorphism that usually results from such views (*De Nat.*I.xxxiv.94). In passing, we may note that both Cicero and Hume refer to the ancient view that the world itself is God (*De Nat.* I.xv.39; D.162; cp. Bayle's definition of 'naturalisme' as "l'opinion de ceux qui ne reconnoissent d'autre Dieu que la Nature", *Oeuvres Diverses*, III.294).

Epicurus argued that men have a preconception of the gods, a kind of mental picture instilled by nature (*De Nat.* I.xvi.43; cp. *Tusc.* I.xvi.36); the mind tries to strengthen this natural belief by trying to discover the form of God, the mode of his activity and intelligence. Epicurus himself held that God is entirely inactive, and that the world was made by nature, without need of an artificer to create or sustain it (*De Nat.* I.xx.53).

Against the Epicurean position, Cotta is made to argue that although it might be impolitic in public to deny the existence of the gods, it is not improper in private, and that the first question is, indeed, "Do the gods exist ?" (I.xxii.61; cp. xxxi. 85 – 7). Hume enjoys and celebrates this point in his own way (D.139, 142). In the past, Cotta remarks, doubters were punished for the mere expression of doubt; contemporaries, it is ironic-ally implied, ought not to behave so barbarously. The question should be treated not merely as an article of faith (*non opinione solum:* I.xxii.62), but as a matter of fact. Epicurus is mistaken in the claim that all mankind agree that the gods exist and have human form, although he may be right to suggest that the representation of gods in human form was adopted by rulers as a device to appeal to the ignorant (I.xxvii.77). Cotta points out that if we accept the existence of nothing save what we have touched or seen, we must sweep aside everything unusual of which science or history informs us (I.xxxi.88). As we shall see in the next chapter, Hume has some difficulty with reports of unfamiliar events. Cotta re-iterates Cicero's earlier insistence that rational intelligence exists only in con-junction with other attributes (I.xxxv.98), and urges that if God is the image of man we need to know about his activities and whereabouts; alternatively, "if the gods appeal only to the faculty of thought, and have no solidity or definite outline, what difference does it make whether we think of a god or of a hippocentaur ?" (I.xxxviii.105). Moreover, claims about the image of God need to be set beside the facts that different people have different images, that we can have images of non-existent things, and that some images are voluntary and some involuntary (ibid., 108).

The design argument, which occupied so much of Hume's critical attention, is outlined in Book II, which opens with a defence of Stoic theology. The spokesman, Balbus, supposedly a pupil of Cleanthes, claims that the existence of the gods is easily proved: "when we gaze upward to the sky, what can be so obvious and so manifest as that there must exist some power possessing extraordinary intelligence by whom these things are ruled ?" (II.ii.4). Further, the judgments of nature (*naturae iudicia:* ibid., 5) concerning such things are confirmed over time. Balbus argues that upon entering a house and observing the regularity within, we cannot suppose such arrangement to have occurred without a cause; similar considerations apply to the heavenly bodies (II.v.15). This famous example, used by almost everybody in the eighteenth century, re-appears in Shaftesbury[119] and several times in Hume. In an important prelude to the argument that all things are under the influence of nature (*subiecta esse naturae:* ibid., xxxii.81), Balbus defines various senses of 'nature':

some persons define nature as a non-rational force that causes necessary motions in material bodies; others as a rational and ordered force, proceeding by method and plainly displaying the means that she takes to produce each result and the end at which she aims, and possessed of a skill that no handiwork of artist or craftsman can rival or reproduce.... Some thinkers [*Epicurus*] again denote by the term 'nature' the whole of existence.... When we on the other hand speak of nature as the sustaining and governing principle of the world, we do not mean that the world is like a clod of earth or lump of stone ... which possesses only the natural principle of cohesion, but like a tree or an animal, displaying no haphazard structure (*temeritas*), but order and a certain semblance of design. (II.xxxii.81–2)

In the final chapter we shall consider Hume's own discussion of senses of 'nature' (see e.g. T.474–5; M.124). Balbus continues by arguing that habit and familiarity diminish our curiosity about the causes of phenomena, but that really nothing is more remarkable than the stability and coherence of the world (*De Nat.* II.xlv.115). He invites his hearers to consider the marvellous structure of the eye, a favourite example in the eighteenth century, and one borrowed by Hume for his own 'Cleanthes' (*De Nat.* II.lvii.142–3: D.154). In an observation on language, which we know expressed Cicero's view and influenced Hume, Balbus claims that speech

enables us both to learn things we do not know, and to teach things we do know to others; secondly, it is our instrument for exhortation and persuasion ... for curbing passion and quenching appetite and anger; it is this that has united us in the bonds of justice, law and civil order, this that has separated us from savagery and barbarism. (*De Nat.* II.lix.148)

Book III is devoted to criticism of the preceding Epicurean and Stoic positions, and at the outset Cotta observes that although everyone began by agreeing over the existence of the gods, their existence is precisely what the arguments sought to prove (III.iii.9). Hume follows both Cicero and Bayle in this regard at the beginning of his own dialogues. Cotta argues against each of Cleanthes's contentions, and claims that the Stoics only resort to god as an explanation (e.g. II.vi.16) when they fail to find any other rational explanation (III.x.24). But the coherence of nature is not due to a divine power, and, furthermore, there are no grounds for ascribing the recognised human virtues or the other traditional properties to God. What need would God have of reason or intelligence, which are faculties used for proceeding from the known to the unknown (III.xi.28; xv.38)? Cotta holds that individual conscience (*conscientia*), capable of distinguishing right from wrong, is a sufficiently powerful force in itself, and without which everything else collapses; there is therefore no need of any assumption of divine design (III.xxxv.85).

The two short works supplementing *De Natura Deorum, De Divinatione*

and *De Fato*, both discuss the nature of causal connections and our knowledge of them, and the alleged conflict between freedom and determinism.
Hume (see e.g. E.viii) was familiar with both works, but was particularly
influenced by the former. In Book ii of *De Divinatione* Cicero contends
that if divination is taken to be "the foreknowledge and foretelling of
things which happen by chance" (ii.v.13), there is no need of divination
to explain things perceived by the senses, and consequently no place for it
in medicine or astronomy, any more than in moral philosophy, logic,
physics or government (ii.iii.9–11). Of course, even those who make
probable conjectures, such as physicians and farmers, sometimes make
mistakes (ii.vi.16), but they do not seek to explain, let alone predict, such
unexpected events by reference to the croak of a raven, the fall of a star or
the utterances of persons in a frenzy. Cicero asks how anything can be
foreseen that, by definition, has no cause and no mark of its coming
(ii.vi.17). In effect, Cicero seeks to argue that: it is logically impossible
to foresee an unforeseeable event; that a chance event is an unforeseeable
event; that divination claims to be the foreseeing of chance events; and
that therefore divination is impossible (ii.vii.18; x.26). It has to be
remembered that we know of countless instances of some natural connection between apparently unrelated objects (ii.xiv.34). Even when the
causes of phenomena are unknown to us, we can still observe and study
the phenomena themselves (ii.xxi.47); usually, indeed, our ignorance of
the causes of frequent occurrences seems not to dismay us, whereas with
a new occurrence ignorance of its cause excites wonder (ii.xxii.49). We
really ought to insist that "the impossible has never happened and the
possible need not excite wonder" (ibid.). Even when a prophecy and an
event agree, how can it be established that the agreement was not due to
chance (ii.xxiv.52)? The general principle is this:

> whatever comes into existence, of whatever kind, has a cause in
> nature necessarily, so that, even if it is contrary to custom, it cannot
> be contrary to nature. Therefore, seek the cause, if you can, of every
> new and strange thing; if you find nothing, be assured, nevertheless,
> that nothing could have happened without a cause. (*nihil fieri potuisse
> sine causa:* ii.xxviii.60)

"There ought to be no place in philosophy for fabricated stories" (*com-
menticiis fabellis:* ii.xxxvii.79). If the subject-matter is dreams, we should
realise that it is possible to think of nothing, however irregular, vague or
strange, that we cannot also dream (ii.lxxi.146).

Cicero concludes by repeating his view from *De Natura Deorum*, that
superstition (*superstitio*) is widespread among men, and that he deemed
it a service to tear up such superstition by the roots: "but it is not true –
for I want this to be carefully understood – that in destroying superstition, religion is destroyed. For it is wise to uphold the institutions of our
forebears by observing their sacred ceremonies" (*De Nat.* ii.lxxii.148).

A final remark declares that the beauty of the universe and the celestial order lead one to confess to a superior and eternal being (ibid.).

In *De Fato* Cicero claims that he means by 'cause' something precedent, effective and necessary to produce the thing of which it is the cause (xv.34–xvi.36). When the positions maintaining free-will and determinism are unfolded, it will be seen that "the difference between them is one of words and not of fact" (xix.44). If differences in men's propensities are due to natural and antecedent causes, it does not follow that our wills and desires are also due to such causes: "if that were the case, we should have no freedom at all" (v.9).

Cicero shows a tendency, later displayed by Hume himself, to dismiss apparently substantive disagreements as 'merely verbal' disputes (see e.g. *De Fin.* IV.xx.57, xxii.60, xxvi.72; *Tusc.* II.xii.29; V.xli.120; *De Fato* xix.44). He also shows a tendency, no doubt traceable to Plato's *Cratylus*, and in which he is not at all followed by Hume, to engage in remarkable etymological speculation (see e.g. *Tusc.* I.ix.19; III.viii.16; IV.viii.19, xi.26: *De Offic.* I.xii.37, xl.142). Cicero prefaces almost every work with a defence of his method (see e.g. *De Nat.* I.v.10; cp. *De Div.* II.lxxii.148), and Hume seems to have Cicero in mind when commenting on method at the beginning of the Introduction to the *Treatise*, and again in the first *Enquiry*. In Cicero the rhetorical requirement to contrast one's own view with that of others (e.g. *De Fin.* v.viii.23; *De Offic.* II.xiv.51) often results in a less than accurate representation of rival views, in spite of the denial of such an accusation (*Tusc.* V.x.31). Truth, or at least probability, is supposed to emerge from attempts to determine the consistency and plausibility of such rival views. Cicero's own views, however, are not always stated; he cannot be identified completely, for example, with any single spokesman in the *Tusculan Disputations* or even in *De Natura Deorum*. It is significant that in his last philosophical work, *De Officiis*, to which we must now turn, Cicero abandons the dialogue form in the urgency of stating his own position and emphasising the practical relevance of philosophical questions; philosophy is indeed the cultivation of the soul (*Tusc.*II.v.13), but it is equally the science of life (*ars est enim philosophia vitae: De Fin.* III.ii.4). In contrast, Hume's own last work represents the apogee of philosophical dialogue.

In his short dissertation, 'Of the nature of virtue', appended to *The Analogy of Religion*, Bishop Butler, citing Cicero, declares that "It does not appear, that brutes have the least sense of actions, as distinguished from events: or that will and design, which constitute the very nature of actions as such, are at all an object to their perception".[120] In *De Officiis* Cicero examines the nature of the supreme good, and the best practical rules for daily life, arguing, as I have already indicated, that there can be no real conflict between moral goodness and expediency. He begins by characterising differences between man and other animals:

the most marked difference between man and beast is this: the beast, just as far as it is moved by the senses and with very little perception of past or future, adapts itself to that alone which is present at the moment; while man – because he is endowed with reason, by which he comprehends the chain of consequences, perceives the causes of things, understands the relation of cause to effect and of effect to cause, draws analogies, and connects and associates the present and the future – easily surveys the course of his whole life and makes the necessary preparations for its conduct. (I.iv.11)

Cicero adds that "nature likewise by the power of reason associates man in the common bonds of speech and life". Such reflections were important to Hume when he turned to the topic 'Of the reason of animals' (T.176; E.112). In contrast to animals guided purely by sensual pleasures, "man's mind is nurtured by study and reflection, and he is always either investigating or doing" (*agit: De Offic.* I.xxx.105). The glory of virtue, indeed, lies in action (*in actione:* I.vi.19). Hume's insistence (E.18) that man is reasonable, sociable, and active, owes much to these tenets.

Cicero argues that the chief bond between men is provided by reason and speech (*De Offic.* I.xvi.50); the foundation of justice in society is fidelity to promises and agreements (I.vii.23), a claim which explains, incidentally, the central place accorded to promise-keeping in natural law theorists of the seventeenth century, such as Pufendorf, and also its prominence in Hume's own discussions of justice (e.g. T.516ff.). Among the other bonds of society is a principle of sympathy, by means of which other men are attracted to *honestum* whenever they detect it (*De Offic.* I.xvii.55). Four related but distinct virtues constitute *honestum* itself, and each is associated with specific duties: (*a*) the detection and pursuit of the truth; (*b*) the conservation of organised society, and the faithful discharge of duties; (*c*) the strength of a noble and invincible spirit; (*d*) order and the mean in all things, wherein consist moderation and self-control (*ordine et modo, in quo inest modestia et temperantia:* I.v.15). This last notion is involved in the idea of *decorum*: what is proper is morally right, and what is morally right is proper (I.xxvii.34). Propriety in moral behaviour has its analogue in the harmonious symmetry of beautiful objects (I.xxviii.98), a view that appealed to the eighteenth century, as is evident in Shaftesbury. The duty prescribed by propriety is to follow nature as our guide in mind and body, although reason should command, and appetite obey; in this way the four virtues mentioned above, wisdom, justice, fortitude and moderation, are achieved (I.xxviii.100). Propriety may thus be understood as uniform consistency in everything we do, and *modestia* or moderation as the art of doing the right thing at the right time (I.xxxi.111; I.xl.142). We should do nothing for which we cannot offer a likely motive (*causam probabilem:* I.xxix.101). In most things, the best rule is the golden mean (*mediocritas optima est:* I.xxxvi.130).

Cicero then emphasises the importance of seeing ourselves from a spectator's viewpoint, and of recognising that the established customs and conventions of a community constitute rules for behaviour (*praecepta:* I.xli.147). He claims that those duties are closer to nature which depend on social instinct, rather than on knowledge, one reason being that the claims of society and bonds which unite it take precedence over individual pursuit of speculative knowledge (I.xliii.153–xliv.154). On the other hand, the social instinct (*communitas:* I.xlv.159) is *not* always to take precedence over temperance and moderation, but "in choosing between conflicting duties, that class takes precedence which is demanded by the interests of human society" (ibid.).

Books II and III of *De Officiis* are largely devoted to establishing the indissolubility of the notions of *honestum* and *utile*. In the course of the discussion Cicero seems to distinguish between self-regarding and other-regarding virtues, and defends the unequal distribution of property as a condition of social stability (II.vi.21; xxi.73). The chief end of all men ought to be the union of the interest of each individual and the whole body politic (III.vi.26).

The aesthetic aspect embodied in the notions of *decorum* and *moderatio* reflects Cicero's views of rhetoric, with which Hume and his contemporaries were familiar both in their theoretical presentation and in the collected speeches; there are more than a dozen references to the speeches in the first volume of Hume's *Essays* (1741). In *De Oratore* Cicero asserts that "eloquence is so powerful a force that it embraces the origin and operation and development of all things, all the virtues and duties, all the natural principles governing the morals, minds and life of mankind, and also determines their customs and laws and rights" (III.xx.76); rhetoric, in brief, embraces the entire field of practical philosophy (*de omni vivendi ratione:* III.xxxi.122). Virtue, Cicero claims in another place, is exhibited either in knowledge or conduct; justice, greatness of mind and moderation are displayed in action, but wisdom requires eloquence. Eloquence, indeed, is nothing but wisdom speaking copiously (*De Partitione Oratoria* xxii.76–xxiii.79). In eloquence, the theory arose from its practice, not the practice from theory (*De Oratore*, I.xxxii.146).

Summary. In this chapter I have considered a number of works studied by Hume, which can be taken as sources of his own views and attitudes. There has been no discussion of what counts as an influence, or of variant interpretations of the works quoted. Sometimes Hume may have misled himself, as well as later readers, by failing to reflect on these issues. The present exercise makes no claim to comprehensiveness. A separate study is planned of Bayle, to whom reference is made throughout the book, and it is time to reassess the influence of Hutcheson, to whom no reference is made. It is quite legitimate for one man to use another's words for his own purposes. This common philosophical approach to Hume's works, however, has diminished our grasp of the context in which Hume saw himself; moreover, it frequently misrepresents the nature and weight of his own claims, and often presupposes a view of truly philosophical ideas as eternal, immutable, and probably *a priori*, which Hume might not have accepted.[121]

We have seen so far that:

1. For the application of "experimental philosophy to moral subjects" Hume needed to understand little more of Newton than the general statements of method in *Principia* and *Opticks*, which were explained by every commentator.

2. Hume's lack of interest in science finds an explanation in his deep commitment to Ciceronian humanism, with its distinctive attitude to man and to philosophy; such views separated him from Newton. Two early letters acknowledge debts to Malebranche and Cicero, and support this contention.

3. The influence of the Port-Royal *Logic*, often mediating Descartes's views to a wide audience, is considerable. A later work, by Crousaz, which attempts to bring the *Logic* up to date by incorporating insights from Locke and Malebranche is instructive, because it illustrates the climate of thought at the time Hume was beginning work on the *Treatise*.

4. Malebranche held that ideas are the immediate objects of perception; they are of a spiritual nature, carrying no existence or resemblance implications to anything else; ideas of sense differ from those of imagination only in degree of force. In the science of man we must judge by probabilities, and also recognise the ubiquity of natural judgments, which are essential to life. We can only discover relations between objects, not what they are in themselves; there are no necessary connections between bodies, only the relations of continuity, contiguity, and union. The social need that men have for each other explains the urge to imitate and agree.

5. Hume adopted as major theses both the insistence on natural judgments, and the analysis of causal connection as observed by us, in addition to most of the other epistemological tenets. Hume rejected Malebranche's attempt to trace both theses to God's efficacy, and found the secular dimension he needed, in Cicero.

6. The French Connection with Hume extends beyond Malebranche, to writers on language and art (see Chapters 3 and 4); the influence of Fontenelle should be noted, especially for his cosmological reflections and the attempt to convey abstract ideas in an elegant literary form.

7. Hume agreed with Cicero that man differs from animals primarily in his capacity to trace causal connections. Although nothing can happen without a cause, we should distinguish what is contrary to our experience from what is alleged, impossibly, to be contrary to nature. Total

scepticism[122] deprives life of all foundations, but fortunately we are aided by habit and by natural beliefs; in the end, nature is too strong for principle or custom. In the absence of absolute certainty, one has to develop probabilities, but these are not incompatible with conviction and action.[123] The proper balance for man is a mixed life of thinking, feeling and acting, the central notion being moderation. Dispensing with theological views both in the field of cosmogony and the field of morals, Cicero set out a secular morality with *honestum* and *moderatio* at its core. Emphasis on the style with which one conducts oneself links with views on the nature and roles of rhetoric.

8. Hume adopts all these views, particularly stressing the social dimension of man, the adoption of limited scepticism only, the importance of moderation, and the nature of the causal connection. He lamented the absence of theoretical support for Cicero's conclusions, and the theological dimension in Malebranche's theory. Book I of the *Treatise* can be seen, in part, as grounded in a secular version of Malebranche's views; and Book III of the Treatise can be seen, in part, as providing theoretical support for Cicero's conclusions.

Hume's early philosophical thoughts were also influenced and directed by his reading of Bayle, particularly on scepticism and religion; moreover, Bayle drew attention to many of the arguments in Cicero which Hume himself admired. But Bayle did more to strengthen Hume's sceptical reflections than to provide the positive theoretical support he wanted for Cicero's secular morality.

TWO

Scepticism in Religion

The special interest of Hume's views on religion and art, which we shall discuss in the next two chapters, is that in both cases he seeks to resist the sceptical challenge by locating a criterion of knowledge in sentiment; in both cases, however, he is forced to consider the notion of appropriateness or justification, and this leads him to supplement a purely causal account of response with a view of the mind as active and constructive. His essentially pragmatic method of resolving disputes is grounded on assumptions about what it is natural for man to do, and these aspects of his thoughts are significantly parallel to views of modern philosophers, as we shall see in Chapter 5.

Hume's predecessors bequeathed him a problem about knowledge, two parts of which are acute in disputes about miracles: when is it reasonable (*a*) to believe third-person reports about past events, and (*b*) to make analogical inferences, especially concerning causes? In this chapter we shall consider Hume's treatment of these issues, and then show how his account of the historical origins and development of religions is mainly a paraphrase and synthesis of familiar classical views.

If the thesis of the first chapter is tenable, we should expect Hume to follow Cicero in some detail, and to support his conclusions with modified arguments drawn from Malebranche: and, in fact, he does. Hume agrees with Cicero that religions are rooted in fear for the future, and that the fear itself is explicable by reference to ignorance of both particular causes and the universal causal principle; such fears generate superstition and dispute, and contribute to struggles for power. The proper office of religion is to enforce morality, which is independent of it and founded in both natural and artificial virtues. An attitude of *moderatio* in life embodies a properly sceptical attitude towards religious claims. Malebranche agreed with Cicero that in practical life we must be governed by probabilities and certain natural judgments, but he also argued that there are no necessary links between bodies, and that ideas carry no pointers or implications to anything else, least of all to their causes; nevertheless, he traced both natural judgments and true causal efficacy to God. In rejecting only this last move, Hume sought to expound a purely secular system. In his view, religious beliefs are not natural beliefs, but can be explained in terms of psychological states and social background; moreover, there are insufficient grounds for postulating God as a cause of phenomena. He says, in a letter of 1743, that the Deity "is not the natural Object of any Passion or Affection. He is no Object either of the Senses or Imagination, and very little of the Understanding, without which it is impossible to excite any Affection" (L.1.51).

Before elaborating on these points, however, it is proper to begin with Hume's philosophical reflections on the nature of testimony, since his failure to find a secure ground or justification for religious claims encourages his search for the causes of religious phenomena. Locke had said that "what I see I know to be so by the evidence of the thing itself: what I believe I take to be so upon the testimony of another" (*Essay*, IV.xix.10). For Hume this view led to a general problem in the following way. Of the four ways in which Hume says that knowledge can be acquired: instinct, education, experience and abstract reasoning, more than half our opinions are due to education; and "the principles, which are thus implicitely embrac'd, over-ballance those, which are owing either to abstract reasoning or experience" (T.117). "Education is an artificial and not a natural cause", according to Hume, "built almost on the same foundation of custom and repetition as our reasonings from causes and effects" (ibid.). We can see its artificial character most clearly "from the effects of discipline and education on animals, who by the proper application of rewards and punishments may be taught any course of action the most contrary to their natural instincts and propensities" (E.113). Since Hume attributes "all belief and reasoning" to custom (T.115), it is inevitable that he should treat education as the inculcation of habits. Moreover, "no man can have any other experience but his own. The Experience of others becomes his only by the credit which he gives to their testimony" (L.1.349). Discussions of education and of testimony thus go hand in hand. By reflecting on the nature of testimony, Hume comes to see the social nature of man, and four main elements characterise his view. Firstly, man is born into a group, which trains him in its ways. Secondly, our claims must be public, because we learn from others and are tested by them. Thirdly, man exhibits "an inclination to truth and a principle of probity" (E.119); this principle secures the possibility of communication. Fourthly, languages are gradually established by human conventions, enabling groups to achieve common goals. Since we shall discuss these last points in the next two chapters, we can now turn to the views of Hume's predecessors, and to his own development of them.

Testimony and analogy: (a) Hume's predecessors

The works of Sextus Empiricus were re-discovered in the late sixteenth century. Montaigne, Mersenne and Gassendi all helped to revive interest in Sextus's arguments, and under the threat of his scepticism the search for a criterion of truth had become a prominent task for theologians by the first half of the seventeenth century.[1] During the Counter-Reformation, Catholics used sceptical arguments as a defence against the individual assertions of faith by the Reformers, and in response Protestants pursued sceptical arguments about the meaning and reliability of historical documents. In fact, theologians before Luther, including Origen, had worried about such issues, and Hume must have known, at least through Bayle or Collins, of the fundamental questions about Biblical interpretation raised by the seventeenth-century Catholic scholar, Richard Simon.[2] Hume recognised that the sceptic challenged the secular philosopher as much as the theologian: "What would become of *history* had we not a dependence on the veracity of the historian according to the experience which we have had of mankind?" (E.99). "If we proceed not upon some fact present to the memory or senses, our reasonings would be merely hypothetical" (E.59). From his allusions and implicit borrowings it is clear that Hume studied the thoughts of his predecessors on the matter with the greatest care.

In the preface to *Novum Organum* Bacon had recommended a middle way between the extremes of dogmatically denying the force of scepticism, and yielding to it completely. His warning that, whereas philosophical systems lead to dogmatism, the errors of the senses, personal idiosyncrasies and misleading language lead to scepticism, was widely canvassed in the seventeenth century; and his emphasis, albeit rather scholastic, on the role of analogies in reasoning about experience and the need to search for causes, was equally well known.[3] Within a few years of the publication of Bacon's work in 1620, and under the initial inspiration of it, a group of liberal English theologians was publicly discussing the nature of religious knowledge and certainty. Among these writers mention should be made of John Tillotson, subsequently Archbishop of Canterbury, because Hume quotes him prominently at the beginning of the essay on miracles (E.117; also LG.23). It is likely that Hume had read the work of others in the group, such as Joseph Glanvill,[4] since he refers to French disputants such as Nicole, Claude and Huet, as well as later British writers such as Collins, Tindal, Foster and Hoadly.[5] Like Grotius earlier, and Locke later, Tillotson distinguishes kinds of evidence, ranging from immediate sense-perception to the testimony of others. In *The Rule of Faith*, 1666, he searches for a criterion of truth, particularly for religious beliefs, and he remarks, possibly under the influence of the Port-Royal *Logic*:

> We are not infallibly certain that any Book is so ancient as it pretends to be, or that it was written by him whose Name it bears, or that this is the Sense of such and such Passages in it; it is possible all this may be otherwise, *that is,* it implies no Contradiction: But we are very well assured that it is not; nor hath any prudent Man any just Cause to make the least Doubt of it. For a bare Possibility that a Thing may

be, or not be, is no just Cause of doubting whether a Thing be or not. It is possible all the people of *France* may die this Night; but I hope the Possibility of this doth not incline any Man in the least to think it will be so: It is possible the Sun may not rise to Morrow Morning; and yet, for all this, I suppose no Man hath the least Doubt but that it will. [6]

Hume made similar remarks in the *Treatise* (e.g. T.124), and certainly agreed with Tillotson and others who made the same point, that one should proportion assent to the evidence available. Tillotson described the kinds of evidence in a sermon of 1664, 'The Wisdom of being Religious':

> *Aristotle* hath long since well observed, how unreasonable it is to expect the same kind of proof and evidence for every thing, which we have for some things. *Mathematical* things, being of an abstracted nature, are capable of the clearest and strictest *Demonstration*: But Conclusions in *Natural Philosophy* are capable of proof by an *Induction* of experiments; things of a *moral* nature by *moral* arguments; and *matters of fact* by *credible testimony*. And tho' none of these be capable of that strict kind of *demonstration*, which Mathematical matters are; yet have we an undoubted assurance of them, when they are prov'd by the best arguments that things of that kind will bear. [7]

Referring explicitly to this passage, Hume says that a distinction between such kinds of evidence was intended

> *only* to mark a Difference betwixt them, not to denote a Superiority of one above another. *Moral Certainty* may reach as *high* a Degree of Assurance as *Mathematical*; and our Senses are surely to be comprised amongst the clearest and most convincing of all Evidences.

Accordingly, one should recognise that a principle such as '*That whatever begins to exist must have a Cause of Existence*'

> is supported by *moral Evidence*, and is followed by a Conviction of the same kind with these Truths, *That all Men must die*, and that *the Sun will rise To-morrow*. Is this any Thing like denying the Truth of that Proposition, which indeed *a Man must have lost all common Sense to doubt of*? (LG.22)

Hume rejects the arguments for the necessity of a cause put forward by Hobbes, Clarke and Locke (T.80). In his chapter 'Of Religion', Hobbes had written that

> men that know not what it is that we call *causing*, (that is, almost all men) have no other rule to guess by, but by observing, and remembering what they have seen to precede the like effect at some other time, or times before, without seeing between the antecedent and subsequent Event, any dependance or connexion at all: And therefore from the like things past, they expect the like things to come. [8]

In the following paragraphs Hobbes repeats the ancient view that men

created their gods out of ignorance of causes and fear of the future, and
he speculates on how men decide which properties to ascribe to God,
concluding that "those Attributes are to be held significative of Honour,
that men intend shall so be".[9] He points out that men wonder at and find
admirable two classes of things: very strange events, and those they can
imagine to have been done only by the hand of God. Many later writers,
including Locke, agreed with Hobbes that "the same thing, may be a
Miracle to one, and not to another".[10] Moreover, men are apt to be
deceived by miracle claims ("false miracles") but, Hobbes adds, "a
private man has always the liberty, (because thought is free,) to believe,
or not believe in his heart, those acts that have been given out for
Miracles".[11] Although Hobbes raises the question of the authority and
interpretation of the Bible, he does not directly confront the issue of
testimony in the way his immediate successors were to do.[12]

We have already discussed some of the basic tenets of the Port-Royal
Logic, but it has not been generally noticed that four chapters of Book IV
are devoted to the following topics:

12. Of what we know through Faith, whether Human or Divine.
13. Some rules for the right direction of Reason in the belief of
    events which depend on human faith.
14. Application of the preceding rule to the belief in Miracles.
15. Another remark on the same subject of belief in events.

The authors assert that "the simple possibility of an event is not a
sufficient reason to make me believe in it"; to determine whether or not
to believe it, it is not necessary to consider it in itself, as one would a proposition in geometry, but it is necessary to take account of all the internal
and external circumstances which accompany it. External factors are
those which belong to the persons by whose testimony we are led to
believe it. Applying this rule to miracle-claims, the authors deplore the
attitudes of both those who doubt none, lest they should be required to
doubt all, and those, like Montaigne,[13] who doubt all because they are
required to doubt some. But the otherwise admirable rule of the free-
thinkers, to believe only what is proportionate to their reason, is too weak
to persuade anyone of a miracle; and it "is no argument that a miracle has
occurred, that something similar happened on other occasions". Arnauld
and Nicole assert that frequently a fact which is scarcely probable, because
of a single circumstance which is usually a mark of falsehood, should be
reckoned certain because of other circumstances. The authors are stressing the importance of establishing the fullest possible context in which
miracle-claims are made, and in the following discussion they urge that
we should content ourselves with moral certainty in contexts where metaphysical certainty is unattainable. When even moral certainty is lacking,
the authors suggest a primitive frequency test, in conjunction with the
notion of common circumstances (*circonstances communes*) which are said

to accompany truth more than falsehood, to determine whether a report is false; such a view was still being canvassed by Chambers in his *Cyclopaedia*. One of the many failings in their brief discussion is that the authors try to use as a criterion of truth for contingent propositions a further set of contingent propositions subject to all the objections they have raised. In the final chapter of the *Logic* a brief account of probability is outlined, concerning belief in future events, and it is to this discussion that Hume refers when lamenting recent failures to sustain reflection on probability (A.184).[14]

In a short but influential chapter on probability, to which Hume refers and from which he and numerous other writers borrowed the example of the East Indian and the ice (E.121), Locke lists six factors to be considered when assessing the testimony of others:

> 1. The number. 2. The integrity. 3. The skill of the witnesses. 4. The design of the author, where it is a testimony out of a book cited.
> 5. The consistency of the parts, and circumstances of the relation.
> 6. Contrary testimonies. (*Essay*, IV.xv.4)

In the following chapters on degrees of assent, Locke echoes Hobbes in asserting that we should "proportion the assent to the different evidence and probability of the thing" (IV.xvi.9; cp. xix.1); adoption of such a maxim is a criterion of loving truth for its own sake. Locke remarks that in the laws of England only a first attested copy of a record is accepted as proof, not copies of copies: "in traditional truths, each remove weakens the force of the proof, and the more hands the tradition has successively passed through, the less strength and evidence does it receive from them". In the case of historical evidence, he asserts that "no probability can arise higher than its first original" (IV.xvi.11), and the testimony of a single witness, however many times it is quoted subsequently, "must stand or fall by its own testimony". Where sensory evidence is not available, analogy is the great rule of probability, as Bacon and others had insisted, but there is one case where the "strangeness of the fact lessens not the assent to a fair testimony given of it": well-attested miracles. Faith is assent given "upon the credit of the Proposer, as coming from God, in some extraordinary way of communication" (IV.xviii.2). But how can we guarantee that a divine revelation has really occurred (IV.xvi.14, xviii.6, xix.9), especially since "faith can never convince us of anything, that contradicts our knowledge" (IV.xviii.5)? Reason is the ultimate judge of whether revelation has occurred and faith is appropriate (IV.xviii.6, xix.14), and reason is the only safeguard against enthusiasm (IV.xix.3). Locke repeats the ancient insight that the "strength of our persuasions are no evidence at all of their own rectitude" (xix.11), a truth which Hume curiously disregards in his own account of the vivacity of belief; as Locke remarks, "if reason must not examine their truth by something extrinsical to the persuasions themselves, inspirations and delusions, truth and falsehood, will have the same measure, and will not be possible to be distinguished" (xix.14).[15]

Two features of passages such as those quoted were quite clear to friend and foe alike: first, no criterion of testimony had been found and no guarantee of miracles established; second, before long it was likely that someone hostile to religion would avoid the circumlocution and would plainly spell out the consequences. Although Hume never cites the work, he must have known John Toland's *Christianity not Mysterious*, 1696, which was generally taken as applying Locke's principles, and as initiating the Deist controversies of the next few years. Toland states that "the Evidence of Fact solely depends upon Testimony" and "whoever tells us something we did not know before, *his Words must be intelligible, and the Matter possible*". Therefore a miracle, defined as contravening the laws of nature, "must be something in it self intelligible and possible, though the manner of doing it be extraordinary".[16] Shaftesbury too, deeply influenced by Bayle, speculated on the credibility of miracles, and the nature of testimony and textual interpretation. He emphasised that any ancient text is liable to corruption through mistakes by copyists, transcribers, editors; we also need to take account of alternative readings, and variations within the texts themselves (*Characteristics*, 1.97). If testimony lacks a guarantee, "the attestation of men dead and gone, in behalf of miracles past and at an end, can never surely be of equal force with miracles present"; so "the truest mark of a believing Christian is to seek after no sign or miracle" (11.90, 88). Moreover,

> whoever is not conscious of revelation, nor has certain knowledge of any miracle or sign, can be no more than sceptic in the case; and the best Christian in the world, who being destitute of the means of certainty depends only on history and tradition for his belief in these particulars, is at best but a sceptic Christian. He has no more than a nicely critical historical faith, subject to various speculations, and a thousand different criticisms of languages and literature. (11.201)

Such a view is confirmed by those competent to judge original texts for themselves, and by the majority who must rely on the "unbiassed and disinterested judges of these religious narratives" (ibid.). But in the latter case, a man's "confidence and trust must be in those modern men, or societies of men, to whom the public or he himself ascribes the judgment of these records"; in all such contexts, "even the highest implicit faith is in reality no more than a kind of passive scepticism". Since the early Gnostics were condemned as heretics for claiming knowledge in the mysteries of faith, the safest opinion "must be the sceptical and modest" (11.202–3).

In its original constitution Christianity was "diametrically opposed" to "philosophy or refined speculation", but as ignorance and its attendant superstition increased in late Roman times, and as philosophical schools dissolved, their inmates became ecclesiastical instructors, with the result that "a sort of philosophical enthusiasm overspread the world" (II.207). Hume incorporated these views into his own essays on religion (G.I.135, 182). Shaftesbury contends that superstition, which is a kind of fear, flourishes in proportion to the number of priests and soothsayers who "receive advantage by officiating in religious affairs" (*Characteristics*, II.184). Many religious faiths, however contradictory or far-fetched, "have been raised on the foundation of miracles and pretended commissions from heaven", and men have co-operated towards imposture (II.219). But terrors, even when accompanied by miracles, are insufficient to explain the "first beginning" of religious belief, even if they do suffice for sustaining beliefs "founded in that natural complacency and good humour which inclines to trust and confidence in mankind" (II.226).

On the authority of the scriptures, Shaftesbury observes that "it belongs to mere enthusiasts and fanatics to plead the sufficiency of a reiterate translated text, derived to them through so many channels and subjected to so many variations, of which they are wholly ignorant". The "collateral testimony of the ancient records, historians and foreign authors" is crucial to establish the authority of the Bible, and if such texts were lost, scepticism would triumph (II.301–2). The most striking remarks, however, occur at the end of *Miscellany III* (Ch.3), where Shaftesbury discusses the nature of textual interpretation, particularly of scripture, and in a way which Leland, subsequently,[17] took Tindal to have expressed even more forcefully, and yet to have been effectively answered by the orthodox. The first question concerns identification of the material to be studied: which texts, or parts of them, are to be counted as canonical, and why; in which languages, translations, copies or transcripts, belonging to which parties or sects? Second, there is the problem of possible variations in interpretation. Even "when the grammatical sense is found out, we are many times never the nearer"; few passages are susceptible of only one interpretation, and "there is no certain mark to determine whether the sense of these passages should be taken as literal or figurative" (II.354–7). In defence of his questions Shaftesbury cites the doubts expressed in 1657, that is, after Hobbes but before the Port-Royal *Logic* or Tillotson, by Bishop Jeremy Taylor. In *The Liberty of Prophesying*, published in 1648, Taylor discussed the freedom of interpretation of sacred literature. He listed the enormous difficulties confronting any interpreter of ancient texts; reason must be the final judge, and "our confidence should be according to our evidence, and our zeal according to our confidence" (quoted II.359n). Although Taylor was quoted, along with Richard Simon, by other free-thinkers such as Collins,[18] Hume himself made only limited use of such views (E.140), and ignored their relevance to literary criticism when discussing that topic.

Shaftesbury offers a formal definition:

> To believe nothing of a designing principle or mind, nor any cause, measure, or rule of things, but chance, so that in Nature neither the interest of the whole nor of any particulars can be said to be in the least designed, pursued, or aimed at, is to be a perfect Atheist. (*Characteristics*, 1.240)

It is doubtful, however, whether anyone is either a "perfect" atheist or theist, according to such strict conditions, especially if a man's opinion is taken to be what is "most habitual to him". Such considerations lie behind the contention that religion "is capable of doing great good or harm, and atheism nothing positive either way" (1.265).

It is necessary to refer only briefly to the views of Berkeley and Butler, from among Hume's predecessors, before turning to his own reflections on testimony and analogy. Berkeley's *Alciphron*, 1732, is an attack on Mandeville, Shaftesbury and other free-thinkers, although no one is actually named.[19] The discussion of testimony in Dialogues VI and VII outlines Shaftesbury's position (*Characteristics*, II.354ff.), with Alciphron observing that reports of miracles have been handed down by tradition, "and tradition . . . gives but a weak hold: it is a chain, whereof the first links may be stronger than steel, and yet the last as weak as wax, and brittle as glass" (VI.222). A man's heart, mind or memory may all distort judgment, and thus "no divine faith can possibly be built upon tradition". At this point he is accused of introducing a general scepticism into human knowledge, and of thereby threatening the stability of civil government; moreover, "suppose you read a passage in Tacitus that you believe true; would you say you assented to it on the authority of the printer or transcriber rather than the historian?" (VI.224). One should distinguish what is unintelligible from mere nonsense. No criteria are offered for such a distinction, but it presumably alludes to requirements of writers such as Toland for intelligible propositions and possible events. Berkeley's characters then insist that when interpreting the scriptures one should seek to "know the intention of the speaker, to be able to know whether his style be obscure through defect or design" (VI.230, 233). Free-thinkers, when reading Horace or Perseus, make due allowance for "transpositions, omissions and literal errors of transcribers", but resist such moves over sacred texts, and in their appeal to reason and common sense they "mean only the sense of their own party" (VI.235, 243). Further, they overlook "how rarely men are swayed or governed by mere ratiocination, and how often by faith, in the natural or civil concerns of the world; how little they know, and how much they believe", and how much better qualified men are "to receive truth upon testimony than to deduce it from principles". "A spirit of trust or reliance runs through the whole system of life and opinion" (VI.255).

Hume, and the free-thinkers, would agree with such observations, but insist that they merely define the problem, and not the solution.

> [T]he main points of Christian belief have been infused so early, and inculcated so often, by nurses, pedagogues, and priests, that, be the proofs ever so plain, it is a hard matter to convince a mind, thus tinctured and stained, by arguing against revealed religion from its internal characters. (VI.258)

There must therefore be examination of both internal and external collateral evidence. But the more Alciphron presses such views, the more his opponents insist that "probable arguments are a sufficient ground of faith" (VI.280); to which he replies that no testimony amounts to a demonstration, "no testimony can make nonsense sense; no moral evidence can make contradictions consistent" (VII.286). "Things obscure and unaccountable in human affairs or the operations of nature may yet be possible, and, if well attested, may be assented unto; but religious assent or faith can be evidently shewn in its own nature to be impracticable, impossible, and absurd" (ibid.). Alciphron maintains that

> all degrees of assent, whether founded on reason or authority, more or less cogent, are internal acts of the mind, which alike terminate in ideas as their proper object; without which there can be really no such thing as knowledge, faith, or opinion. (VI.288)

In reply it is urged that words have many uses apart from that of exciting ideas in our minds, and several kinds of words cannot be said to stand for ideas. Whereas we may have picturable ideas of corporeal objects, we may be said to have non-picturable *notions* of mental phenomena; and terms such as *gravity* and *vis inertiae* have frequently been used, notwithstanding difficulties over their proper explanation (VII.294).[20] A man may thus show a practical faith in his actions, even in the absence of "precise, distinct ideas" (VII.299). Sceptics, like other people, are members of the community, and their capacity to distinguish good from evil may well serve them through life. For some energetic minds, it is no doubt proper to "examine and compare the differing institutions of religion" and to "consider their rise and progress" (VII.326). Hume accepted the challenge.

Joseph Butler's *The Analogy of Religion*, to which Hume alludes in the *Treatise* (e.g. T.424), was published in 1736, but it makes no reference to Berkeley. It begins with the avowedly Lockean affirmation that "to Us probability is the very guide to life" (3) but urges that, in spite of Locke's work, the subject of probability "has not yet been thoroughly considered". Hume's agreement on this point (A.184) may have prompted him to send Butler the first two volumes of the *Treatise* (L.I.27), as I suggested in the first chapter. Butler himself, however, offers little new thought on the topic.

Butler assumes without argument "an author of Nature" and a doctrine of final causes (38–9), but begins with reflections on personal identity, in order to support his further assumption that "mankind is appointed to live in a future state" (10):

> there is in every case a probability, that all things will continue as we experience they are, in all respects, except those in which we have some reason to think they will be altered. This is that *kind* of presumption or probability from analogy, expressed in the very word *continuance*, which seems our only natural reason for believing the course of the world will continue tomorrow, as it has done so far as our experience or knowledge of history can carry us back. (15)

Hume agreed with Butler that "there is not any action or natural event, which we are acquainted with, so single and unconnected, as not to have a respect to some other actions and events" (*Analogy of Religion*, 131; cp. Hume, E.98); further, "experience also shows many means to be conducive and necessary to accomplish ends, which means, before experience, we should have thought would have had even a contrary tendency" (135). A miracle, Butler declares, "in its very notion, is relative to a course of nature", but when considering miracles, it should be remembered that "there be the presumption of millions to one, against the most common facts", for example, "against the story of Caesar, or of any other man" (174–7). In the religious context, "the only material question is, whether there be any such presumption against miracles, as to render them in any sort incredible" (ibid.). Butler's main point seems to be that, of the countless possibilities we may entertain in our "thoughts" (177), very few are actualised, and we require experience as "proof" of those which are; it is in this sense that there is a presumption against what actually happens, and against all contingent reports. He adds that, given our ignorance of nature on the one hand, and the occurrence of strange phenomena such as comets or the effects of powers such as magnetism and electricity on the other, it cannot be said that miracles are incredible. Nevertheless, he agrees that "it is from our finding, that the course of nature, in some respects and so far, goes on by general laws, that we conclude this of the rest"; we always assume the operation of general laws, because we all agree that there is no such thing as chance (201).

It is true that any single fact of such antiquity as is related in the New Testament "may have *general doubts* raised concerning it, from the very nature of human affairs and human testimony". But we believe human testimony, partly because men are "naturally endowed" with a capacity to distinguish truth from falsehood, and partly because they are "as naturally" "endowed with veracity or a regard to truth in what they say" (254, 261). Until proof or probability be brought against the evidence of testimony, "the *natural* laws of human actions require, that testimony be admitted" (263). In fact, in daily life, we often "act upon evidence much lower than what is commonly called probable" (249), although, Butler adds, when they are available "probable proofs, by being added, not only increase the evidence, but multiply it" (290).

Summary. The discussion so far may be summarised as follows:

1. With the revival of interest in scepticism, seventeenth-century writers returned to the ancient search for criteria of truth and certainty, often, like Descartes, merging the two. Adopting the old distinction between mathematical and empirical truths, they all recognised the importance of insisting that the mere possibility of an event was an insufficient ground for belief or disbelief (Tillotson, Port-Royal).

2. It was reasonable to believe that the sun would rise tomorrow, because of the general rule that it is reasonable to expect like things in the future when there have been like things in the past (Bacon, Hobbes). Strange things happen, however, although the strangeness is essentially due to our ignorance of causes. Such ignorance itself causes fear, which leads to superstition, religion, and often to claims of miracles. The nature of the causal connection must clearly be a fundamental question (Hobbes: cp. Cicero and Malebranche, in the previous chapter).

3. To establish the truth of miracle-claims it is necessary to examine in detail the context in which they are made, as well as the internal nature of the claims themselves. The Port-Royal introduced a criterion of truth for contingent propositions which consisted of a further set of contingent propositions subject to all the original objections.

4. Locke, while accepting a standard distinction between intuitive, demonstrative and sensitive knowledge (*Essay*, IV.ii.I), held, like Descartes, that without appeal to self-evidence somewhere, a search for a criterion leads to an infinite regress (IV.vii.19). Nevertheless, in assessing testimony, he lists six factors to be considered, and urges that "no probability can arise higher than its first original". Reason must be the ultimate judge of whether revelation has occurred.

5. Shaftesbury extends reflection on the authority and reliability of ancient texts, pointing out the need to identify the canonical versions as well as the preferred interpretations. The difficulties might be taken to cast doubt on the wisdom of grounding so much on so little. He points out that since faith is contrasted with and substituted for knowledge, it must count as a form of scepticism; but he admits, with his predecessors, that no one can be an absolute sceptic, or, indeed, a "perfect Theist".

6. If there are difficulties over testimony and ancient texts, there are also difficulties in how theological claims are to be understood; one can be asked to believe only intelligible claims about possible events (Toland). Berkeley tries to make theological use of his view that not all ideas are derived from sensory evidence, and not all words stand for ideas (cp. Port-Royal). The latter point does more to underline than to reduce the problems of assessing testimony and interpreting texts.

7. In everyday life we have to make do with all kinds and degrees of

evidence (Tillotson, Locke, Butler), and we believe testimony because we can generally distinguish truth from falsehood, and because people generally tell the truth. But the general rule does not help us to determine whether a particular case falls under it.

8. The central questions therefore remained: under what conditions is it reasonable to believe in or assent to an empirical claim? what techniques are appropriate for assessing claims about the past? Such questions might well presuppose others about the source and nature of the ideas expressed in such claims, and the conditions of meaningful utterance. Hume thought so. The question of testimony, therefore, although acute for theologians, was not confined to them; it is central in any attempt to deal with scepticism.

Testimony and analogy: (b) Hume

Hume discusses testimony on three main occasions. Observations in the *Treatise* (I.iii.9), which is possibly the place from which the original essay on miracles was excised, are incomplete and need to be supplemented in the light of what is said in Books II and III about the social nature of man. Hume incorporates those views in his modified account in the first *Enquiry*, and his practical attitude towards testimony is revealed in an unpublished essay. His clearest views on analogy are expressed in the *Dialogues concerning Natural Religion*.

It would be natural for Hume to reflect on the nature of testimony whenever he addresses a problem which, in its most general formulation, requires a solution from any sceptically minded philosopher, and which manifests itself most obviously in religious contexts: why do men believe what logic shows to be suspect, and fail to believe what logic shows to be incontrovertible? By an examination of the "nature", "causes" and "effects" of belief (*Treatise*, I.iii.7, 8, 10), Hume initially tries to argue that belief and logic are essentially independent of each other. His explicit conclusions about testimony are unsatisfactory, however, not only because of his views on belief, but because of confusion about several other basic notions which bear on the topic, such as experience, custom, sentiment, resemblance, evidence, reasoning, probability. Eventually, as a result of reflection on the roles of reason and sentiment in moral and aesthetic judgments, Hume formulates a notion of appropriate response, which usefully amplifies earlier remarks on many related topics, including the assessment of testimony. We shall consider that revised notion of a response in the next chapter.

Hume's first thoughts on testimony reveal the directions of his enquiry, and they should be quoted at length:

> No weakness of human nature is more universal and conspicuous than what we commonly call CREDULITY, or a too easy faith in the testimony of others; and this weakness is also very naturally

accounted for from the influence of resemblance. When we receive any matter of fact upon human testimony, our faith arises from the very same origin as our inferences from causes to effects, and from effects to causes; nor is there any thing but our *experience* of the governing principles of human nature, which can give us any assurance of the veracity of men. But tho' experience be the true standard of this, as well as of all other judgments, we seldom regulate ourselves entirely by it; but have a remarkable propensity to believe what is reported, even concerning apparitions, enchantments, and prodigies, however contrary to daily experience and observation. The words or discourses of others have an intimate connection with certain ideas in their mind; and these ideas have also a connection with the facts or objects, which they represent. This latter connection is generally much over-rated, and commands our assent beyond what experience will justify; which can proceed from nothing beside the resemblance betwixt the ideas and the facts. Other effects only point out their causes in an oblique manner; but the testimony of men does it directly, and is to be consider'd as an image as well as an effect. No wonder, therefore, we are so rash in drawing our inferences from it, and are less guided by experience in our judgments concerning it, than in those upon any other subject. (T.112–3)

Hume claims that because our imagination tends to operate beyond its proper limits once it gets under way, we often assume a greater resemblance than in fact exists between the present and the past, as is clear when we too readily believe another's testimony. Although the assumption of resemblance is grounded in experience, so is our knowledge of its limits; because that knowledge fails to check the imagination, Hume concludes that testimony can only be weighed through the calculation of probabilities.[21] It is not necessary here to discuss Hume's account of probability, but we do need to reflect briefly on his remarks about belief, which, as his comments in the Appendix testify, he regards as of great importance.

Hume sharply separates himself from the Port-Royal *Logic*, and from Malebranche, in claiming that there are not three "acts of the understanding", namely conception, judgment and reasoning, but only one; there are only different "ways of conceiving". His view is that belief is "only a strong and steady conception of any idea, and such as approaches in some measure to an immediate impression" (T.96n; cp. 164). The peculiarities of his view, as Hume would be the first to admit, are largely due to his previous definitions and his precise goals; in the present context Hume wants to prove that man is not motivated by his reasoning faculty, while conceding that beliefs can function as causes of actions. To enable an agent to discern the cause of his action Hume assumes that there must be an experientially detectable item in the mind, and he thus concentrates on the "merely internal" experience of belief (T.102); moreover, he restricts his attention to causally efficacious beliefs, that is, the beliefs on which it can be said we act, and that partly explains why he equates belief with assent and a feeling of conviction. "The chief spring and moving principle of all" the actions of the mind is the perception of pleasure and pain, but perceptions themselves are divisible into impressions and ideas, each of which can vary in strength, vivacity or intensity (T.118); only the most vivid ideas have the force or "power of actuating the will" (T.119). Indeed, without the mind's capacity to enliven "some ideas beyond others (which seemingly is so trivial, and so little founded on reason) we cou'd never assent to any argument" (T.265). If it be asked, however, "by what criterion" the "truth" can be distinguished, "no reason" for assent can be given; all that an individual can find is a feeling or propensity to consider certain things "strongly" (ibid.). Thus: "belief consists merely in a certain feeling or sentiment; in something, that depends not on the will, but must arise from certain determinate causes and principles, of which we are not masters"; in this sense, *belief is more properly an act of the sensitive, than of the cogitative part of our natures*" (T.624 Appendix; 183).

An aesthetic analogy which echoes Bayle and in the end leads Hume towards a slightly better account, is stated at the outset of his discussion:

all probable reasoning is nothing but a species of sensation. 'Tis not solely in poetry and music, we must follow our taste and sentiment, but likewise in philosophy. When I am convinc'd of any principle, 'tis only an idea, which strikes more strongly upon me. When I give the preference to one set of arguments above another, I do nothing but decide from my feeling concerning the superiority of their influence. (T.103)

Hume contends that "the degree of evidence" is "proportion'd" to the "degree of force and vivacity" of the sentiment (T.153). There is an important factor, however, which is central to Hume's philosophy, although it is rarely formulated: "The mind, as well as the body, seems to be endow'd with a certain precise degree of force and vivacity, which it never employs in one action, but at the expence of all the rest" (T.186). That is why "conviction, which arises from a subtile reasoning, diminishes in proportion to the efforts, which the imagination makes to enter into the reasoning", and why "sceptical reasonings" are "destroy'd by their subtility" (ibid.). The sustained and subtle reasonings of philosophers lack impact because they are essentially unnatural and forced, and cannot offset the customary responses of man which have been proved by experience to be sufficient for common life. "Belief, being a lively conception, can never be entire, where it is not founded on something natural and easy" (ibid.).

Because of his insistence that "abstract or demonstrative reasoning" "never influences any of our actions", reason being "inert" or "inactive in itself" (T.414; 457), and that the "motions of the mind" depend on "certain peculiar sentiments of pain and pleasure" (T.574), Hume has to associate beliefs with such sentiments if he is to avoid the paradoxical conclusion that beliefs cannot influence action either. Hume, so far, has defined assent or conviction as an involuntary, but detectable, feeling or impulse or disposition to act, which co-exists easily with our other dispositions (cp. T.185); thoughts which lack intensity sufficient to activate the mind presumably ought not to be classified as beliefs, and the notion of suspended belief ought to be analysed in terms of one disposition dominating another. But if Hume sets aside such questions when considering the experience of belief from the first-person standpoint, along with all the cognitive questions of the meaning, truth and verification of the content of beliefs, he acknowledges such questions when considering man as a social being; had he not done so, indeed, his view of belief would have been identical with Locke's definition of faith as "nothing but a firm assent of the Mind" confirmed by reason, and, worse, to the view that "persuasions are right, because they are strong" (Locke, *Essay*, IV.xix.9; xvii.24).

Although Hume is concerned to "explain the *causes* of the firm conception", and to show that "the *effects* of belief, in influencing the passions and imagination, can all be explain'd from the firm conception" (T.626), he faces the problem, recognised by most of his predecessors from Cicero to Locke, of whether any inner experience can be an adequate criterion of knowledge; Locke, it will be recalled, insisted that reason must be able to distinguish between "inspirations and delusions" by reference to "something extrinsical to the persuasions themselves" (IV.xix.14). In his constant battle against superstition, Hume must differentiate his notions of belief and faith. In the next chapter we shall see how he realised that he could afford to give only very qualified support to the claim that "all sentiment is right; because sentiment has a reference to nothing beyond itself, and is always real, wherever a man is conscious of it" (G.I.268). In the *Treatise*, Hume claims that "a passion" can only "be call'd unreasonable, but when founded on a false supposition, or when it chuses means insufficient for the design'd end"; and it is "not the passion, properly speaking, which is unreasonable, but the judgment" (T.416). His account is almost always causal; one can displace another man's belief or conviction only by exposing him to causes which will produce new beliefs. Later, Hume implicitly acknowledges the active and cognitive roles of belief in perception, whereby a man can think of phenomena under differing descriptions; the germs of such a view appear in Books II and III, but are not evident in Book I of the *Treatise*.

At the outset of his discussion in that book, Hume asserts that most men do not "really believe" "what they pretend to affirm" about a future state and the immortality of the soul. Indeed, they *cannot* believe, because "the want of resemblance" between our present life and "our future condition" permits ideas that are too faint to count as belief. Only those who "have taken care by repeated meditation to imprint in their minds the arguments for a future state" can be said to have a belief parallel in intensity to one "deriv'd from the testimony of travellers and historians" (T.114). The question to ask is whether the repetition of experiences or thoughts necessary for such conviction is customary or in any sense natural. In due course, Hume tries to establish that religious beliefs are not natural, in any significant sense. When, however, a few sections later he returns to the topic of testimony in the present context, he acknowledges two problems, the first of which we met in the reflections of his predecessors: is it possible to prevent the increasing unreliability of information re-iterated over a period of time, and is it possible to offset the fact that our ideas become less vivid, and thus less convincing, as they recede in time from their original, exciting impressions? (T.144). The latter problem arises in connection with all phenomena subject to the principle of decaying sense. Hume declares that "there is no point of ancient history, of which we can have any assurance, but by passing thro' many millions of causes and effects, and thro' a chain of arguments of almost an immeasurable length"; indeed, "if belief consisted only in a certain vivacity, convey'd from an original impression, it wou'd decay by the length of the transition, and must at last be utterly extinguish'd". It would seem to follow, as in the present example, that "the evidence of all ancient history must now be lost" (T.145). Hume's reply does not meet the force of the objection. He asserts that if we assume both the reliability of the connection between the original fact and impression, and "the fidelity of Printers and Copists" without variation, "the evidence of history" is preserved. But even theologians had doubted the second assumption, and the first assumption begs the question, as Hume gradually realises as a result of reflection on miracle-claims, the nature of historical interpretation, and the assessment of analogies. Anxiety about historical reports is parasitic upon confidence about present-tense reports, but Hume offers no guidance on how their appropriateness is to be judged. He merely asserts, with respect to the former:

> If all the long chain of causes and effects, which connect any past event with any volume of history, were compos'd of parts different from each other, and which 'twere necessary for the mind distinctly to conceive, 'tis impossible we shou'd preserve to the end any belief or evidence. But as most of these proofs are perfectly resembling, the mind runs easily along them, jumps from one part to another with facility, and forms but a confus'd and general notion of each link. By this means a long chain of argument, has little effect in diminishing the original vivacity, as a much shorter wou'd have, if compos'd of

parts, which were different from each other, and of which each
requir'd a distinct consideration. (T.146)

Hume barely avoids saying, vacuously, that the links are sufficiently
resembling to ensure enough vivacity for belief. Hume next turns to a
notion which he has recently introduced, and which comes to play an
increasingly important part as the *Treatise* progresses: "*general rules*".
Our imagination passes "by a natural transition, which precedes reflection" between ideas having some resemblance almost as easily as it passes
between exactly resembling ideas; hence that "unphilosophical" "species
of probability, deriv'd from analogy, where we transfer our experience in
past instances to objects which are resembling, but are not exactly the
same with those concerning which we have had experience. In proportion
as the resemblance decays, the probability diminishes" (T.147). Hume
then adds, in a passage reminiscent of the Port-Royal, that although
custom is the foundation of our judgments, it sometimes works on the
imagination in opposition to them. That happens when the usual
surrounding circumstances of an event, although in no way necessary or
sufficient conditions of its occurrence, seduce the imagination to run
"away with its object", as when, safely secured, we still tremble on
looking over a precipice. Only general rules can resolve such conflict
between judgment and imagination: "by them we learn to distinguish the
accidental circumstances from the efficacious causes" (T.149). Although
these rules are themselves the products of custom, they are needed to
counteract the contrary effects of custom on our promiscuous imagination; such conflict and oscillation, Hume believes, should delight those
sceptics who wish to argue that man is not essentially governed by reason.
He later declares that "in every judgment, which we can form concerning
probability, as well as concerning knowledge, we ought always to correct
the first judgment, deriv'd from the nature of the object, by another judgment, deriv'd from the nature of the understanding" (T.181).[22] But each
judgment or check is subject to another, which introduces yet further
doubt, "and so on *in infinitum*" until, in the end, there is "a total extinction
of belief and evidence" (T.183). To explain why, in fact, we do not
experience "a total suspense of judgment", Hume develops his view that
such arguments are too strained to displace our natural responses. In
contrast to those who offered metaphysical or theological explanations of
why men's actions manifestly fail to accord with the conclusions of
reason, Hume starts from the fact that man is evidently capable of living
and surviving in apparent ignorance of even elementary philosophical
principles; and that where such principles help us to understand what
man does, they should be thought of as his essentially implicit principles
whose acquisition can be causally explained (cp. T.552, 573), and
which require no ascription to the faculty of *a priori* reason.

Hume's comments on testimony in Book I of the *Treatise* are markedly incomplete, and no account is offered there of appropriate or justified belief; the importance of general rules and of an aesthetic analogy are announced, but not explained. In the first *Enquiry*, to which we must now turn, most of his remarks on probability are omitted, belief is still treated as a sentiment, but rules are assigned a place in a more complex view of the formulation and estimation of testimony; the aesthetic analogy remains undeveloped until the essay on taste, which we shall discuss in the next chapter.

In 1846 Burton[23] suggested that a more accurate title for the essay on miracles might have been 'The Principles of Belief in Human Testimony'. The term *testimony* occurs almost fifty times in little over twenty pages, and it is clear from his locating the discussion in the context of probability judgments and his assertion that he will "apply these principles to a particular instance" (E.119), that Hume's interest is mainly in the epistemic status of miracle reports, not in the ontological status of alleged miracle events. A later passage, in which he assesses the miracle reports in the Pentateuch, in a manner now familiar to us from his predecessors, also reveals where his interest lies;[24] in addition, it reveals his occasional synonymy between "extraordinary" and "miraculous". Hume asks whether the falsity of primitive tales would be more extraordinary than the events they claim to relate (E.140). It is important to see that the assessment of probability rests on the content of the reports as well as on the context of their utterance.

In the *Treatise*, the section entitled 'Of the reason of animals' (1.iii.16) concludes the overall discussion 'Of knowledge and probability', and precedes consideration of scepticism; in the first *Enquiry*, 'Of the reason of animals' follows the more abstract discussion of causation and precedes its application in the sections 'Of Miracles' and 'Of a particular providence and of a future state'. After Descartes and Hobbes almost everyone over the next century speculated on the reasoning capacity of animals, including Malebranche, Fontenelle, Bayle and Shaftesbury from among Hume's own mentors.[25] As is well known, Hume argues that "all our reasonings concerning matter of fact are founded on a species of *analogy* which leads us to expect from any cause the same events which we have observed to result from similar causes", and that the accuracy of the analogy rests on the degree of the resemblance (E.112). Since it can be said that animals learn from experience, and in this sense infer beyond the present, but cannot by definition be said to be "directed by any such relations or comparisons of ideas as are the proper objects of our intellectual faculties", Hume concludes that "custom alone" enables us to infer. In this sense, all experimental reasoning is "a species of instinct or mechanical power that acts in us unknown to ourselves" (E.116; cp. T.327). Hume's aim, it must be remembered, is to show that man is not governed by his "understanding"; the non-*a priori* reasoning he engages in, however self-consciously, must be allocated to a source other than the understanding.

Because we can make mistaken inferences from the "supposed causes" of events, it is important to adhere to the principle of proportioning belief to the evidence (E.118). Hume begins the section on miracles by discussing the nature of evidence. He emphasises that we have to rely on testimony, that is, reports by others, not simply because no individual has enough experience to get very far but because knowledge is a social phenomenon and cannot be acquired alone. In this sense, to be further explored in the final chapter of this book, testimony is "necessary to human life". Four main points should be made. First, Hume states that our reliance on testimony is founded on the variable, and therefore non-causal, conjunction of reports and the events they report. Certain assumptions about language underlie this view, but we can re-formulate Hume's point in the following way: testimony is in general reliable, by definition, because, in a given society, only when there has been experience of conformity between kinds of events and kinds of reports are conventions developed or sanctioned which authorise the notion of testimony as something generally reliable. Hume cannot yet tell us how such general assurance aids us in a particular case of doubt, and his further points do not help. His second claim about testimony, which we met in Butler but which is essentially Ciceronian, is that our confidence in witnesses is based on an inclination in men "to truth and a principle of probity", on their shame if detected in a falsehood, and on the moderate reliability of memory (cp. T.405). Third, there is no "necessary" or "*a priori*" connection between testimony and reality, language itself being conventional. Moreover, there can be variations in both the type and amount of evidence given, and in the manner and motive in giving it, all of which are relevant in assessing its probability (E.120, 121, 124, 134). Witnesses with an interest in the matter, or of doubtful character, are to be treated with caution, as are those who deliver their reports in an uneven or unusual manner. All of this shows the importance of conventions for picking out and classifying what is going on and, even more importantly, that testimony necessarily involves interpretation both by the giver and by the receiver. Hume explicitly calls upon interpretation (E.94; M.92), but does not explain it.

The fourth point Hume makes about testimony is that "the ultimate standard by which we determine all disputes that may arise concerning them is always derived from experience and observation" (E.120). This seems to mean that we appeal to experience in order to test reports of experience, in which case we want to know whose experience is to count and why, and how the test is to be performed, a point which Leland later makes forcefully against Hume.[26] *Ex hypothesi*, we cannot appeal to our own experience to test reports by others of experiences unlike our own;

and in weighing reports we neither appeal indiscriminately to anyone, nor require the assent of everyone. Hume envisages an assessment of the context of the report in comparison with its content, as we have already indicated: is it more likely that the testimony is mistaken than that the laws of nature have been violated? (E.139). Hume relies implicitly on a notion of qualified observers to whom appeal is made in order to resolve particular disputes. On this matter he may have been influenced by Bayle's remarks on "Le jugement des experts".[27] The identity of those qualified to judge can be learned by members of the community, usually during the process of learning the procedures governing reports of the relevant kind. We shall see that in the context of art Hume adopts such a view, urging that critics exercise authority and constraint over others, but are neither infallible nor irreplaceable. Locke's East Indian prince who doubted reports of the effects of frost "reasoned justly" from his own "constant and uniform experience"; the reports he rejected, however, were not in fact "contrary to his experience", but only, in a phrase Hume borrowed from Bayle,[28] "not conformable to it" (E.121). To someone who wants to know whether an apparently singular and anomalous experience, of which he hears reports, can be subsumed together with his own experiential reports under a higher level hypothesis, Hume can offer advice only in terms of familiar general empiricist principles. Because we follow the maxim that "objects of which we have no experience resemble those of which we have" (E.124), we initially suspect observations and claims about anomalous events, and our subsequent treatment of them depends on our knowledge and interests in the context. Hume follows Cicero in observing that doctors never cite the "irregular events" they encounter as "proof that the laws of nature are not observed with the greatest regularity" (E.97).

It must be agreed that Hume had neither the scientific knowledge nor interest of writers such as Fontenelle or, later, d'Alembert, and did not discuss the nature of laws and principles, or the *ceteris paribus* condition implicit in their statement; he tends to treat them as both falsifiable empirical generalisations, and as procedural rules, in either case something whose displacement we resist for primarily methodological reasons. Hume claims that ignorant peoples, identifiable by their overall cultural behaviour and beliefs in comparison with eighteenth-century northern Europe, are more credulous than others, and that enthusiasts may persist in propagating tales they know to be false "for the sake of promoting" a holy cause. He also suggests that the pleasure of wonder or surprise, caused by miracle stories, can induce belief in them (E.125), presumably because the secondary impression of pleasure heightens the original impressions derived from the reports.

The essay on miracles is concerned with the assessment of testimony about events which fall outside Hume's account of how we learn about causal connections, since Hume takes miracle reports to be reports of unique events, the cause of which is allegedly known, even though none of the standard conditions for establishing causal connection have been fulfilled. Of course, the cause of such events, God, is 'known' only by inference, and that is why Hume turns to the question of analogical arguments in the next section of the *Enquiry*. Before looking at that discussion, however, it is important to remind ourselves briefly of some fundamental tenets in Hume's epistemology.

At the beginning of the *Treatise* Hume stressed that the relation of resemblance was part of the foundation of his whole system; resemblance is necessary to reasoning because "all kinds of reasoning consist in nothing but a *comparison*", and there can be no comparison without some degree of resemblance (T.14, 73, 142). Hume's views are initially confusing. On the one hand, impressed by the speed with which we sometimes detect resemblances, Hume asserts that the role of a percipient on those occasions is passive and non-cognitive (T.73), even instinctive (E.116); on the other hand, he says that we discern resemblances "by a distinction of reason" or "kind of reflexion", and in this sense resemblance strikes "the mind" rather than the eye (T.25, 70; cp. 165). Usually, however, he associates the detection of resemblances with the very act of thinking (T.637 Appendix insertion to T.20), and regards the relation of resemblance itself, like those of contiguity and succession, as existing "independent of, and antecedent to the operations of the understanding" (T.168). But since "even different simple ideas . . . admit of infinite resemblances upon the general appearance and comparison" (T.637) and difficulties arise from the fact that "resemblance admits of many different degrees" (T.142), it is unclear whether there are differences in type, or merely in degree, between resemblances detected instinctively, and those discerned by the more self-conscious acts of our intellectual faculties. Hume treats resemblance as both a natural and a philosophical relation, that is, as a real detectable relation between "several objects" (T.20), and as a condition of thought about any two items. It is central to his position that "probability is founded on the presumption of a resemblance betwixt those objects, of which we have had experience, and those, of which we have had none" (T.90); but it is real resemblance that he needs here, in the relevant respects and degrees, and to determine these he offers no guidance. His logical point, that without a notion of sameness there could be no concepts, and hence no reasoning, is important but separate.

A minor difference in terminology between the *Treatise* and the *Dialogues* may indicate a slight change in Hume's position. 'Resemblance' is the key term in the *Treatise*, although 'similarity' and 'analogy' (T.142) also occur; in the first *Enquiry* 'similarity' and 'analogy' (E.112) become more prominent, and in the *Dialogues* 'analogy' is the dominant term. We generally talk of observing, detecting, discovering resemblances and similarities; but of drawing, thinking up, considering and proposing analogies, activities which imply that the mind is creative. And the creative role of the mind had been emphasised rather more by French writers familiar to Hume, such as Fontenelle and most clearly Diderot, than by their British contemporaries. In the first *Enquiry* and in the *Dialogues* Hume asks several questions that he failed to raise in the *Treatise*, particularly the question of how we decide between competing analogies, and how we determine the criteria of relevance. It is likely that his reflections on these issues arose from examining the role of hypotheses in factual reasoning.

In Hume's view, to "account for" any phenomenon is to give a story of its causes and effects, which cannot be done merely by examining "the qualities of the objects as they appear to us" (T.70, 111) because, taken by itself, no object implies the existence of any other, and only by experience of causal relations can we get "beyond the immediate impressions of our memory and senses" (T.89, 86, 139). Although custom is adduced as the psychological explanation of reasonings about cause and effect (LG.8), their logical foundation is secured by a number of assumptions, variously called 'principles', 'maxims', 'rules', 'hypotheses'. "The supposition, *that the future resembles the past*", and that objects continue to exist unperceived, are two of the most important such principles in the present context, and neither is "founded on arguments of any kind" (T.134). Hume accepts that the main role of hypotheses is to render phenomena intelligible, and this means that a genuine explanation should embody a prediction beyond our present experience (cp. T.499, 551, 572). For example, "the simple supposition" of the continued existence of objects "gives us a notion of a much greater regularity among objects, than what they have when we look no farther than our senses" (T.198). Our coherence-enabling hypotheses are so important that, as he insists in the first *Enquiry*, we "still suppose a degree of uniformity and regularity" (E.95; cp. T.362) even when we have not found it. Indeed, the postulate of the uniformity of nature, which is a logical condition of all factual reasoning, would alone suffice, in Hume's view, to establish the falsity of miracle-claims. One danger of such assumptions, however, is that they are imaginative constructions or 'fictions' (from *fingo*, to feign), and the natural impetus of imagination can lead us astray. For example, having postulated the coherence of appearances, we need also to postulate constancy, and in this way come to suppose that "interrupted perceptions are connected by a real existence, of which we are insensible" (T.199). Something similar occurs in our ascriptions of identity to variable or interrupted objects (T.255). The only way to control the impetus of imagination, and thereby forestall hypostasisation, is for the judgment or understanding to impose a principle of parsimony on our hypotheses, along with a requirement of universality in their scope. The goal is to operate with as few general principles as possible, "it being an inviolable maxim in philosophy" that we "ought not to multiply causes without necessity" (T.578; cp. xxi, 282; E.45, 112). One way to achieve parsimony is to postulate analogies between phenomena, thereby enabling them to be brought under a single category or principle. The question then arises of how to control the analogies and estimate the legitimacy of inferences from them. At this point we can return to Section xi of the first *Enquiry*.

In that section Hume discusses the general principle of inferring a cause, and the particular issue of ascribing properties to an inferred cause. Those who suppose "the order of nature" to be the chief argument "for a divine existence" use thereby "an argument drawn from effects to causes". But "if the cause be known only by the effect" we are entitled to ascribe to the cause only qualities that "are exactly sufficient to produce the effect" (E.145–6). Moreover, where we infer only a sufficient condition, we cannot "by any rules of just reasoning, return back from the cause and infer other effects from it, beyond those by which alone it is known to us" (ibid.: refers to E.94). The application of this point to theology is central, and Hume repeats the passage: "While we argue from the course of nature and infer a particular intelligent cause which first bestowed and still preserves order in the universe, we embrace a principle which is both uncertain and useless" (E.151). It is useless, because of the rule just cited, and uncertain "because the subject lies entirely beyond the reach of human experience". Not only is it illegitimate to infer other effects from a merely hypothetical cause, but there is no reason to suppose that any other effects exist (E.154n).

Several points need to be made here. Hume's formal definition of the causal relation is in terms of a sufficient condition and a necessary condition; the latter, which is expressed in the subjunctive-conditional form (E.87), is suddenly introduced without warning or explanation. By definition alone, therefore, the supposition of a mere sufficient condition is not the supposition of a cause. Secondly, many theologians, as Hume well knew from contemporary debates, urged that God must be a necessary condition and First Cause, even if not the immediate efficient cause of every subsequent event. Hume by-passes all such discussion by insisting that the only causal relation is efficient (T.171: "all causes are of the same kind"), and that it can be known only through experience of ordered pairs of events. When a cause is inferred, but not known, the inference is probable to the extent that there is a relevant and determinable resemblance between the alleged effect and effects where the relation has been established; that is because the "sensible qualities" of matter, taken singly, neither reveal nor "give us ground" to suppose any causal connection (E.75). Because Hume defines the causal relation as holding between kinds of events, he seems to debar himself from admitting such a relation between allegedly unique events. He accepts, however, that "one experiment" must sometimes suffice for our causal claims, but only in virtue of the general principle, itself grounded in "millions" of experiments, *"that like objects, plac'd in like circumstances, will always produce like effects"* (T.104–5). But Hume failed to link recognition of this point with two others necessary to any adequate account. The conjunction of his two principles that "every thing in nature is individual" and that resemblance is a necessary condition of perception in a full sense (T.19, 73), implies that unique phenomena cannot be perceived in that sense. Notoriously, in spite of his discussions of identity and unity (see e.g. T.14, 30, 200), Hume offers no guidance on how to individuate and identify events or objects. Moreover, non-trivial uniqueness is relative to descriptions, and descriptions are governed by our interests and knowledge, as well as by social and linguistic conventions. It is quite contingent whether, at a given moment, any thing or event satisfies or falls under a particular description in our current or available repertoire. Descriptions are among the devices we use to structure the information we receive from the world about us, and questions about the appropriateness of a particular description require analysis of the contexts in which it is used, and the principles and theories in operation.

Hume argues that if the Deity "is a single being in the universe" and "is known to us only by his productions", then he is "not comprehended under any species or genus, from whose experienced attributes or qualities we can, by analogy, infer any attribute or quality in him" (E.153). "So far as the traces of any attributes at present appear, so far may we conclude these attributes to exist" (E.146), but, *ex hypothesi*, we have not here experienced any phenomena as traces, the description of some phenomena as 'traces' being part of the case to be established. Moreover, we must not falsify the apparent evidence in order to legitimise our desired hypothetical cause. It is therefore futile to attempt "to justify the course of nature upon suppositions . . . of which there are to be found no traces in the course of nature" (E.148). In connection with the search for unequivocal traces, it is worth recording that in the *Treatise* Hume claims that "fore-thought and design" or "intention" show "certain qualities" which remain "after the action is perform'd", and detection of such qualities is a condition of our love or hatred for the agent (T.349; cp. T.411, E.107).

"It is a maxim in all philosophy, that causes which do not appear, are to be considered as not existing" (G.1.249). These words, from an addition of 1770 to an earlier essay, reveal no essential change in Hume's view. Indeed, he concludes Section XI by expressing the "doubt whether it be possible for a cause to be known only by its effect", "or to be of so singular and particular a nature as to have no parallel and no similarity with any other cause or object that has ever fallen under our observation"; inferences are legitimate only between species of objects, and therefore "both the effect and cause must bear a similarity and resemblance to other effects and causes which we know, and which we have found in many instances to be conjoined with each other" (E.156). We lack experience to warrant any inference about what a unique god might do.

If Hume is not once again defining his opponents' views as inadmissible, there are nevertheless several points that need to be clarified. Perhaps only some mystics have claimed that God bears no resemblance to anything ever experienced; few would accept, however, that the alleged effect falls under no known species. Things are countable in virtue of belonging to kinds, and even in the absence of discussion about classification it seems likely that Hume would have regarded it as grounded in conventions; he certainly denies the intelligibility of seeking for the cause of a whole set whose members have been individually explained already, on the ground that "the uniting of these parts into a whole" is performed "merely by an arbitrary act of the mind" (D.190). Aside from these points, however, is another.[29] Precisely the excellence of the concept of gravity, an hypothetical concept Hume and his contemporaries admired for its yield, is that one can infer other effects from it although, as Newton continuously stressed, it is not itself observable. There are, of course, many concepts in common use whose analysis eludes us, but which function within limits. Hume includes different kinds within his own class of so-called 'fictions': concepts like 'chimera', which are conscious products of imagination; concepts like 'substance' which are also constructs, but often unconscious; and a group of concepts containing such members as "matter, cause and effect, extension, space, time, motion" (D.131). These last characteristically appear at the terminal points in our analyses; like "our vulgar methods of reasoning", "we cannot account for them", "even in common life and in that province which is peculiarly appropriated to them" (D.135; cp. 178). Terminal concepts mark problems for subsequent analysis, and reflect our present state of knowledge and methodology; they must not be confused with the "ultimate principles" sought by rationalists, and constantly repudiated by Hume (see e.g. T.xxi, xxii, 91, 159, 267; A.183). It is quite contingent which concepts function terminally, but necessary that some do; the important point is that all terminal concepts are in principle supersedable, and open to progressive improvement or rejection, as happened with the notion of the aether. They are coherence-enabling constructs, temporarily resistant to analysis, casting light elsewhere but themselves shrouded in gloom. These features explain why Hume omits 'God' from the set. To traditional theologians 'God' denotes a solution, not a problem for subsequent disposal, nor a concept marking our temporary ignorance. In order to show the impropriety of allowing 'God' to function as a terminal explanatory concept, Hume devotes considerable time in the *Dialogues* to such questions as: what is gained by the hypothesis of God as cause (D.160, 162, 175), what are the advantages of the view (163, 177, 183), what consequences flow from the argument (180, 183), how is arbitrary choice among hypotheses to be avoided (166, 177, 179)?

It is relevant here to consider only four of the analogies proposed in the *Dialogues*. In order to underline the importance of examining the analogies on which the religious hypothesis is based, Philo appeals to Cicero's popular example of a man who sees a house and assumes that its arrangement has resulted from quite specific causes (D.144; cp. Cicero, *De Natura Deorum*, II.v.15). Philo insists on the dissimilitude between a single house, inferences about which are grounded in our experience of other houses, and the universe taken as a whole. He introduces an important passage which can be summarised as follows: repeated experience is necessary to establish that two items are causally related, rather than merely casually conjoined; considered singly or abstractly, neither events nor ideas point to their origins or connections; only by experience can we establish which of the possibilities conjured up by imagination are actualised (D.145–6). It follows that any 'order' we find can be deemed an effect of 'design' or intention only if we have actually experienced the causal relation between the two.

The other three analogies occur at the beginning of Part III. Hume had used the first one twice before (T.225; E.41), and may have derived it from Berkeley's *Alciphron* (IV.161), although it was popular in the previous century, and even appears in Locke (*Essay*, IV.xix.15); its Biblical inspiration is obvious. In both of his earlier uses of the example, Hume argued that one "reasons justly" if, on hearing an articulate voice in the dark one concludes that someone is near. The present case differs:

> Suppose, therefore, that an articulate voice were heard in the clouds, much louder and more melodious than any which human art could ever reach: Suppose, that this voice were extended in the same instant over all nations, and spoke to each nation in its own language and dialect: Suppose, that the words delivered not only contain a just sense and meaning, but convey some instruction altogether worthy of a benevolent Being, superior to mankind: Could you possibly hesitate a moment concerning the cause of this voice? And must you not instantly ascribe it to some design or purpose? (D.152)

Cleanthes begs the question by having the "instruction altogether worthy of a benevolent Being", since it has not been established what that would be like. More seriously, neither "the cause" nor the identity of such a variously exemplified voice could be established without a great deal more experience and information than that provided; the progressive withdrawal of the characteristic features of a man's voice shows that the proper answer about its source is, as Cleanthes naively suggests, that we do not know: perhaps "from some accidental whistling of the winds" (D.153). To infer a man in the dark is to infer something with determinable properties; to describe a phenomenon as "a rational, wise, coherent speech" is not, if such a thing is possible, a purely phenomenal description, but one which presupposes a restricted range of causes. To wonder what caused the noise is not to "instantly ascribe it to some design or purpose", but merely to reveal the ubiquity of our assumption that every event has a cause.

The second example shows what may happen in an attempt, not merely to extend the boundaries but, to alter the core of a concept. Cicero had quoted Zeno's plane-trees which generated well-tuned lutes (*De Nat.* II.viii.22), and Cleanthes imagines the occurrence of books which are organically generated but which, because they are indeed books, allow us to infer the "thought and design" of their "parents". The normal inference from books to authors rests on the necessary condition that books are human products, and removal of that condition removes the legitimacy of the inference. The substitution of a new causal story of how books come about creates a new concept of book, and leaves us so far ignorant what to say about their content, let alone the properties of their causes; and a purely materialist account of their propagation might be taken to diminish the plausibility of supposing their First Cause to be, in some sense, "mind and intelligence" (D.153).

Although the first two examples are assumed to admit of straightforward interpretation and to produce immediate assent, they both involve covert conceptual revision. The third example, again from Cicero (*De Nat.* II.lvii.142), was popular among orthodox divines and freethinkers alike, and Cleanthes's version closely follows one in Maclaurin; it was supposed to be one of "the arguments for natural religion" which strike a man "with so full a force, that he cannot, without the greatest violence, prevent it" (D.154):

> Consider, anatomize the eye: Survey its structure and contrivance; and tell me, from your own feeling, if the idea of a contriver does not immediately flow in upon you with a force like that of sensation. The most obvious conclusion surely is in favour of design; and it requires time, reflection and study, to summon up those frivolous, though abstruse, objections, which can support infidelity.

Once again to "survey its structure and contrivance" is to think of the phenomena in a certain way, not merely to look at its discrete phenomenal properties; and to conclude that the idea of a contriver follows from thinking of something as a contrivance, if not a merely verbal move, is legitimate only if teleological descriptions of events presuppose agents behind those events, and if other descriptions of them are not equally "natural" and "convincing", given a proper background. The weighing of analogies itself presupposes a clear understanding of what responses are, in the relevant senses, natural. In the *Treatise*, Hume observed that in complex issues "there seldom is any very precise argument to fix our choice, and men must be contented to be guided by a kind of taste or fancy, arising from analogy, and a comparison of similar instances" (T.504n). But if this is meant as a general answer, it needs to be filled out, and Hume gives at least one hostage to fortune:

> In what sense we can talk either of a *right* or a *wrong* taste in morals, eloquence, or beauty, shall be consider'd afterwards. In the mean time, it may be observ'd, that there is such an uniformity in the *general* sentiments of mankind, as to render such questions of but small importance. (T.547n)

Hume did not publish his answer until his essay on taste, almost twenty years later, although some guide lines are evident in the *Treatise*. Although one general rule can never reveal whether a doubtful case falls under it (T.563), we can sometimes appeal to other general rules for assistance; and while there can always be borderline cases, it is equally necessary that the majority of cases covered by the rule are non-borderline. Hume very early insists that we "form a *general rule* against the reposing any assurance in those momentary glimpses of light, which arise in the imagination from a feign'd resemblance and contiguity"; and he later adds that "the imagination adheres to the *general* views of things, and distinguishes the feelings they produce, from those which arise from our particular and momentary situation" (T.110, 587). In the end, therefore, Hume has to define the conditions for objective judgment; and he does so by reflecting on the standard of taste, as we shall see in the next chapter.

Two letters set the context for Hume's practical assessment of testimony. In 1761 Hugh Blair sent a manuscript of George Campbell's *Dissertation on Miracles* to Hume, asking for comments, in spite of the severe criticism of Hume in it. In reply, Hume asks:

> whether the medium by which we reason concerning human testimony be different from that which leads us to draw any inferences concerning other human actions; that is, our knowledge of human nature from experience? Or why is it different? I suppose we conclude an honest man will not lie to us, in the same manner as we conclude that he will not cheat us. As to the youthful propensity to believe, which is corrected by experience; it seems obvious that children adopt blindfold all the opinions, principles, sentiments and passions, of their elders, as well as credit their testimony; nor is this more strange, than that a hammer should make an impression on clay.
>
> No man can have any other experience but his own. The experience of others becomes his only by the credit he gives to their testimony; which proceeds from his own experience of human nature. (L.1.349)

Two years later, in 1763, Hume was again in correspondence with

Hugh Blair, this time about James Macpherson's presentation of the Ossian poems. Hume requests proof that the poems are not recent forgeries, confirmation from more than one reliable Gaelic speaker that there is an original manuscript of which the poems are a faithful translation, and positive, particular testimony that these very poems have for a long time been "vulgarly recited in the Highlands"; as he said on another occasion: "the same story, coming from different canals, without any dependence on each other, bears a strong air of Probability" (L.1.218). Hume adds that publication of all the evidence, including anything unfavourable to the claim, would serve to convince the public of impartiality, and persuade them that "no arguments are strained beyond their proper force" (L.1.399–400).

In fact, Hume wrote but never published a review of Macpherson's work, citing ten points which convinced him that it was a forgery. Hume listed the following factors as relevant, and leading to such a conclusion:

1. the manner in which the work was presented to the public, unsupported by publicly checkable sources;
2. the great length of the poems (over 20,000 verses), allegedly transmitted by oral tradition over fifteen centuries;
4. the "insipid correctness, and regularity, and uniformity" of the style, together with the manners of the characters, in contrast to what may be observed in other works of parallel alleged antiquity;
4. "the general tenor of the narrative", including the absence of monsters and giants, who normally appear in works of this type;
5. the absence of anything to do with religion, which usually appears in such works;
6. the anachronistic representation of skills such as building, metal work, etc.;
7. the conflict with present traditions, especially in Irish versions;
8. the pretence that oral traditions concerning the characters in the poems still exist in the Highlands, in spite of the fact that "without the help of books and history, the very name of Julius Caesar would at present be totally unknown in Europe";
9. the fact that earlier compilers never came across the stories, although they are allegedly still current in the Highlands, after fifteen centuries;
10. the character of the author himself, who has supported inconsistencies and wild speculations only by indignant affirmations.

Hume adds that Highlanders of his day were no doubt delighted to receive poetry allegedly from antiquity, but "on such occasions, the greatest cloud of witnesses makes no manner of evidence. . . . [A]s finite added to finite never approaches a hair's breadth nearer to infinite; so a fact, incredible in itself, acquires not the smallest accession of probability by the accumulation of testimony" (G.11.424).

Hume here examines internal and external evidence, in both cases assessing probabilities in relation to the resemblances between the present case and others deemed to be relevant; this point lies behind the reference to "a fact, incredible in itself". He adopted similar tests in his discussion of the so-called Casket Letters, allegedly evidence for a conspiracy between Mary Queen of Scots and Bothwell to murder Darnley (*History of England*, Ch.39).

It suffices to conclude that Hume's analysis of the nature and estimation of testimony is incomplete, and in places seriously flawed. In spite of this, many of his criticisms are strong enough to remove the plausibility of the theological claims he considers, and that is often all that a mitigated sceptic strives for. Moreover, Hume has indicated the directions in which a fuller analysis can be found. Before considering such an undertaking, however, we should look briefly at Hume's remarks on the origins of religion.

Summary. In this section we have seen that:

1. Apart from our instinctive assumptions and attitudes, education is the main source of our beliefs. An analysis of the nature of belief on the one hand, and of testimony and evidence on the other, is essential to determining when it is proper to accept other people's claims. Belief or conviction is a sentiment and as such can be a motive to action; reason, by contrast, is inert, cannot be an impulse to action, and is independent of belief. Man's uncritical reliance on testimony is largely due to the impetus of imagination which assumes too much resemblance between the present and the past.

2. If belief is a sentiment, can there be a notion of justified or appropriate belief? Justified belief in testimony can result only from the assessment of probabilities, which themselves rest on the degrees of resemblance between the cases compared. But if, as earlier writers urged, probabilities are subject to diminution over time, all historical evidence, including religious evidence, becomes increasingly suspect, and is eventually lost. To check the customary sallies of imagination, the understanding operates with certain general rules, which are also the offspring of custom; but the understanding itself can be stopped from generating its checks *in infinitum* only by certain natural tendencies of the mind. Meanwhile sceptics take delight in the conflicts between imagination and understanding, and the disastrous results of either one getting out of hand; and they cite such facts in defence of their view that man is not governed by *a priori* thought or deductive reasoning.

3. We have to rely on the testimony of others because, in a crucial sense to be explored later, knowledge is a social phenomenon: (*a*) testimony is generally reliable because of experienced conformity between kinds of reports and kinds of events; (*b*) there is a general inclination to truth in men; (*c*) there is no necessary connection between testimony and

reality, which means that interpretation is unavoidable, and that we must learn the conventions governing the type of report in question; (*d*) experience must itself provide the test for reports about experience. This last move is intended as a means to avoid appeal to a non-empirical criterion, and is not circular; but it does confirm the grip of the past over the present, and once more reveals the necessity for the relation of resemblance.

4. The chapter on miracles is concerned with the nature of evidence and proof in one kind of allegedly factual argument. Hume contends that resemblance is necessary to all reasoning, but confuses the discussion by treating it as both a detectable natural relation, and a logical condition of joining two items in thought; he needs the former for his claims that probability rests on resemblance, but offers no guidance on how to determine the relevant respects and degrees of resemblance. Having postulated resemblance, Hume next argues that knowledge of causal relations is necessary for extending our awareness beyond present impressions. A continued life depends, in part, on the assumption that the future will resemble the past; such general principles, together with particular hypotheses, help us to structure sensory data in our efforts to understand them. A rule of parsimony is needed to prevent the proliferation of hypotheses, by means of which the creative imagination is directed towards the supposition of analogies; the appropriateness of analogies again depends on the degree of resemblance.

5. In spite of his definitional dismissal of miracle events, Hume's main interest is in miracle reports, which raise the general question of how to deal with alleged anomalies. His treatment of the issues is marred by taking general laws to be both falsifiable empirical generalisations and as procedural rules, although he is right to insist that we use both. Hume engages in further definitional dismissal by excluding final causes from any definition of cause, by defining the causal relation in terms of necessary and sufficient conditions and then arguing that theologians cannot infer the cause of the universe, because they are restricted to the inference of only sufficient conditions. Hume accepts that we do postulate causal relations between single pairs of events, provided they exhibit relevant resemblance to other kinds of pairs. Those who claim the order of nature to be an argument for the existence of God, are inferring possible causes from alleged effects; if legitimate inference is restricted to sufficient conditions, we are left with little more than a re-description of the events awaiting explanation. Nothing is gained by the mere hypotheses of a cause, of which, by definition, no properties can be known.

6. All explanatory theories make use of terminal concepts, that is, concepts which help us to understand other phenomena, but which are

themselves, temporarily, not understood; 'gravity', for Newton, 'cause, space, time', for Hume, function in this way and indicate problems for future solution. This fact at once separates them from the traditional concept of God, however variously it was understood, because that was never intended as a potentially disposable terminal concept, but as an ultimate concept in the rationalists' sense which Hume utterly repudiated.

7. Hume's central concepts in the discussion remain undefined: resemblance, experience, testimony. He fails to offer criteria for individuating, counting, or classifying events or objects, and although he worries about the transmission of reports, he overlooks the basic problem of criteria for appropriate descriptions of the original data. By reflection on the part played by general rules in objective judgments, and on the nature of moral and aesthetic verdicts, Hume discovers that the criteria for appropriate responses and judgments are to be found and learned by each individual in his social context, and are to be underwritten by certain natural reactions. Sceptics have been prevented from recognising these points by their residual, if unacknowledged, rationalist assumptions.

Hume on the origins and development of religion

In Hume's *Early Memoranda* there are brief comments on atheism, proofs for the existence of God, the first cause, freedom and evil, and all of them seem to record notes made during selective reading of Bayle's *Réponse aux questions d'un provincial* in which the entries are to be understood in a pyrrhonist context.[30] Bayle's extensive speculation on the reliability of historical testimony, and on *l'évidence* as a criterion[31] of truth, may have influenced Hume in his choice of entries in Section III of the *Memoranda*, if those entries are seen as part of a search for the principles governing man's social conduct. Although Hume told Hutcheson that Book III of the *Treatise* might give offence to the orthodox (L.1.37), the anti-religious dimension of the earlier books was quickly detected.[32] In *A Letter from a Gentleman*, of 1745, Hume lists the charges made against the *Treatise* by those who sought to prevent his appointment to the University of Edinburgh:

1. Universal Scepticism. See his Assertions . . . where he doubts of every Thing (his own Existence excepted) and maintains the Folly of pretending to believe any Thing with Certainty.
2. Principles leading to downright Atheism, by denying the Doctrine of Causes and Effects . . . where he maintains, that the Necessity of a Cause to every Beginning of Existence is not founded on any Arguments demonstrative or intuitive.
3. Errors concerning the very Being and Existence of a God. For Instance . . . as to that Proposition, *God is*, he says (or indeed as

to any other Thing which regards Existence) "The Idea of Existence is no distinct Idea which we unite with that of the Object, and which is capable of forming a compound Idea by Union".

4. Errors concerning God's being the first Cause, and prime Mover of the Universe: For as to this Principle, That the Deity first created Matter, and gave it its original Impulse, and likewise supports its Existence, he says, "This Opinion is certainly very curious, but it will appear superfluous to examine it in this Place, &c."

5. He is chargable with denying the Immateriality of the Soul, and the Consequences flowing from this Denial. . . .

6. With sapping the Foundations of Morality, by denying the natural and essential Difference betwixt Right and Wrong, Good and Evil, Justice and Injustice; making the Difference only artificial, and to arise from human Conventions and Compacts, Vol.2.

Hume always denounced attempts to check philosophical speculation "by a pretext of its dangerous consequences to religion and morality" (T.409, repeated E.105; cp. T.250),[33] and in the Introduction (T.xxi n) aligned himself with Mandeville and Shaftesbury, and thus with the free-thinkers; indeed, only Butler on Hume's list was free from that taint, since Hutcheson had had trouble in Glasgow, and Locke had been violently attacked on the ground that his doctrine of substance under-mined the notions of the Trinity and the immateriality of the soul.[34] Moreover, to orthodox divines even discussion of scepticism implied sympathy with it – Shaftesbury deplored criticism of Cudworth on this very point[35] – and "atheist and sceptic are almost synonymous" (D.139). Thus, even the standard Protestant abuse of Catholicism (see e.g. T.99, 515, 524) could not atone for the clear implications of Hume's questions about how an idea could be acquired of an immaterial substance (T.240; cp. NL.20), or of the Deity (T.94, 160, 172, 248; A.193; E.28); or for the implications of his account of how causal connections are known.

Following Locke and others, Toland was only one of many writers to urge a distinction between "the way whereby we come to the knowledge of a thing" and "the grounds we have to believe it".[36] Because of his view of belief as a sentiment, however, Hume generally saw himself as trying to establish the causes and effects of beliefs on the one hand, and the grounds of judgments, which he sometimes treats as the content of beliefs, on the other. Two claims clearly emerge from Hume's observations on religious topics in his early essays. Firstly, he adopts Cicero's view, which had been widely accepted in France by such writers as Fontenelle and Bayle, and in Britain by deists and others such as Shaftesbury, that religions have their roots in ignorance of causes, and fear of the future. Secondly, he accepts Cicero's view, which was widely disseminated by Fontenelle and Bayle, that such fears feed, and are in turn fed by, quasi-explanatory tales; as they become popular, such tales become systematised and widespread, and the powers of the story-tellers increase, engendering rivalry and faction.[37] If the first view required an account of how causal connections are known, the latter required reflection on the nature of testimony and its effects on individuals and society. In the 1741 *Essays* Hume presupposes, but does not allude to, his earlier analyses of these issues; moreover, all of his substantive claims about religion in those essays are subsequently incorporated within *The Natural History of Religion*, of 1757. It is therefore only necessary here to refer to some general observations in the essays.

Hume claims that defenders of "established and popular opinions, are always the most dogmatical", whereas their opponents always exhibit moderation; Fontenelle, in his defence of the moderns against the ancients, or Collins and Tindal, among "our *free-thinkers*", provide examples of such moderation (G.1.118n).[38] An effort to retain power is only one factor in such situations. "Impatience of opposition" is to be explained by the nature of the human mind, which "always lays hold on every mind that approaches it; and as it is wonderfully fortified by an unanimity of sentiments, so it is shocked and disturbed by any contrariety". This universal principle of attraction and repulsion "seems to have been the origin of all religious wars and divisions" (G.1.131). In the present context Hume does not refer us to his principle of sympathy, which explains why agreement between persons is mutually re-enforcing (cp. T.365), or to the psychological and social needs for agreement, which itself brings peace of mind and re-assures men of their normality. On the other hand, Hume declares that "a controversy about an article of faith, which is utterly absurd and unintelligible, is not a difference in sentiment, but in a few phrases and expressions, which one party accepts of, without understanding them; and the other refuses in the same manner" (G.1.130). This remark is clearly about the alleged content of a belief, as is evident from the subsequent remark that in the ancient world everyone "was disposed to receive, with implicit faith, every pious tale of fiction, which was offered him". Hume suggests three reasons why Christendom became "the scene of religious wars and divisions": the authority of the priests, the separation of the ecclesiastical and civil powers, and the alliance of an outmoded speculative philosophy with "traditional tales and fictions" (G.1.131-2). In the following essay Hume adds that "liberty of thinking, and of expressing our thoughts, is always fatal to priestly power, and to those pious frauds, on which it is commonly founded" (G.1.135).

Hume closely follows Shaftesbury,[39] and less directly Locke and Voltaire, although without acknowledgment to any of them, in his important essay 'Of Superstition and Enthusiasm'. Hume's central claim is that man is subject to states of both extreme gloom and terror, and extreme elation. In the former, unaccountable methods ("ceremonies, observances, mortifications, sacrifices") are taken in order to appease "invisible and unknown" enemies; in the latter, man attributes his raptures "to the immediate inspiration" of "the object of devotion", and even judges himself to be a special "favourite of the Divinity", reason and morality being "rejected as fallacious guides" (G.1.144–5). Only philosophy can conquer the terrors which give rise to superstition, but in this essay Hume does not indicate what kind of philosophy, or which tenets are particularly effective. Readers who sensed the influence of *De Divinatione*, of course, recognised that at least a knowledge of causes would be required, even if they did not know of Hume's own account of such knowledge.

In a subsequent essay, 'Of the Rise and Progress of the Arts and Sciences', Hume repeats Shaftesbury's view that Roman catholicism, in combination with Peripatetic philosophy, suppressed various sects which, through mutual challenge, had earlier ensured the progress of learning. Because the repetition of any experience is the beginning of custom, the closest scrutiny is necessary to prevent doctrines achieving unchallenged authority; under such scrutiny, Newtonian theory has survived, but Cartesian has not (G.1.183). Hume does not indicate who is to undertake the scrutiny, with what qualifications, and for how long; mere survival under attack, irrespective of the motives and arguments for the opposition, can be no criterion of the truth or value of a position. Many, but not all, of Hume's claims are compatible with the view that members of a given society or group learn who the experts are in a given field, while learning the procedures in that field; the judgments of the experts are accepted as true, and their judgments, accordingly, function as standards which are modifiable over time. Modifications are often called for and justified by reference to the diminished utility of the existing standards, but Hume offered no general precept for the proper balance between standards, which tend to ossify and to inhibit new thought, and change, which can needlessly overturn tradition and dissipate energy. The utility that Hume is prepared to grant to religion and its institutions, however, is a great deal less than religion itself would claim, and less even than Cicero, in antiquity, or most secular critics, in the eighteenth century, were willing to concede. In the suppressed preface of 1756 to Volume 2 of his *History of England*, Hume wrote:[40]

> The proper office of religion is to reform men's lives, to purify their hearts, to inforce all moral duties, and secure obedience to the laws and civil magistrates. While it pursues these useful purposes, its operations, tho' infinitely valuable, are secret and silent; and seldom come under the cognizance of history. That adulterate species of it

alone, which inflames faction, and animates sedition, and prompts rebellion, distinguishes itself on the open theatre of the world.

Hume incorporated a version of the first sentence in his *Dialogues* (D.220), and a comment of his, published posthumously in 1777, expresses a similar view: "even the clergy, as their duty leads them to inculcate morality, may justly be thought, so far as regards the world, to have no other useful object of their institution" than the administration of justice (G.1.114).

There are many adverse comments on priests throughout Hume's works, but it is necessary here only to quote remarks from an essay of 1748. "Though all mankind have a strong propensity to religion at certain times and in certain dispositions; yet are there few or none, who have it to that degree, and with that constancy, which is requisite to support the character of this profession" (G.1.246n). The clergy must often "feign more devotion" than they really feel, must not "give scope to their natural movements and sentiments", and must exercise considerable restraint "in order to support the veneration paid them by the multitude"; moreover, they must indulge in hypocrisy in order to "promote the spirit of superstition", and in order to satisfy their own ambition for power (ibid.). It is significant that Hume denies a constant and uniform "propensity to religion", because this is alone sufficient to rule out a view that man has a natural belief of religious dimensions. Hume realised, of course, that serious study would be needed to substantiate such a dismissal, and the complementary works of *The Natural History of Religion* and the *Dialogues*, can be seen as constituting that study.

In what appears to be an adaptation of Locke's argument against innate ideas, *The Natural History of Religion* both opens and closes with the central claim that the non-uniformity and non-universality of "belief of invisible, intelligent power" shows that "this preconception springs not from an original instinct or primary impression of nature, such as gives rise to self-love, affection between the sexes, love of progeny, gratitude, resentment" (N.21; 75). Philo expresses a similar view in the *Dialogues*:

> A man's natural inclination works incessantly upon him; it is for ever present to the mind; and mingles itself with every view and consideration: Whereas religious motives, where they act at all, operate only by starts and bounds; and it is scarcely possible for them to become altogether habitual to the mind. (D.221)

He adds that superstition or enthusiasm, as a principle of action, "not being any of the familiar motives of human conduct, acts only by intervals on the temper, and must be roused by continual efforts" (D.222).

An entry in Hume's *Early Memoranda* paraphrases a comment by Bayle: "'Tis a stronger Objection to the Argument against Atheism drawn from the universal Consent of Mankind to find barbarous & ignorant

Nations Atheists than learned & polite ones".[41] Given the existence of both monotheism and polytheism, Hume in *The Natural History* sets himself the problem of determining which was prior, temporally and logically. He divides the problem into two, following Shaftesbury's distinction;[42] the first concerns the principles "which give rise to the original belief", the second "those accidents and causes" which "direct its operation" (N.21).

Because "the mind rises gradually from inferior to superior", men are able to abstract the notion of perfection from their experience of imperfection (cp. T.48, 198, 510n). "Nothing could disturb this natural progress of thought, but some obvious and invincible argument, which might immediately lead the mind into the pure principles of theism"; although such an argument might be provided, as Shaftesbury had surmised,[43] by "the order and frame of the universe, when accurately examined", there are two reasons why that argument could not occur in the beginnings of religion (N.24). In his earliest and presumably most necessitous state, it is the irregular that excites man's curiosity and alarm; he "has no leisure to admire the regular face of nature, or make enquiries concerning the cause of objects, to which, from his infancy, he has been gradually accustomed". On the other hand, "if men were at first led into the belief of one supreme being, by reasoning from the frame of nature, they could never possibly leave that belief, in order to embrace polytheism" (N.25). The need to find the particular causes of the problems before us, must be prior to the luxury of reflecting on the possible causes of things that do not immediately concern us; but only the latter kind of reflection can provide grounds for the pure principles of theism. In partial support of this claim, Hume immediately contrasts the dissemination of historical facts and speculative opinions, echoing his remarks on testimony in the *Treatise*. All ideas diminish in vivacity over time; experientially based ideas, however, are subject to the drawback that the vivacity of the original impressions can never be literally re-charged, but only matched by succeeding and resembling impressions. Moreover, empirical reports decrease in reliability over time, through inaccurate repetition, particularly if the testimony is transmitted orally. On the other hand, the original vivacity of *a priori* ideas or "clear and obvious" arguments, albeit less intense than the vivacity of experiential ideas, can be re-charged merely by renewed "contemplation of the arguments". But, the more abstruse the arguments are, the more need there is for constant contemplation of them if they are to have any effect at all on conduct. Hume's position is thus: if religious claims are historically grounded, they are subject to the diminishing reliability of all experiential reports; if religious claims are grounded in abstruse speculative opinions, they are unavailable to the vulgar, whose practices, whether monotheistic or polytheistic, cannot then be ascribed to corruption of those opinions; if religious claims are grounded in arguments "so clear and obvious as to carry conviction with the generality of mankind", they would still carry conviction and there could be no explanation of polytheism or superstition (N.25–6). In an earlier essay, Hume's 'sceptic' had observed:

> an abstract, invisible object, like that which *natural* religion alone presents to us, cannot long actuate the mind, or be of any moment in life. To render the passion of continuance, we must find some method of affecting the senses and imagination, and must embrace some *historical*, as well as *philosophical* account of the divinity. Popular superstitions and observances are even found to be of use in this particular. (G.1.220)

The term *invisible* is conspicuously emphasised throughout *The Natural History*, because the crucial hypothesis, as in the parallel reflections in the first *Enquiry*, concerns an inferred cause; as before, therefore, one question is how such an idea is acquired, from experience or reason.

Hume contends that by restricting contemplation to "the works of nature" men could be "led into the apprehension of invisible, intelligent power", even of "one single being, who bestowed existence and order on this vast machine, and adjusted all its parts, according to one regular plan or connected system"; but if attention is extended to "the various and contrary events of human life, we are necessarily led into polytheism". The variety of unfamiliar and unexpected events leads, no doubt necessarily in Hume's view, as a consequence of the assumption of the uniformity of nature, to the supposition of varied and possibly disanalogous causes. Moreover, Hume thinks that mere speculative curiosity is an insufficient "motive" for the supposition of invisible, intelligent power; "the first obscure traces" of such a view must be assigned to "the ordinary affections of human life; the anxious concern for happiness, the dread of future misery, the terror of death, the thirst of revenge, the appetite for food and other necessaries" (N.26–8). The "*unknown causes*, then, become the constant object of our hope and fear". But although the ignorant multitude cannot do so, were they to "anatomize nature, according to the most probable, or at least the most intelligible philosophy, they would find that these causes are nothing but the particular fabric and structure of the minute parts of their own bodies and of external objects" (N.29). Passages such as this imply that there is no need to postulate a cause outside phenomena; they are self-sufficient and in principle understandable in terms of their own make-up. Because men not only conceive all beings like themselves, but also "transfer to every object those qualities, with which they are familiarly acquainted", they often unjustifiably assume that all the unknown causes are "of the same kind or species" (N.29–30; cp. T.224; E.153–4; L.1.155). Superstition is proportional to the extent that a man's life is governed by accident; and, Hume ironically adds, those barbarous men who remain ignorant of astronomy, anatomy and final causes (N.30, 47) are incapable of conceiving "that infinitely perfect spirit, who alone, by his almighty will, bestowed order on the whole frame of nature". On the contrary, such men conceive of many limited beings, resembling the human species, and this is an understandable result of their attempt to determine the causes of their happiness and misery.

Stressing his aim to trace the various aspects of polytheism "in the principles of human nature", Hume contends that anyone who "learns, by argument, the existence of invisible, intelligent power, must reason from the admirable contrivance of natural objects, and must suppose the world to be the workmanship of that divine being, the original cause of all things" (N.38). This observation is about inferring causes, rather than about the impossibility of establishing existence by any means other than experience. Vulgar polytheists deify "every part of the universe" because of their "opposite inclinations" to believe in invisible power and to rest attention on visible objects; these inclinations are reconciled by uniting "the invisible power with some visible object" (N.38). Hume held that in such a move lay the seeds of superstition. In the previous year, 1756, he distinguished between "pure" worship and what seems necessary to "human infirmity":

> The idea of an infinite mind, the Author of the Universe seems at first sight to require a worship absolutely pure, simple, unadorned; without rites, institutions, ceremonies; even without temples, priests, or verbal prayer and supplication; yet has this species of devotion been often found to degenerate into the most dangerous fanaticism. When we have recourse to the aid of the senses and imagination, in order to adapt our religion, in some degree to human infirmity; it is very difficult, and almost impossible, to prevent altogether the intrusion of superstition, or keep men from laying too great stress on the ceremonial and ornamental parts of their worship.[44]

Hume refers to the view, discussed by Cicero (*De Natura Deorum*, I.xlii) but also widely canvassed by such writers as Fontenelle and Toland, that men deify heroes and leaders, or promote formerly limited deities to sovereign positions; or, alternatively, humanize their gods in order to make them "sensible object[s] of worship" (N.40).[45] But even when encouraged in such moves by priests, the assent of the vulgar is "merely verbal", because "they are incapable of conceiving those sublime qualities, which they seemingly attribute to the deity" (N.45). Hume here gives no reasons for the last claim, but two can be found in the *Treatise*. Although our imagination enables us to extrapolate from imperfect experience to the idea, say, of perfect straightness, or perfect equality (T.48), experience of a finite property cannot give rise to an idea of that property in an infinite instantiation; secondly, since "belief is an act of the mind arising from custom", there can be no belief where there is no experience (T.114). By definition, therefore, the vulgar cannot believe what they claim to believe either about the infinite and sublime qualities of the deity, or about a future life. Moreover, the vulgar never cite final causes in defence of their belief in an omnipotent creator, but rather unexpected disasters, which are ascribed "to the immediate operation of providence" (N.41, repeating E.96); indeed, the vulgar cite as "the sole arguments for" the belief the very events which, "with good reasoners, are the chief difficulties in admitting" it (N.41). The "irrational" opinions of vulgar theists are not arrived at "by any process of argument" but by more inconsequential trains of thought.

Hume repeats his view that "the origin" of religion, idolatry or polytheism should be located in the "confused image" or "abstract conception" of unknown causes; and that in order to particularise such conceptions men inevitably "clothe them in shapes more suitable" to their natural comprehension, and represent the unknown causes as "sensible, intelligent beings, like mankind" (N.47). There is no discussion in the present context of the general problem of ascribing properties to unknown causes, or the particular problem of anthropomorphism, but Hume's reflections elsewhere on these topics show his familiarity with contemporary debate. For example, at the beginning of Part II of the *Dialogues*, Hume follows the practice established by Cicero, in making Philo apparently agree with Demea that their discussion concerns not "the *being*, but only the *nature* of the Deity", the former being "unquestionable". This transparent device, which Hume had used before (E.145), and which, indeed, would deceive only "the most careless, the most stupid thinker" (D.214), was needed to avoid jeopardising the whole enquiry at the outset. But Philo then makes two important moves. First, he suggests that "the original cause of this Universe (whatever it be) we call God; and piously ascribe to him every species of perfection" (D.142). This view, which occurs in many writers from Hobbes onwards, is taken up later (D.158, 217) and echoes the contemporary view of liberal thinkers that it did not matter whether one called the being 'God', or 'Blictri' with Toland, or even 'Hippocentaur' with Cicero (*De Nat.* I.xxxviii.105). Locke (*Essay*, IV.x.6) made the point, and Berkeley makes Alciphron express the view that "men frame an idea or chimera in their own minds, and then fall down and worship it"; to which Lysicles later adds the view: "I wish indeed the word *God* were quite omitted, because in most minds it is coupled with a sort of superstitious awe, the very root of all religion" (*Alciphron*, IV.141, 163). Philo's second move in the *Dialogues* is to warn us that because "all perfection is relative", that is, to kinds or species, we should beware of attributing human predicates to the divine being; he then outlines an incomplete syllogism, the unstated conclusion of which is that we have no ideas of divine attributes, because all our ideas are derived from our finite, mundane experience (D.142). Berkeley clearly stated the problem: if "the words *knowledge, wisdom, goodness,* when spoken of the Deity, must be understood in a quite different sense from what they signify in the vulgar acceptation", there is a danger not only of depriving those terms of all meaning, but of having no attributes at all by means of which to characterise God. To deny that the attributes belong to God in "any known particular sense or notion" is "the same thing as to deny they" belong at all; but all who take this line of "denying the attributes of God . . . in effect denied His being, though perhaps they were not aware of it" (*Alciphron,* IV.164). "The belief that there is an unknown subject of attributes absolutely unknown is a very innocent doctrine" (ibid. cp. v.175), but it has an important consequence: "you cannot argue from unknown attributes, or, which is the same thing, from attributes in an unknown sense". A principal source of such views was the extended discussion by Bayle, with which Hume was very familiar, in *Pensées diverses sur la comète* and *Continuation des Pensées Diverses.* Bayle observes:

> Une chose considerée en general & sans aucune limitation individuelle peut bien exister objectivement dans nôtre esprit, mais elle ne peut exister réellement hors de nôtre esprit. Il faut que ce qui existe réellement hors de nôtre esprit soit precisement ceci ou cela.[46]

Hume's own position is unequivocal (G.I.220; D.158): without experience of God's properties, we are without means to individuate God; without means to individuate, we are without means to verify claims that God exists. Indeed, in Part II of the *Dialogues,* Cleanthes concedes that discussion of properties is implicitly discussion of existence: "By this argument *a posteriori,* and by this argument alone, we do prove at once the existence of a Deity, and his similarity to human mind and intelligence" (D.143).

In Section IX of *The Natural History* Hume turns to the advantages and disadvantages of polytheism. First, he claims that polytheism is essentially tolerant, in contrast to the intolerance of theism. One reason is that it limits the powers of its deities; but, because it is "founded entirely in vulgar traditions" it tends to condone or authorise almost any practice or opinion. Second, polytheism encourages emulation of its limited deities, in contrast to the abasement and mortification associated with an infinitely superior deity; activity and liberty also generally accompany polytheism (N.52). Third, the mythologies attending polytheism are quite "natural" (N.53), although they lead to superstitious practices rather than to "philosophical argument and controversy"; here, as elsewhere (T.271), Hume treats superstition as a natural consequence of ignorance of causes. Because theism is "conformable to sound reason", philosophy is apt to be incorporated in and thus to corrupt the system "to serve the purposes of superstition" (cp. G.I.132, following Shaftesbury); there is, for example, "no tenet in all paganism, which would give so fair a scope to ridicule as this of the *real presence*" (N.54–5, echoing the opening of the chapter 'Of Miracles'). The fourth point is a consequence of polytheistic tolerance, since Hume contends that man's "loose and unsteady" views accorded better with familiar traditional stories, not all of which they were required to believe in as articles of faith. Hume re-asserts that "the conviction of all religionists, in all ages, is more affected than real, and scarce ever approaches, in any degree to that solid belief and persuasion, which governs us in the common affairs of life" (N.60). "The usual course of men's conduct belies their words"; in any case, "the empire of all religious faith over the understanding is wavering and uncertain" (N.62). That is why "a *traditional, mythological* religion", however groundless its stories, "sits also so easy and light on men's minds", in contrast to "a *systematical, scholastic* one", where the stories are likely to imply "express absurdity and demonstrative contradiction" (N.65). Hume pointedly commends Cicero for his attitude towards religion, remarking that in his time "it was the great business of the sceptical philosophers to show that there was no more foundation" for one part of the national religion than for another. It should be observed that Hume tends to deny the reality of religious beliefs, as he denies the reality of extreme sceptical beliefs, on the grounds that they are and can be affirmed and acted on only intermittently if life is to continue, and that they are not basic or necessary in the way that our natural life-sustaining instincts are. In addition, however, Hume claims that the propositional content of most religious beliefs is unintelligible, and that in the absence of appropriate and repeatable experiences the reactions that occur are not genuine beliefs.

But why has not the practice of morality, rather than superstition, formed the core of religion, since "there is no *man* so stupid, as that, judging by his natural reason, he would esteem virtue and honesty the most valuable qualities, which any person could possess" (N.71)? Here, Hume repeats a claim from his 1752 essay, 'Of the Original Contract', that there are two groups of duties and virtues, to the first of which "men are impelled by a natural instinct or immediate propensity, which operates on them, independent of all ideas of obligation, and of all views, either to public or private utility. Of this nature are, love of children, gratitude to benefactors, pity to the unfortunate" (G.1.454). In contrast to such duties performed "without any effort" is the second group, consisting of those "more founded on reflection", such as public spirit and temperance (N.72); in both groups, however, the moral obligation "removes all pretensions to religious merit", because "the virtuous conduct is deemed no more than what we owe to society and to ourselves". But a superstitious man finds nothing in this "which he has properly performed for the sake of deity, or which can peculiarly recommend him to the divine favour and protection". He fails to see moral action as serving his deity, because a practice seems to be "more purely religious" the more it "proceeds from no mixture of any other motive or consideration"; consequently, a superstitious man adopts practices which serve "to no purpose in life" (N.72). That is one reason, Hume asserts, why one cannot safely infer a man's morals "from the fervour or strictness of his religious exercises".[47]

"The natural undisciplined suggestions of our timid and anxious hearts" spring "from the essential and universal properties of human nature", such as the instinctive assumption that the future will resemble the past; only "a manly, steady virtue" will help us to avoid or survive accidents, and only the exercise of "our natural reason" can help us resist "the artifices of men" who "aggravate our natural infirmities" by encouraging the "depraved ideas of mankind" (N.73). Hume accepts the view, canvassed by Bayle, Shaftesbury and Fontenelle, that men "exalt their idea of their divinity" in proportion to their fear of the future, but that they progressively augment the deity's power and knowledge, not his goodness; the result is really "a species of daemonism" (N.67).[48]

In 1752 Hume carefully distances himself from the design argument: "That the Deity is the ultimate author of all government, will never be denied by any, who admit a general providence, and allow, that all events in the universe are conducted by an uniform plan, and directed to wise purposes" (G.I.144). The conclusion to *The Natural History*, which purports to draw a 'General Corollary' from the preceding discussion, is formulated with equal care. "When once it is suggested" to a man

a purpose, an intention, a design is evident in every thing; and when our comprehension is so far enlarged as to contemplate the first rise of this visible system, we must adopt, with the strongest conviction, the idea of some intelligent cause or author. The uniform maxims, too, which prevail throughout the whole frame of the universe, naturally if not necessarily, lead us to conceive this intelligence as single and undivided, where the prejudices of education oppose not so reasonable a theory. Even the contrarieties of nature, by discovering themselves every where, become proofs of some consistent plan, and establish one single purpose or intention, however inexplicable and incomprehensible. (N.74)

Three points should be underlined here. First, the idea of "some intelligent cause" requires the stimuli of suggestion, and also the broadening of our reflection to embrace "the first rise of this visible system"; second, when we reflect on the maxims which obtain throughout the universe, we are led, naturally but not necessarily, to conceive of this intelligence as single, unless our education counteracts such a view. In the penultimate section of the *Dialogues*, Philo suggests that "the conducting of the world by general laws" "seems nowise necessary to a very perfect Being"; an omniscient Being could easily intervene with "particular volitions", without "discovering himself in any operation" (D.206). Part of Philo's intention is to underline the tenet that events may carry no mark indicating the precise nature of their cause, and that it is therefore possible for a benevolent deity to have created a good world, without our being able, justifiably, to infer the former from the latter. The third point to notice in the passage from *The Natural History* is that the notion of a single purpose, "however inexplicable and incomprehensible", receives support from the established or supposed repetition of almost any phenomena, but *also* from our failure to find such repetition. In other words, the notion is undiscriminating, and to that extent, vacuous. On the one hand, the irregular course of events excites alarm, and the supposition of special causes; on the other hand, all causal reasoning is grounded on the relation of resemblance, and we can only suppose the unknown to be somewhat analogous to the known; no other ideas are even possible. "The universal propensity to believe in invisible, intelligent power, if not an original instinct" is "at least a general attendant of human nature" (N.75); but the propensity need be no more than an aspect of the basic assumption that every event has a cause, and its common but unjustifiable corollary that the causes we have not found must resemble, in significant ways, those we have. In the 1741–2 *Essays*, Hume wrote: "an abstract, invisible object, like that which *natural* religion alone presents to us, cannot long actuate the mind, or be of any moment in life" (G.I.220); the subtly phrased conclusion to the *Dialogues* does not depart from that view. "Plain, philosophical assent" can be accorded to the "ambiguous" and "undefined proposition, *that the cause or causes of order in the universe probably bear some remote analogy to human intelligence*"; but the proposition seems to be incapable of "extension, variation, or more particular explication", or of affording any "inference that affects human life", or of being "the source of any action of forbearance" (D.227). Philosophical assent to the proposition is thus devoid of religious significance, and parallels the detachment recommended at the conclusion of *The Natural History*. There, he states that although the pressures of life and society make it difficult to sustain "doubt, uncertainty, suspence of judgment", doubt is easier to uphold in the face of conflicting superstitions; our goal should be "the temperate and moderate" course of life, "which maintains, as far as possible, a mediocrity, and a kind of insensibility, in every thing" (N.75–6): Cicero's *mediocritas* (cp. M.59).

We have seen that Hume tries to establish polytheism as more primitive, and in this sense more natural, than monotheism. In the *Dialogues* he assesses the fashionable two-pronged argument, *to* design as a cause of experienced phenomena, and then *from* design to a designer in whom the cause resides. A major problem concerns the initial descriptions of the universe from which the first inference is drawn, because unless our hypotheses are based upon agreed descriptions and determinate predictions, we shall be unable to distinguish speculations merely consistent with the data, from those established by them. One set of data cannot be both the source and verification of a supposition, but it is precisely this double duty that is often required of the order supposedly detectable in the universe. Hume canvasses at least two separable notions of order, one referring to the adaptation of means to ends, and the adjustment of final causes, the other to uniformity of appearance or proportion and arrange-ment of parts.[49] But if our groupings are governed by our beliefs, needs and interests, nothing follows about the possible cause of the external world from our mental capacity to group things; indeed, on occasion (D.190), Hume treats ordering as part of the process of making things intelligible, and 'order' then suffers from the same ambiguity as 'resem-blance', being both a condition of thought, and a real property of, or relation among, things. Such ambiguity lurks beneath a claim which Hume made in 1752 (G.1.381), and which re-appears in the *Dialogues* (D.174), that, despite the changes we observe, we experience the universe as proceeding "from one state of order to another". To this popular view, which Hume could have found in Diderot[50] and Maclaurin, among others, Philo is made to add the following observation:

> Chance has no place, on any hypothesis, sceptical or religious. Every thing is surely governed by steady, inviolable laws. And were the inmost essence of things laid open to us, we should then discover a scene, of which, at present, we can have no idea. Instead of admiring the order of natural beings, we should clearly see, that it was abso-lutely impossible for them, in the smallest article, ever to admit of any other disposition. (D.174)

Admiration is inappropriate because there are no alternatives between which choice can be exercised, and Hume denies the intelligibility of a First Cause which might deserve credit for the initiation of the whole causal chain.

In conclusion, only two further observations need be made. Hume agreed with Bayle that religious controversy cannot be resolved by refer-ence to sentiment, because in the religious context there is no way clearly to distinguish the influence of sentiment from that of education.[51] While composing the *Dialogues*, in 1751, Hume wrote to his friend Gilbert Elliot about the dispute between members of the Port-Royal and their Protestant opponents in the 1660s:

> The Comparison of these controversial Writings begot an Idea in some, that it was neither by Reasoning nor Authority we learn our Religion, but by Sentiment. And certainly this were a very convenient Way, and what a Philosopher wou'd be very well pleas'd to comply with, if he coud distinguish Sentiment from Education. But to all Appearance the Sentiment of Stockholm, Geneva, Rome ancient & modern, Athens, & Memphis, have the same Characters. And

no thinking man can implicitly assent to any of them; but from the general Principle, that as the Truth in these Subjects is beyond human Capacity, & that as for one's own Ease he must adopt some Tenets, there is more Satisfaction & Convenience in holding to the Catechism we have been first taught. Now this I have nothing to say against. I woud only observe, that such a Conduct is founded on the most universal & determin'd Scepticism, join'd to a little Indolence. For more Curiosity and Research gives a direct opposite Turn from the same Principles. (L.I.151–2)

Traditionally, appeals to religious sentiment were appeals to faith. As a transition, therefore, to our discussion of the roles of sentiment in criticism, it will be useful to summarise the main grounds on which Hume, usually by implication rather than direct statement, rejects the propriety of appeals to faith. As Hume understands them, expressions of faith are not put forward as verifiable or revisable empirical claims; moreover, although testimony is in general reliable, language is purely conventional and there is no necessary connection between testimony and its alleged referent; expressions of faith, however, are often declared immune from the normal tests for testimony. Next, if faith is identical or associated with an internal impression, it must be remembered that no impression points beyond itself to its possible cause; the mere occurrence of an impression can be no guarantee of its cause. Man is a thinking, feeling and socially active being; to require faith is to set an arbitrary limit to his thinking capacities (cp. N.73), and to substitute dogma for experience.[52] Bayle held, indeed, that to act according to the kind of faith required of the religious was to act like a mechanism, not as a fully conscious human being; and he frequently casts doubt on appeal to "preuves de sentiment", which are often claimed to express the Word of God.[53] For Hume, even if a criterion for genuine cases of faith could be found, there remained the question of the significance for an individual himself of his inner sentiments. In the next chapter we shall see that Hume takes our sentiments to depend both on external causes, and on our physiological and psychological make-up. But, as social beings, we seek re-assurance that our experiences do not differ radically from those of our peers, and to find that out we must attend and respond to publicly identifiable phenomena.

Summary.

1. In his early *Essays* many of Hume's observations on religion occur during his advocacy of political toleration and individual peace of mind; he held that, historically, religions had generally contributed to neither. He accepts Cicero's view, widely adopted by free-thinkers of the time, that religions have their roots in ignorance of causes, and fear for the future; such fears feed, and are in turn fed by, pseudo-explanations, which are systematised and fostered by factions seeking power.

2. Only philosophy can conquer the fears which give rise to super-stition and its attendant unintelligible articles of faith; only philo-sophy can help man to achieve a balance between the otherwise extreme conditions of gloom and elation, between which he is likely to oscillate. Conscious effort and care are needed to achieve the best explanations, to inject life into abstract principles whose impact is otherwise negligible, and to prevent the creation or spread of unchallenged dogma.

3. The proper office of religion is to reform men's lives, enforce moral duties and secure obedience to the laws; but morality has not formed the core of religion because both natural and artificial virtues and duties can be understood and exercised quite independently of it.

4. Priests must feign more devotion than they really feel, because a propensity to religion is found only at certain times and in certain dispositions. While an idea of an infinite mind might seem to require a pure and unadorned worship, this is rarely found, because the conditions for acquiring the idea are rare; even belief in "invisible, intelligent power" is neither universal nor uniform, and must, in any case, be supported by visible phenomena in order that men may reach some determinate idea.

5. Polytheism arises from the practical need to establish the causes of puzzling phenomena; it must therefore precede monotheism, his-torically. The single cause, supposed by monotheism to be the explanation of all things, could be based on the relatively detached contemplation of the universe as a whole; but even if the suggestion of an "inexplicable and incomprehensible" purpose or intention is easy to accept when one learns of the apparent uniformity of the maxims in the universe, such a notion cannot occur to peoples at the lowest levels of subsistence, and with no leisure for reflection. In any case, the notion is really non-explanatory and suspense of judgment is the proper attitude, associated with Ciceronian *mediocritas*.

6. Since all reasoning about experience is founded on the relations of resemblance and analogy, it is proper to ask what analogies the religious hypothesis is based on. If we suppose the universe exhibits some species of order, and further suppose that the order was caused by something resembling human agents, it does not matter what name is assigned to the supposed cause, but it does matter what properties we believe it to have. We can assign non-explanatory properties, parallel to the occult qualities or powers of former times, or invent worship-worthy attributes; but if, in the end, we have no known experience of the thing's properties, we cannot pick it out, and thus cannot verify that it exists. Discussion of inferred properties of God is therefore implicitly discussion of his existence.

7. The advantages of polytheism over monotheism are that it is sociable,

tolerant, encourages emulation of its limited deities, and is attended with mythologies which sit easily on men's minds, and which are quite natural to the extent that they embody primitive explanatory hypotheses. But religious beliefs are never as strong as those which govern everyday life, and always involve some degree of simulation and bigotry, as can be seen by observing men's lives.

8. At least two motions of 'order' are used in Hume's *Dialogues*: one refers to the adaptation of means to ends, and the adjustment of final causes, the other to uniformity of appearance or arrangement of parts. 'Order', like 'resemblance', is in danger of being taken as both a condition of intelligibility, and as a real relation between things.

9. Religious controversy cannot be resolved by appeal to sentiment, on analogy, perhaps, with judgments about beauty, because the influence of sentiment cannot be unequivocally separated from that of education. No impression, by itself, reveals its cause; so, although belief, as a sentiment, is a motive to action, its causes can be established only by investigation of experience. Such investigations must abide by the public conventions for enquiry and communication.

10. Apart from a few references to recent travellers and historians, Hume's acknowledged sources for his speculations on religion are ancient writers; it is clear, however, that Hume was equally familiar with the parallel observations of writers such as Fontenelle, Bayle, Toland, Shaftesbury and others. He does not pursue his own remarks on fables and allegories (N.39), to the extent of considering the roles of metaphor and symbolism (cp. T.515–16; E.65),[54] as Fontenelle had done, or Shaftesbury's hints on the sublime, to which there are oblique allusions in the *Treatise*. Hume tends to deny the reality of religious beliefs, both on the ground that they can be held only intermittently, and on the ground that their content is unintelligible. As a humanist he was dismissive of practices associated with fear and mortification.[55]

THREE

Scepticism in Criticism

In this chapter I shall establish the French influence on Hume's views about the nature of criticism, and the conditions under which art may grow and flourish; I shall also discuss Hume's views on the nature of beauty, and in the next chapter his views on language. There are, of course, no explicit theories of beauty, art, criticism or language to examine, because Hume never published his promised treatise on "criticism" (T.xii, xx).[1] A reader who wishes to construct even a tentative theory can do so only on the basis of usually passing comments, and his understanding of Hume's general aims and tenets. The separate subject-matter of aesthetics had not been acknowledged when Hume was writing, and even the term 'art' still led an uneasy life in the 1740s;[2] but we shall find that Hume's reflections on aesthetic topics occur in contexts where man is considered as a social being, because only there is reasoning possible. In the previous chapter we saw how Hume tried to find a first-person criterion of knowledge, or at least belief, in feeling or sentiment, without aligning his view with traditional notions of religious faith; defined as one of the feelings which cause a man to act, belief, from his standpoint, cannot be said to be true or false. From a spectator's view-point, however, questions of appropriateness and justification, if not also of truth and falsity, are unavoidable. In the aesthetic context we shall see that Hume amplifies his account of the causes of human responses by assigning to the mind overtly constructive tasks, including the task of achieving, under external guidance, appropriate sentiments. Further-more, we shall discover Hume's view that an effective social institution presupposes the possibility of communication between its members; the conventions and rule-governed nature of language secure both the intelligibility and objectivity of such communication. On these matters we can discern Hume's constructive and often effective defence against general scepticism.

The French Connection again: Dubos

In 1719 the Abbé J-B. Dubos published *Réflexions critiques sur la poésie et sur la peinture*. For at least fifty years it was the most influential work of its kind, and an English translation appeared in 1748.[3] From 1723 until his death in 1742 Dubos was Secretary of the French Academy; he was a

friend of Bayle, whose philosophical scepticism he found increasingly
congenial, and of Locke, whose *Essay* he had helped to publicise, in
Coste's French translation, at the beginning of the century. Like Fontenelle, whose work he admired, Dubos was a learned and cultured man, and
his volumes abound in references to ancient and modern works, and in
allusions to recent scientific discoveries. Hume referred to Dubos's work
in his own *Early Memoranda* and its impact is discernible both in the early
essays, especially when the topic is art, and most dramatically, as we shall
see, in 'Of the Standard of Taste'. Dubos's debts to Bayle would have
been obvious to Hume.

The *Réflexions*, among other things, is a contribution to the debate
between the ancients and the moderns, Hume's interest in which is
everywhere apparent in his own 1741 *Essays* (and cp. G.1.282). Bacon
had argued that the ancients relied on reason rather than observation for
their claims, and had failed to amass the data which might serve as a
proper basis for general laws. In France,[4] where the debate had a longer
life and greater impact, Descartes had also challenged the methods of the
ancients and, like Bacon, rejected appeal to authority as a criterion.
Between 1687 and 1689 Charles Perrault and Fontenelle powerfully
advanced the cause of the moderns, and although not the first man in his
age to do so, Fontenelle expounded a theory of climatic influence on the
progress of culture.[5] In fact, Thomas Sprat, official historian and
apologist of The Royal Society, had used the notion in 1667, but other
English writers often took their lead from the French debate; this is
evident, for example, in the dispute between Sir William Temple and
William Wotton, who defended the ancients and moderns, respectively,
in the 1690s.[6] In the wake of Perrault several issues were canvassed in the
debate, including the nature of judgments of taste and the influence of
history and society on such judgments; the limits of criticism and the role
of rules in it; the nature of beauty and the respective roles of experts and
the public in its determination; overall comparison between the ancients
and moderns, with particular dispute over the stature of Homer; the
nature of progress, particularly as revealed in modern institutions and
practices and in relation to Christianity. Hume expressed views on all
these matters, although it is clear that his own inclinations pulled him in
opposite directions. His limited knowledge of, and sympathy with,
science, together with his hostility towards Christianity as practised led
him towards the ancients; his admiration for recent political progress,
and reluctance to appeal merely to authority, together with recognition
of material advance, aligned him with the moderns. In presenting the
case for either side, however, what he demanded was moderation; and,
in spite of a surprising footnote (G.1.118n), moderation was what he
found in both Fontenelle and Dubos. To demonstrate the influence of
Dubos it will be necessary to outline the theses of the first two volumes,

which Hume clearly studied with care; from the third volume, on ancient theatre, Hume derived less.

Dubos sets out to tackle six questions in the first two volumes: (*a*) what the beauty of a picture or poem chiefly consists in; (*b*) the role of rules in the determination of beauty; (*c*) the relation of different arts to each other; (*d*) the qualities, natural or acquired, necessary to being a great artist; (*e*) how the reputations of artists are established; (*f*) why some ages seem to be more artistically fertile than others. Dubos begins the first volume by offering an account of how a man's sentiments (*sentiments*) arise, as a way of accounting for approbation and disgust for certain works of art.

For Dubos, natural pleasures are always the satisfaction of needs, and the greater the need, the greater the pleasure in its satisfaction. One of man's greatest needs is to be occupied, in order to avoid *ennui* (cp. Pascal). Of course, many factors can bring about *ennui*, including mental exhaustion, and that is why a properly balanced attitude, or moderation (*moderation*) is important; such remarks must have appealed to Hume, especially during his own mental breakdown. Works of art raise artificial passions (*passions artificielles*) which differ from real passions in three respects: they are less deep, less serious, and of less duration. Works of art present imitations of objects capable of exciting real passions, but the passions excited by the imitations are weaker (*moins fortes*); and, because they do not affect our reason, they are less serious and of shorter duration. Dubos holds that the most useful discoveries in society have been made by chance (*Réflexions*, Vol. I, Ch.iii: he does not consider the constructive role of hypotheses), but whether or not art developed by chance, it satisfies our natural need to be employed and to avoid *ennui*. Only fellow practitioners (*les gens du métier*) and students at college regularly study poetry; everyone else reads it for amusement rather than instruction. For even if lessons can be drawn from poems, it is not for the sake of those lessons that one reads the poem (I.xxxiv).

Words are arbitrary signs which arouse ideas that our imagination can order into affecting pictures. The sequence of operations, however mechanical and rapid, is nevertheless complex and, precisely because the signs are arbitrary, partly artificial (I.xl). In contrast, objects in representative paintings are natural signs, and affect us in a quicker and stronger fashion. Although sight has a greater impact than the other senses, no illusion is involved in the pleasure we derive from art. We are moved by plays although we know we are in a theatre, and we are pleased by paintings although we only see a piece of canvas (I.xliii), and in both cases we are very often unable to enjoy a work on first acquaintance, because we are dazzled by its beauties, or are too restless in our attention. We cannot derive pleasure from such works, of course, unless we have some understanding of what is going on, and that is why we constantly look for some order (*ordre*) in what is presented (I.xxxi). In the case of fictional characters, however, we are provided with a special clue. In ordinary life, we have to guess at a man's true thoughts and motives, and we are often wrong, not only about others, but even about ourselves. But in a tragedy, for example, characters throw off the mask in our presence (*quittent le masque devant nous*) and inform the audience of their most secret projects and sentiments (I.xliv). Dubos adds, hastily, that he is not advocating dramatic poems as a universal remedy in morals, notwithstanding this quality of transparency. In any case, tragedies do not aim to excite the emotions they represent; usually the contrary.

Now what governs our predilection for one part of a work, or even for one work, above another, is our taste (*goût*), conceived in a physical way as the organisation, present inclination and situation of our mind (*esprit*). Only physical changes (*changement physique*) can alter taste, however insensible we may be at the time of such changes. One such causal factor is a man's age. At sixty a man may prefer Molière, at thirty Racine, and when younger, La Fontaine; these particular tastes or *préférences* do not prevent a man from just estimation of the merit of other good authors. The point is, however, that whoever would seek to alter those sentiments which depend purely on a man's taste, must first change his organs (I.xlix). What place is there for reasoning, then, and how may just estimates be achieved?

Dubos begins the second volume by comparing and contrasting social and physical influences on the rise and development of the arts. The fundamental physical condition for art is the right quality of a man's blood, and the happy disposition of his internal organs, most particularly of his brain. Aside from Harvey, whom he mentions later on, Dubos also seems to be following Descartes (*Les passions de l'âme*, 1644) at this point. In view of our scientific ignorance, perhaps all that can be said, he suggests, is that the springs (*ressorts*) of our imagination are conditioned by the quality of the blood in the brain (*Réflexions*, II.ii), since, in general, the character of our mind or soul (*esprit: l'âme spirituelle*) depends on the conformation of the organs of our brain (II.vii). No effort of will on our part can effect any physical alteration in these organs (ibid.). The quality of our blood depends essentially on the quality of the air we breathe, which, in turn, depends on the quality of the earth beneath us and its emanations (II.xiv–xv). Dubos spends some time explaining how this happens, but it is significant that Hume follows him at this point no more than he followed Malebranche in his physiological speculations.[7]

One can usefully consider man (*la naissance des hommes*) in two ways: either in terms of his physical condition and natural inclinations, or in terms of social factors (II.iii: *conformation physique, et des inclinations naturelles qui dépendent de cette conformation: de la fortune et de la condition dans laquelle ils naissent comme membres d'une certaine société*). Social factors, such as education, can never over-rule physical factors of the kind already mentioned, but they are important nevertheless.

The public can attend to the arts in such a way as to promote their success, only if its basic needs are already satisfied. Fundamental conditions for general attention to pleasure are absence of war, of insecurity and of threats to the constitution of the society (*la constitution de la société*) (I.xii). Two positive factors in the progress of the arts are attention by one's countrymen, and encouragement by the sovereign. Fontenelle[8] was right in maintaining that ideas, like plants, do not flourish equally in every climate; but, Dubos contends, there are three important facts to be noted. First, there are some countries in which, although the social conditions are favourable, the arts and sciences do not flourish; second, the arts and sciences seem to make sudden progress, not slow advances; third, great painters have always had great poets as contemporaries, which suggests some mutual influence (II.xii). On the last point at least, Dubos himself presents counter-evidence, when lamenting the absence of notable English painters to match their poets. He also subscribes to the apparently tautologous thesis of *la révolution des siècles* (II.xii), according to which periods of great success are inevitably followed by periods of decline.

The chief end of poetry is to move us (*toucher*), and its value depends on its moving and engaging us (*émouvoir: attacher*, II.xxii). Following Shaftesbury, no doubt,[9] Dubos contends that those best able to discern such value are *le public*. There are two, crucial, reasons for this. First, *le jugement du public est désintéressé* (II.xxi). But not only does it judge disinterestedly (*avec désintéressement: sans intérêt*), *il en juge par sentiment* (II.xxi), *par la voie du sentiment, et suivant l'impression que le poème ou le tableau font* (II.xxii). Now the sense (*le sens*) whose province it is to judge whether we have been moved by a poem is the sixth sense we all have within us, and which is generally called *le sentiment* (II.xxii). Reason (*le raisonnement*) ought not to influence us in answering the question whether a work pleases; its role is only to determine why it pleases, or fails to please. In brief, the role of reason is to justify the verdict of sentiment by determining the causes of our pleasure; tasks that are properly undertaken by critics who engage in discussion and analysis (*justifier le jugement que le sentiment a porté: les causes*). Dubos adds that what he means by *esprit* in this context is *la justesse et la délicatesse du sentiment* (II.xxii).

Three brief points should be made here. Dubos was not the first writer to use the notion of disinterested judgment. Arnauld and Nicole, at the beginning of the *Logic*, had claimed that any really disinterested writer abandons all proprietary claims over his work in making it public, and Shaftesbury, as is well known, used the notion a dozen times or so in his *Characteristics*.[10] But Dubos seems to have been the first to assign the notion a central role in criticism. Second, Dubos did not invent the notion of a sixth sense; Fontenelle had used the notion in the Troisième Soir of his *Entretiens*, and it was commonplace to refer to Cicero for allusions to inner sense, at least in the moral realm.[11] But Dubos again seems to have been the first to assign the notion a specific role in critical response, even if it amounted to little more than the ancient view that poetry was judged by the heart. It should be remembered that Hume found it quite natural to talk of looking for reasons to justify a passion, as when he refers to "a clear proof, that, independent of the opinion of iniquity, any harm or uneasiness has a natural tendency to excite our hatred, and that afterwards we seek for reasons upon which we may justify and establish the passion" (T.351). The third point to notice is that the ambiguity in the French term *sentiment*, deplored by French and English writers alike, is precisely mirrored in Hume's term 'sentiment', by which he sometimes means 'emotion, passion', and sometimes 'judgment, opinion';[12] indeed, for him, the term treacherously covers both feeling and thought, which are otherwise often kept apart by the notions of impression and idea (cp. A.185).

Dubos contends that the heart is agitated by itself, independently of all deliberation, when it confronts genuinely affecting phenomena; that is the main reason why discussion cannot affect its essentially mechanical movements, and why the public can be introduced as the true arbiter of value. For, as Cicero remarked, all men are capable of judging by means of their inner sentiment, even though some have perfected it by use (*l'usage*) and experience (II.xxiii). The last point is central in Dubos's designation of *le public*, since this term covers only those who have acquired, mainly through experience, that special discernment known as the 'taste of comparison' (*goût de comparaison*: II.xxii). Some equivocation takes place here, however, because Dubos wants his specialised public to displace the authority of critics, while urging at the same time, that even the most ignorant man can say whether a work is pleasing or not. This aside, Dubos suggests that as we gain in experience of these matters, the less trust we place in philosophical reasoning, and the greater confidence we have in sentiment and practice (*la pratique*), especially if we understand by 'philosophy' sets of general principles or chains of argument. In brief, we believe in man, rather than philosophy, because the latter is more easily imposed upon than the former (II.xxiii). General principles are often too vague to help us when confronting a particular work and, moreover, they commonly distract us from the impression a work has made on us. No reasoning, however, can offset the total absence of pleasure, and sentiment cannot judge the extrinsic merit of a work (II.xxiv).

Several points emerge here. The field of art is peculiar in that the practitioners are not to be judged primarily by their peers (*leurs pairs:*

II.xxiv); indeed, artists are unreliable judges for three reasons, even though they are often instrumental in establishing the reputation of a fellow artist in the first place. First, the sensibility of most artists is usually blunted with time; second, artists usually judge by means of discussion and analysis, involving reference to rules and principles, rather than by their natural taste (*goût naturel*), improved by comparison and experience (II.xxvi); third, they very often ignore the whole for the parts, and pay especial attention to the execution (*l'exécution mécanique*) rather than to its effects (II.xxv). The public, precisely because it thinks it has no essential interest (*intérêt essentiel*) in determining the value of works of art, and because it does not wish to differ from those who, it believes, ought to have more experience in these matters, mistakenly defers to the arguments of artists and the authoritative pronouncements of critics (II.xxvi). Only the passing of time dispels the prejudices (*préjugés*) thus constructed by artists and critics.

During what is clearly a search for a standard of taste, Dubos asserts that posterity has never overturned the verdicts of qualified contemporaries, and that the public never changes its sentiment (II.xxvi, xxviii); he suggests that some works owe their short-lived popularity to their being viewed less as works of art than as pamphlets or propaganda (*en qualité de gazettes*). We saw above that the public must acquire the taste of comparison, and Dubos mentions several conditions of such a taste, three of which should be recorded. First, a spectator must have had the frequent opportunity to see outstanding works of a given kind, especially when he is young and forming his taste, and he must, moreover, view a particular work several times before being in a position to gauge its worth. Second, he must acquire a certain tranquillity of mind, itself dependent on serenity of imagination; exhaustion and business, alike, undermine the proper attitude of contemplation. Third, he needs *la liberté d'esprit*, associated with disinterestedness and with the freedom from prejudices erected by the judgments of fellow artists (II.xxix). There is no general answer to how long it takes to determine the worth of a given work, except to say that time will tell, as classical authors such as Cicero and Quintilian rightly maintained (II.xxxi); this view is consistent with his former claim that, in retrospect, we find that the judgments of qualified contemporaries have never been subsequently reversed, although it now seems as if only posterity determines who was qualified. We shall see that Hume is better able to avoid circularity here. One test of merit, Dubos contends, is that people go on reading a work. At this point, he introduces an important distinction between the real and the comparative merit of a given work (*réel: de comparaison*), an idea that had been canvassed by Perrault.[13] Real merit consists in pleasing and moving, and contemporaries can judge this as well as any; comparative merit consists in moving more than other works of the kind or genre, and here contemporaries must leave the verdict to time and experience. Taken literally, of course, this will not do, since any given epoch must defer to some subsequent posterity, and comparative merit then becomes impossible to determine. Neither Dubos nor Hume mentions this point. One other claim by Dubos may be noted: the vote of our neighbours is as disinterested as we could wish, and we should attend to their verdicts (II.xxxii).

Dubos here remarks that in questions where all the facts are known, what distinguishes one judge from another is not learning, but sense and justness of mind (*sens ou plus de justesse d'esprit:* II.xxxiii), and in such matters we cannot assert the relative superiority of the moderns over the ancients. Indeed, the modern age is superior only in *les sciences naturelles*, success in which is due to chance and happy experiments (*hazard et à l'expérience fortuite*); we do not reason better than the ancients in politics, history or morals. Here, Dubos agrees with Fontenelle. The reputation of a poem is determined by the pleasure it affords, and is established by sentiment; the reputation rests on an inner conviction among those who have experienced it (*la conviction intérieure et émanée de la propre expérience de ceux qui la reçoivent*), and that is why the longevity of such a reputation is a ground for believing it to be based on the truth (II.xxxiv). There is only one supposition beneath this claim, Dubos contends, which is that in matters of the heart men are alike (*semblables par le coeur*). We cannot be deceived when we judge by sentiment, and we immediately suspect those arguments designed to counter our convictions. The emotions we feel when confronting a work of art amount to proof as strong as demonstration in geometry, and no man will change his opinion based on them until his internal springs are altered (*les ressorts de la machine humaine*). This is part of the explanation why the reputation of a system of philosophy may be ruined, whereas that of a poem cannot be, notwithstanding the fact that we often mark as defects in past works what contemporaries required, or cultural idiosyncrasies that we find alien (II.xxxvii). The best way to remain immune to specious learning, or to the artificial arguments of those who despise antiquity, is to trust to sentiment (II.xxxv), and to recognise that a proper philosophical spirit is nothing but reason strengthened by reflection and experience (II.xxxiv). The most that critics can do is to teach us the causes of effects we have already felt (*la cause d'un effet qu'on sentait déjà:* II.xxxii).

We must, of course, understand the language of a poem before our sixth sense, sentiment, can respond to the work; just as we must have the same internal physical make-up as our fellows (II.xxxv). In general, however, Dubos writes as if disputes over interpretation (*la construction de la phrase: interpréter*) occupy and divide only the learned, not the public, whose pleasurable impression is to be derived from the whole (II.xxxii). Whereas the learned dispute the meaning of isolated passages resulting from defective texts (1.xl), the public's unpremeditated response (*pas préméditée*) seems to presuppose a certain clarity of meaning in a work (1.xli), not forgetting that membership of the specialised 'public' itself presupposes acquired competence. There is, perhaps, even a muted suggestion that those whose business it is to 'understand' art, the connoisseurs, may easily lose touch with the public whose criterion of merit is the pleasure it feels (11.xxix).

Dubos is confessedly eclectic, and in many respects unoriginal in his views. For example, Descartes, at the opening of the *Discours de la Méthode* had declared: "le bon sens est la chose du monde la mieux partagée", and the notion of *bon sens* achieved wide currency, being understood as both the faculty of judging, and as the wisdom thereby gained. The Port-Royal *Logic* refers to "le bon sens et la justesse de l'esprit", and many French critics adopted the notion as a condition of proper response; under their influence British writers, most prominently Shaftesbury, refer to "good sense" in criticism, and Hume also took up the notion.[14] Shaftesbury also helped to popularise the idea of good taste, associated with good sense, which had been revived by writers such as Saint-Evremond and La Bruyère. 'Taste' denoted both the ability to discern beauties which caused pleasure, and the judgements on them. Pascal had distinguished those who judge "par le sentiment" and those who reason "par principes",[15] and Hobbes, although he set apart matters of taste, had reintroduced comparative judgment into critical practice. Learned readers of Dubos, such as Hume, certainly knew most of these sources, but it was Dubos who received credit for combining so many fashionable critical concepts into a single comprehensive account. It may be suggested that Hutcheson's views on art owe something to Dubos, over and above the acknowledged debt to Shaftesbury. In the present context, at least, Hume's thoughts about art were stimulated primarily by studying Shaftesbury and above all Dubos, not Hutcheson, as we shall now see.[16]

The influence of Dubos is clear in Hume's essay of 1742 entitled 'Of the Rise and Progress of the Arts and Sciences'. The topic was fashionable during the debate over the Ancients and Moderns, and writers as diverse as Addison and George Cheyne all had their say.[17] Hume contends that even if it is futile to speculate on why Homer, as an individual, lived and flourished where and when he did, we may profitably ask why one nation is more learned and artistic than its neighbours, at a given time (G.1.177), presumably because general causal patterns are easier to discern than singular causal links. Although poets form a minority in any society, they do not live and work in a complete cultural and social vacuum, and it is instructive to reflect on "the taste, genius, and spirit" of the people among whom they live (ibid.). Hume makes four points, three of which occur in Dubos. First, Hume agrees with Longinus and,

more recently, Milton, Shaftesbury and Addison, that in general the arts
and sciences can arise only among peoples who possess a free government; one reason is that the "freedom of thought" constitutive of science
breaks "the progress of authority", and is thus a potential threat to it
(G.1.180n, 182, 184; cp. 158).[18] Second, "neighbouring and independent
states, connected together by commerce and policy" (G.1.181), help to
foster learning, because they check any ambitions towards expansion of
power, and at the same time constitute a source of emulation. Third,
although a free state is the "only proper *nursery*" of the arts and sciences,
they may be transplanted subsequently into any government, a republic
being most favourable to the growth of science, and the patronage of a
restrained monarchy to that of the arts. Fourth, as Bouhours, Fontenelle
and Dubos all held, the perfection of any art or science is "naturally, or
rather necessarily" followed by its decline (G.1.195). There is something
"accidental" in the first rise and progress of the arts in any nation
(G.1.170), but the liberal arts which "depend on a refined taste or sentiment" are not hardy plants like the law, but are easily lost, since they "are
always relished by a few only, whose leisure, fortune, and genius fit them
for such amusements" (G.1.185). The "coarser and more useful arts"
more readily influence other nations, and develop more quickly than the
refined arts, even if they originate after them. There is a "connection"
between all the arts that contribute to pleasure, such that they mutually
aid each other's progress (G.1.187n). Because monarchies have commonly received "their chief stability from a superstitious reverence to
priests and princes", they "have commonly abridged the liberty of
reasoning, with regard to religion, and politics, and consequently metaphysics and morals. All these form the most considerable branches of
science. Mathematics and natural philosophy, which only remain, are
not half so valuable" (G.1.187). Consequently, the arts tend to succeed
in monarchies, especially if politeness of manners prevail, and sciences
in republics. Hume suggests that an important factor in the rise and
progress of the arts might be the possession "of patterns in every art,
which may regulate the taste, and fix the objects of imitation" (G.1.195).
But he then wonders why classical Greek models did not benefit the
Romans, but did inspire the Renaissance; and two considerations occur
to him. A nation can be discouraged by the conspicuous success of its
neighbours, and fail to develop its own talents; similarly, artists can be
over-awed by their models. Above all, as Fontenelle implied, "the arts
and sciences, like some plants, require a fresh soil" (G.1.197).

Hume agrees with Dubos that "a false taste in poetry or eloquence" is
rarely, if ever, "preferred to a true, upon comparison and reflection";
when men have access to the proper models, "they soon unite all
suffrages", because "the principles of every passion, and of every sentiment is [*sic*] in every man; and when touched properly, they rise to life,

and warm the heart, and convey that satisfaction, by which a work of genius is distinguished from the adulterate beauties of capricious wit and fancy". Here, indeed, the field of eloquence or oratory is a model for the other liberal arts: "Whoever, upon comparison, is deemed by a common audience the greatest orator, ought most certainly to be pronounced such, by men of science and erudition" (G.1.172; cp. T.552 on morals, and A.182). Hume also agrees with Dubos that the arts, and learning in general, can neither rise nor progress in conditions of war or political and social insecurity, and his early essays constantly insist on the central value to be ascribed to law (cp. G.1.180, 185): "happiness cannot possibly exist, where there is no security; and security can have no place, where fortune has any dominion" (G.1.207). Echoes of Dubos occur in the two essays 'The Epicurean' and 'The Sceptic'. In the former he asserts that my will has little power over its internal condition, and "in vain should I strain my faculties, and endeavour to receive pleasure from an object, which is not fitted by nature to affect my organs with delight" (G.1.198). 'The Sceptic' is the more important essay, however, because many passages in it foreshadow the main argument in 'Of the Standard of Taste', which we shall discuss in the next section. Hume states that "there is a sufficient uniformity in the senses and feelings of mankind" to ensure the intelligibility and propriety of talk about beauty, since a property is no less real for being a dependent or relational property (G.1.219n). These remarks, in which beauty and virtue are likened to colours, to the extent that they are "the objects of art and reasoning" in spite of their relation to sentiment, echoes Hume's letters to Hutcheson of 1739 and 1740, and the well-known discussion at the beginning of the *Treatise* Book III; moreover, the passage is re-iterated in both *Enquiries* (E.23n; M.110), and yet again in 'Of the Standard of Taste' (G.1.268, 272). A passage which occurs six times presumably held some importance for the writer. The 'sceptic' asserts that "beauty and worth are merely of a relative nature, and consist in an agreeable sentiment, produced by an object, according to the peculiar structure and constitution of that mind";[19] "there are no direct arguments or reasons" by means of which we can alter a man's "value for an object", because "the value of every object can be determined only by the sentiment or passion of every individual" (G.1.217, 224). But because men invariably consider objects in their contexts, and do not consider each object "simply, as it is in itself", there is room for discussion of "views, and considerations, and circumstances, which otherwise would have escaped us" (G.1.224). In contrasting "the sentiments of the mind" with the "feelings of the body", Hume is already trading on the ambiguity of the term 'sentiment'; and in this essay of 1742, although the domain of "reasoning" is severely circumscribed, it continues to play a part in bringing about the proper causal relation between an object and a man's sentiments. Such a view is central to his essay on taste, published fifteen years later.

Hume seems to concede to Dubos that the sentiments associated with art are, in a sense, "artificial", because he states that "sentiments, which are merely natural, affect not the mind with any pleasure, and seem not worthy of our attention"; that is why art should concern itself with improved nature, "*la belle nature*" (G.I.240). He agrees with Dubos's criticism of Fontenelle, that critics who merely cite rules and principles are rarely illuminating, since "no criticism can be instructive, which descends not to particulars" (G.I.242). In 1748, Hume again takes up the distinction between 'moral' and 'physical' causes – a topic which still interested him in 1754[20] – using the same definitions as Dubos, but he asserts against Dubos, without naming him, that the physical aspects of climate cannot "work upon those finer organs, on which the operations of the mind and understanding depend" (G.I.258; cp. T.317).

In the political essays of 1752, Hume extends his reflections on the rise of the arts, and argues that only when man emerges from his first "savage state", in which all are hunters, to one of self-sufficiency in which production from agriculture exceeds consumption, do superfluous hands become available to develop pleasurable activities for society as a whole; in this way "the finer arts, which are commonly denominated the arts of *luxury*" are born (G.I.289). Both "history and experience" (G.I.290) show that, thereafter, the ambitions of the state or of its sovereign and the luxury of individuals act as mutually restraining influences. The liberal arts flourish in times of peace and successful foreign trade, and have effects "both on *private* and on *public* life" (G.I.300). "Human happiness", Hume asserts, "seems to consist in three ingredients: action, pleasure, and indolence", some balance between which is necessary for a healthy life; "no one ingredient can be entirely wanting, without destroying, in some measure, the relish of the whole composition" (ibid.). Following Dubos, he contends that, carried very far, indolence destroys all enjoyment, and adds that "*industry, knowledge,* and *humanity*, are linked together by an indissoluble chain"; "the spirit of the age affects all the arts", and "refinements in the mechanical arts" commonly produce refinements in the "liberal". "The more these refined arts advance, the more sociable men become" (G.I.301–2).

Hume draws a moral and a political conclusion from such reflections. First, "the more men refine upon pleasure, the less they indulge in excess of any kind; because nothing is more destructive to true pleasure than such excesses"; second, it is advantageous to society to "multiply those innocent gratifications to individuals" because they "are a kind of *storehouse* of labour, which, in the exigencies of state, may be turned to public service". The inter-connection of Hume's tenets is important: "knowledge in the arts of government naturally begets mildness and moderation, by instructing men in the advantages of human maxims above rigour and severity, which drive subjects to rebellion" (G.1.302–3). Contrary to the views of Latin writers such as Sallust, "whom we peruse in our infancy", the arts neither enervate mind nor body, nor do they beget corruption; on the contrary, "a progress in the arts is rather favourable to liberty, and has a natural tendency to preserve, if not produce a free government", and the Roman state, for example, declined because of bad government, not because of the arts (G.1.305–6). Only where luxury ceases to be innocent, that is, only when it engages a man's complete attention to the exclusion of his other duties, does it cease to be beneficial, and threaten political society (G.1.307). In brief, the provision of a moderate amount of pleasure is necessary to the physical well-being of the individual, and the political well-being of society.

Dubos influenced Hume, however, not only in his reflections on the physical, social and political conditions for the rise and progress of art, but also in his reflections on the conditions for the proper response to works of art. To that topic, we must turn next.

Summary

1. J-B. Dubos (1719) argues that works of art arouse artificial passions which help dispel *ennui*; everyone except scholars and fellow artists reads poems for amusement and pleasure. We suffer from no illusion in our response to art, but we derive no pleasure unless we understand in some way what is going on. Our taste, an essentially physiological mechanism, determines our predilections, but taste itself is affected by physical changes, such as those associated with ageing. We can consider man in terms of physical or social conditions; the former are paramount, although there are important social conditions for art, such as national encouragement and absence of war or strife. Each man's condition, however, depends on his blood and his brain, themselves dependent on the air and the emanations from the earth.

2. The end of poetry is to move us, and its value is judged thereby; those best able to discern the value are the public, because they are disinterested, and judge by sentiment, a sixth sense. The role of reason is to justify the verdict of sentiment by determining the causes of our pleasure; these causes are usually discerned by critics, who engage in discussion and analysis. The public is a restricted group of people who have acquired, through experience, a taste of comparison. General principles are too vague to help when we confront a particular work. Artists themselves are unreliable judges, because their sensibility is commonly blunted, they often judge by means of analysis, and attend to technical execution rather than effects. Critics and artists in this way erect prejudices.

3. In acquiring a taste of comparison, one needs frequent exposure to good works, a tranquillity of mind, and freedom from prejudices. Then one can judge real merit; comparative merit is judged only by

posterity. In this respect, we are no better off than the ancients, whose judgments in politics, history and morals are equal to ours. The reputation of a work rests on the inner conviction of those who have experienced pleasure from it; hence the importance of longevity of reputation. The only supposition beneath these claims is that in matters of the heart, all men are alike. To remain immune to specious reasoning in this sphere, we need only trust to sentiment. In general, matters of interpretation occupy only the learned; there is a danger of connoisseurs losing touch with the public who are the true amateurs.

4. Following Dubos, Hume claims that the arts and sciences arise only among peoples who have what he calls a free government; second, strong rival states constitute a stimulus to invention and a check on territorial expansion; third, the arts and the sciences may be transplanted from a free state, and the sciences are likely to flourish best in a republic, whilst the arts are likely to flourish best in a civilised monarchy; fourth, the perfection of any art or science is necessarily followed by its decline. Hume also agrees with Dubos that the arts can arise only in conditions of social security.

5. There is nothing one can do to alter one's internal constitution; it is beyond our will, although it influences our taste. But reason is also important, because it governs the descriptions under which we view things, as we shall see in greater detail in the following sections. As soon as men have the proper models in art, they rarely judge amiss, because the principles of taste are in every man.

6. Presupposing certain physical data, Hume wishes to stress the influence of social or 'moral' causes. Only when production exceeds demand can superfluous labour provide enjoyments for society; in such conditions art may grow. Happiness, consisting in a balance between action, pleasure and indolence, is necessary to the physical well-being of an individual, and the political well-being of society.

'Of the Standard of Taste'

'Of the Standard of Taste' is Hume's most interesting essay on aesthetics. It appeared in 1757 as a substitute for a piece on geometry, now lost, which Lord Stanhope persuaded Hume to withdraw. Although Hume told a correspondent that he never intended to publish the essay on taste (L.II.253), perhaps because of its closeness to Dubos, whose name appears in the preceding essay 'Of Tragedy', he may not have been altogether unhappy to see it in print. Alexander Gerard's *Essay on Taste*, in an outline version, had won the gold medal of *The Edinburgh Society* in 1756 for the best essay on taste, and Hume had been party to a recommendation that the whole work be published. Gerard's full version was published in 1759, in a volume containing 'three dissertations on the same subject',[21] by Voltaire, d'Alembert and Montesquieu, which were, in fact, unacknowledged translations from entries under 'Goût' in Vol. VII (1757) of the *Encyclopédie*. Like Hume, Gerard discusses: the need for attention and comparison in order to determine the ends, and merit, of a given work; the need for good sense, reasoning, and models; parallels between taste and virtue; the need to lay the foundations of our conclusions in experience. Gerard refers to Dubos half a dozen times, overtly following him at times, as well as to other French writers such as Bouhours and Crousaz, and the usual classical authors; he even draws attention to Hume's brief discussion of the sublime (T.423ff.).

Hume's essay, whatever tactics lay behind its publication, was by no means the first work on the topic in English or French, and he would have expected readers to recognise allusions. The essay is condensed and sometimes confusing, but there lies behind it, of course, a comprehensive system to which we can appeal in order to resolve difficulties. It is in respect of this system that Hume's essay differs from Dubos's.

The opening remarks on the respective roles of reason, sentiment and general principles, echo the beginning of the second *Enquiry* of 1751, and illustrate Hume's favourite rhetorical method of mediating between two apparently contradictory views. He states that in morals and so-called matters of taste the evaluative language, and the prescriptive nature of the general claims made, disguise major disagreement over the particular cases allegedly covered by the general terms. Thus, everyone applauds justice, but no one agrees which acts are just. The proper method, of course, is to begin with particulars, and to take general principles only as generalisations from them (cp. M.8, 37). The aim of the essay is to undertake what Hume deems to be a "natural" search for "a rule, by which the various sentiments of men may be reconciled" (G.1.268, 281). A dispute is said to be reasonable only if it "can be decided" by appeal to a "standard". In the context of taste a central problem is to determine whether a "criterion" can, or need, be found "in sentiment" (G.1.281, 279). The conclusion will be that "the difference . . . between judgment and sentiment" is not as wide as commonly supposed: each must contribute to any proper judgment, verdict or sentiment (terms used with equal promiscuity). Hume needs to "restrain" acceptance of the proverb that it is "fruitless to dispute concerning tastes" (G.1.269), because that view ultimately threatens not only his account of moral judgment, but also his central epistemological position. On the other hand, he must insist that any "general rules of art are founded only on experience and on the observation of the common sentiments of human nature"; they are not established by *a priori* reasoning, which is restricted to "comparing those habitudes and relations of ideas, which are eternal and immutable" (G.1.270, 269).

One of Shaftesbury's characters maintained that "there can be no such thing as real valuableness or worth; nothing in itself estimable or amiable, odious or shameful. All is opinion. 'Tis opinion which makes beauty, and unmakes it".[22] Among other writers, Hutcheson subsequently asked what reasons might be offered in response to such a view, and what reasons might be used in disputes about taste.[23] In the present essay, Hume maintains that, notwithstanding great diversity in matters of taste, "the taste of all individuals is not upon an equal footing"; moreover, no one consistently accepts "the principle of the natural equality of tastes" (G.1.279, 269). In explaining why it is right to reject such a principle, he seeks to determine the nature of the proper judges, and also of that special group of people, *le public* – in Dubos's term, which he may have borrowed from Bayle (Gerard draws particular attention to Dubos's notion).[24]

Hume recognises that at least two problems confront those who "found morality on sentiment". First, as Shaftesbury saw,[25] if "no sentiment represents what is really in the object", it seems to follow that "a thousand different sentiments, excited by the same object, are all right", and it would be fruitless "to seek the real beauty, or real deformity" (G.1.268–9). Second, by thus implying that "the difference among men is really greater than at first sight appears" from their common language (G.1.266), the view seems unable to explain why we reject the principle of equality of tastes. Hume's general goal can be stated simply, although he never defines his central terms, and they are used very casually. By showing that disputes can be resolved, he aims to establish the rational nature of criticism; it is a matter of fact that certain qualities please qualified observers, and that certain works are valued because they possess those qualities and thereby come to function as models; the so-called "rules of beauty" are generalisations "drawn from established models, and from the observation of what pleases or displeases, when presented singly and in a high degree" (G.1.273); there must be an agreed method, for judgments of any kind to be possible, and a description of that method reveals that the referents are matters of fact; emphatically, the rules are not discovered "by reasonings *a priori*" (G.1.269); empirically grounded rules have a scope of sufficient generality to be genuine substitutes for the *a priori* standards unjustifiably canvassed by opponents.

Hume's general causal thesis about sentiments holds that objects of certain sorts, if perceived in definable ways, cause normal people to have sentiments of certain sorts: "some particular forms or qualities, from the original structure of the internal fabric, are calculated to please, and others to displease; and if they fail of their effect in any particular instance, it is from some apparent defect or imperfection in the organ" (G.1.271). But the causal relation between objective properties of a work and the appropriate calm passions, or sentiments, requires a finely tuned mind; in particular, we need three traits mentioned by Dubos, "a perfect

serenity of mind, a recollection of thought, a due attention to the object".
If any one of these is missing "we shall be unable to judge of the catholic
and universal beauty. The relation, which nature has placed between the
form and the sentiment, will at least be more obscure; and it will require
greater accuracy to trace and discern it" (G.I.270-1). The passage shows
that the mind must pay proper attention to the work as a condition of the
relevant causal relation being established; the crucial notion of attention
leads Hume to the view that one must perceive or think of the work in a
certain way or under a restricted set of descriptions. Initially, however, he
merely remarks, following Dubos (*Réflexions*, II.xxxv), that a man in a
fever or with jaundice, is immediately disqualified as a normal observer.
On the other hand, "if, in the sound state of the organ, there be an entire
or a considerable uniformity of sentiment among men, we may thence
derive an idea of the perfect beauty" (G.I.272), judgments of beauty
resembling those of colour in this respect. As social beings, we often know
already the repute of certain works, and this serves the double purpose of
alerting us to the need for special attitudes to the works in question, and of
allowing us to check upon the presence and nature of any sentiment of
pleasure we may happen to feel. We may note that reference to "the force
of any beauty" in the quotation above should be taken as reference to the
vivacity of the secondary impression, or pleasurable calm passion.

Hume always distinguished the problems confronting a spectator, and
those confronting the agent himself, when both are trying to estimate the
agent's performances. The agent, obviously, is likely to be too involved
with the object to be estimated (G.II.152; E.103n), but he may possess
knowledge difficult for the spectator to obtain; conversely, at the beginning of his career, at least, a man's talents are "as much unknown to himself as to others" (G.I.195), and Hume asserts that "in all questions with
regard to morals, as well as criticism, there is really no other standard, by
which any controversy can ever be decided", than by "an appeal to
general opinion" (G.I.460). In art the problem is complex, however: "in
order to judge aright of a composition of genius, there are so many views
to be taken in, so many circumstances to be compared, and such a knowledge of human nature requisite, that no man, who is not possessed of the
soundest judgment, will ever make a tolerable critic in such performances" (G.I.93).[26]

At this stage of 'Of the Standard of Taste', Hume examines several
"cause"[s] why people do not feel the proper sentiment (G.I.272), and
suggests some "condition"[s] (G.I.277) that must be satisfied by "a true
judge in the finer arts" (G.I.278). Hume lists three main causes of failure
to feel the proper sentiment, and each notion seems to be derived directly
from Dubos: lack of delicacy (*la délicatesse*), lack of good sense (*bon sens*),
and prejudice (*le préjugé*) (G.I.272, 277, 276). What are needed to overcome such failure are, again from Dubos, practice and comparison (*la*

pratique: goût de comparaison) (G.I.274, 275). *Practice*[27] is necessary because "there is a flutter or hurry of thought which attends the first perusal of any piece, and which confounds the genuine sentiment of beauty. . . . Not to mention, that there is a species of beauty, which, as it is florid and superficial, pleases at first" (G.I.275). As Shaftesbury[28] and Dubos insisted, any "very individual performance" should "be more than once perused by us, and be surveyed in different lights with attention and deliberation", for only in this way can we determine "the relation of the parts" and their respective merits (G.I.275; cp. T.294, 446; L.I.452). *Comparison* between "the several species and degrees of excellence" and "the different kinds of beauty" is essential, because "by comparison alone we fix the epithets of praise or blame, and learn how to assign the due degree of each" (G.I.275). The reference to "learning how to" is important, and I shall return to it; it suffices to record here, that most writers, not least Shaftesbury[29] and Dubos, argued that most of us have to learn how to respond. A *prejudiced* critic fails to place "himself in that point of view, which the performance supposes" (G.I.277); indeed, he "obstinately maintains his natural position", and thus fails to respond with what Dubos called *désintéressement*; Hume does not use the English equivalent in this essay. In Hume's view, "every work of art, in order to produce its due effect on the mind, must be surveyed in a certain point of view, and cannot be fully relished by persons, whose situation, real or imaginary, is not conformable to that which is required by the perform-ance" (G.I.276). Three points should be remembered here: this rule is an empirical generalisation based on observation of causal connections between observer and work of art, under certain conditions; but, because it is a rule, it can guide an artist's intentions, as well as a spectator's attitudes. Second, the notion of viewpoint is clearly to be understood not only in the literal sense, but in a metaphorical sense, covering attitudes and beliefs. Third, there is a clear need to "fix our attention" (T.449; cp. 452), which Hume described as one of "the most pleasant and agree-able" "exercises of the mind". Although, in one place, Hume says that "effort of thought disturbs the operation of our sentiments" (T.185; cp. 153), his reference there is to the abstruse arguments of excessive scepticism; his other view is that "what is easy and obvious is never valu'd", and that is why history engages the mind more than poetry: "whatever is important engages our attention, fixes our thought, and is contemplated with satisfaction" (T.613). He adds, in the Appendix, that even if "a poetical description may have a more sensible effect on the fancy", "the ideas it presents are different to the *feeling* from those, which arise from the memory and the judgment"; and "there is something weak and imperfect amidst all that seeming vehemence of thought and sentiment, which attends the fictions of poetry" (T.631; cp. 626). Hume therefore valued poetry and drama which required and sustained attention, in a degree appropriate to the genre.

Hume originally defined "delicacy of taste" as sensibility to beauty (M.83; cp. G.1.91, 187n) and he continues to ground it on "the organs of internal sensation" (G.1.278). There can be no doubt, however, that, as in Dubos and other writers, the notion embodies a judgmental element which ensures that the perception is discriminating. The judgmental element is equally evident in the notion of *good sense*, the chief task of which is to guard against prejudice, that is, false judgment: "in this respect, as well as in many others, reason, if not an essential part of taste, is at least requisite to the operations of the latter faculty" (G.1.277). In order "to discern the beauties of design and reasoning" good sense attends to four aspects of the situation: the ends for which a given work has been calculated, the effectiveness of the means to those ends, the mutual relations of the parts and the parts to the whole, and the intelligibility of the whole (G.1.277–8). For example, "the object of eloquence is to persuade, of history to instruct, of poetry to please by means of the passions and the imagination. These ends we must carry constantly in our view, when we peruse any performance"; further, "every kind of composition, even the most poetical, is nothing but a chain of propositions and reasonings", and "the persons introduced in tragedy and epic poetry, must be represented as reasoning, and thinking, and concluding, and acting, suitably to their character and circumstances" (ibid.). If we use Hume's own term 'interpretation' here (M.92), which incorporates the notions of comparison and assessment, we can say that prejudice is combatted by the understanding achieved through interpretation. Such a view remains faithful to Dubos's claim that the proper sentiment presupposes an understanding of the work in question.

To support this construction we should consult the long, and subsequently suppressed, footnote to Section III of the first *Enquiry*, where Hume argues that the principles of human agency are carried across into the products of such agency. For Hume, causation is a condition of intelligibility in the empirical world, and he asks causal questions about each of the three separable issues he raises later in 'Of the Standard of Taste': the issues of the artist and the conditions of creation, of the art product itself, and of the audience and the conditions of response. Like Dubos, Hume's interest centres on broadly representational works of art, and he asks causal questions of the items represented, in order to determine the consistency of the work's content. We can say that there are both external and internal questions: external questions concern the relations between a work and other things, such as the artist, audience, society at large, morality – and Dubos had held that sentiment cannot judge such extrinsic issues (*Réflexions*, II.xxiv); internal questions concern the consistency of the work itself, detection of which quality presupposes an external causal issue of the proper viewpoint. These views are best explained by reference to the text. Hume insists that "as man is a reasonable being . . . he seldom acts or speaks or thinks without a purpose and intention" (E.33n). "In all compositions of genius, therefore, it is requisite that the writer have some plan or object"; "there must appear some aim or intention in his first setting out, if not in the composition of the whole work. A production without a design would resemble . . . the ravings of a madman" (ibid.). In "narrative compositions", it is a rule that "admits of no exception", that the narrated events "must be connected together by some bond or tie", must "form a kind of *unity* which may bring them under one plan or view, and which may be the object or end of the writer in his first undertaking" (ibid.). Again, in epic and narrative poetry, it "is incumbent on every writer to form some plan or design before he enter on any discourse or narration, and to comprehend his subject in some general aspect or united view which may be the constant object of his attention" (E.37). It is a necessary requirement that such works "have a sufficient unity to make them be comprehended" (E.39). Hume concludes the passage by asserting that "the three connecting principles of all ideas are the relations of *resemblance, contiguity,* and *causation*" (ibid.). He had earlier observed that the unity of action "which is to be found in biography or history differs from that of epic poetry, not in kind, but in degree" (E.35); in all of these endeavours "by introducing into any composition personages and actions foreign to each other, an injudicious author loses that communication of emotions by which alone he can interest the heart and raise the passions to their proper height and period" (E.39). Three observations should be made at this stage.

1. In the *Treatise* Hume argued that consistency of ideas ensures their "easy transition . . . and consequently of the emotions or impressions, attending the ideas" (T.379); the natural requirement for such easy transitions lies behind demands for consistency of treatment and tone in literature (ibid.), and for balanced figures in painting and statuary (T.364; M.70). The matter can be clarified further. "The designs, and projects, and views of men are principles as necessary in their operation as heat and cold, moist and dry" (T.474); such "principles" are conditions of human agency, and knowledge of them is a condition of understanding what a man does. It is precisely because art is a human activity, that we require that it should be intelligible; "durable" pleasure is dependent on understanding the work in the relevant way (T.353; cp. E.34n; T.123, 451). Indeed, our affections are aroused only if the actions of our fellows possess what might be called a certain *transparency.* Shaftesbury had accused "certain grotesque painters" of avoiding "a coherence, a design, a meaning" (*Characteristics,* II.160), and Hume's own critical principles can readily make sense of such a view.

2. Even if the "final sentence depends on some internal sense or feeling

which nature has made universal in the whole species" (M.6), "judgment on any work" (G.I.278) involves more than a mere report of such a feeling. Judgment involves identifying the causes of the pleasurable sentiment, and these causes are to be found among the properties of the work itself. But they are perceivable only from certain viewpoints. Like Sancho's kinsmen who were vindicated by the discovery of the leather thong (incidentally, Hume gets the story slightly wrong),[30] a critic who identifies the causes of his sentiment will have "justified the verdict" (G.I.273); he will have established its appropriateness by establishing its repeatable causal conditions. Dubos had claimed that the role of reason was *justifier le jugement que le sentiment a porté* by determining *les causes* of our pleasure; critics, indeed, can only tell us *la cause d'un effet qu'on sentait déjà*, on Hume's view, if the antecedent is identifiable, and the relation repeatable. "Reason", therefore, that is inductive, experimental reasoning, not *a priori* demonstrative reasoning, is "requisite to the operations" of taste (G.I.277) because the proper sentiment depends on the proper discernment, which in turn involves thinking of the work in certain, determinate, ways. "Critics can reason more plausibly than cooks and perfumers" (G.I.217) because cooks are concerned solely with the physical causes of sensations; critics require *good sense* or sound judgment to discern the consistency of a human performance, and to understand it. It must be stressed, however, that a genuine man of taste must experience a pleasurable sentiment when he attends to a work in a specifiable way, because that is the sentiment whose cause and justification he wishes to locate in the work itself; Dubos, it will be remembered, held that a felt sentiment was the only sure defence against specious reasoning and impressive learning (*Réflexions*, II.xxxv). For Hume, critical judgments are objective triadic relational judgments; 'triadic' because they depend on the work, the critic and the viewpoint.

3. Hume's references to the different ends of eloquence, history and poetry, show that he recognised different genres and that his account in no way confines the field of art. He tells us, for example, that the story of a poem is "the least essential part of it" (G.II.433), a remark that underlies his view of fiction (cp. G.I.269) and also functions in his explanation of why tragedy pleases (G.I.258ff.; M.82). In the context of eloquence, the judges must be the public at large since the goal is to persuade them of something (G.I.172). In history there are special difficulties for the imagination, because of the temporal references involved, but to some extent the causal sequence of the narrative offsets the difficulty of having to think into the past, and there is the additional factor that distance tends to increase our esteem (T.431, 433). Finally, since our attitudes to animate and inanimate objects differ (M.41n), the artist and audience must each take account of the fact in their separate tasks.

While outlining causes of failure to feel the proper sentiment, Hume raises two important questions, although he directly answers only one of them. First, he asks how we should "silence the bad critic, who might always insist upon his particular sentiment, and refuse to submit to his antagonist" (G.I.273). His answer is that we must appeal to consistency and acknowledged parallel cases:

> when we show him an avowed principle of art; when we illustrate this principle by examples, whose operation, from his own particular taste, he acknowledges to be conformable to the principle; when we prove, that the same principle may be applied to the present case, where he did not perceive or feel its influence; He must conclude, upon the whole, that the fault lies in himself, and that he wants the delicacy, which is requisite to make him sensible of every beauty and every blemish. (G.I.273)

It is worth separating two issues here. Hume wants to maintain that "no sentiment represents what is really in the object", but also to deny that all sentiments are "right", in the sense of being publicly justifiable.[31] The present problem arises in the absence of established models and general principles. Hume's view is that the facts ultimately vindicate or damn any critical judgment; someone with unusual powers of discrimination may fail to convince his peers, although it is to be hoped that the truth triumphs in the end. Hume may have recalled here a favourite example of Bayle's in the context of experts and testimony: Copernicus did not abandon his thesis in the face of apparent counter-evidence, and although initially alone in his conviction, he was subsequently accepted as right.[32] The problem is that, according to Hume, "many men, when left to themselves, have but a faint and dubious perception of beauty"; however, "though men of delicate taste be rare, they are easily to be distinguished in society, by the soundness of their understanding" (G.I.280). Hume would concede that even if this is plausible, and helps an established critic convince his audience about a new case, it helps neither an unestablished critic, nor an individual himself. Unless such an individual does convince someone else, he must remain doubtful about the propriety of his sentiment. This point leads to the second issue.

A modern philosopher may object that Hume has given no account of how someone detects even the presence of a pleasurable sentiment, unless it is taken as a self-warranting experience (pleasure and pain being the two primitive categories of experience); and no indication of how a precise description of it is settled. It might be argued that if sentiments can be picked out only by means of publicly learned, rule-governed concepts, reference to internal sentiments in discussions about art or beauty could be dropped altogether. Such an objection misrepresents Hume's position by trading on his failure to deal with all the questions that arise in this context. Hume's "proper", appropriate, or justifiable sentiment is not a brute, pleasurable, but otherwise indeterminable feeling, which is caused by identifiable external stimuli. Rather, it is a complex *response to* something attended to in specifiable ways; the attention is actively and consciously controlled, and the required causal relations exist only between objects with certain dispositional properties, and minds which think of those objects in restricted ways. The pleasures, if any are detectable, are tied to the beliefs and attitudes which constitute the viewpoint necessary for the required causal interaction to take place. And the critic's task includes the articulation of the viewpoint, as a means to bringing others to perceive, and thus to derive pleasure from, the work in his way; thereby, he justifies his own verdicts. We have to discover by experience which sequences are genuinely causal, but Hume never held that different effects could follow from one particular cause; on the contrary, he held that cause and effect are uniquely tied in every case (T.173; E.91), and that contention is crucial in his account of criticism and the proper sentiment. There could be no question for Hume of the proper response resulting from different conditions, unless, in a particular case, a restricted range of differing responses were accepted as equally appropriate.

These points aside, however, the modern objection just cited overlooks the second, crucial question that Hume raises: in the context of art criticism, how can pretenders be detected? In contrast to the *bad critic* who insists on his own sentiment, the *pretender* says what others say, but either experiences no pleasure, or derives it from properties other than those he picks out. Pretenders to revelation had been a longstanding problem for theologians, of course, and the issue arose whenever authority was claimed for private states. Malebranche railed against *les faux savants*, and Shaftesbury, Dubos and Hutcheson all raise the question of pretending.[33] Hume's subtle question (G.1.279) forces us to clarify the role of calm passions in his theory. Since a pretender can remain undetected by confining himself to already publicised judgments, the only way to establish the insecurity of his remarks is to see how he deals with cases where he needs to modify existing criteria. But here he is in the same position as everyone else, since everyone "must produce the best arguments, that their invention suggests to them", and then appeal to their peers as jurymen (G.1.273). Only time will tell which arguments, about the proper viewpoints and the work's properties, achieve authority, and that is one reason why Hume, like Dubos, places such weight on the longevity of a work's reputation (G.1.195, 271). Repeated experience is necessary to establish the truth of causal claims, and public conventions are necessary for objectivity in any context. If, as is quite possible, a pretender's judgments gain acceptance, they do so in the absence of his own inner sentiments; he has somehow characterised a way of pleasurably attending to a work although he himself finds no pleasure in thus perceiving it; on the other hand, his converts in the audience do have sentiments whose objective causes they believe him to have isolated. Several points are at issue here.

First, it may be said that what matters to others is the articulation of viewpoints, literal and metaphorical, from which objective properties of a work may be discerned; whereas a man's internal sentiments are of interest primarily to himself, since their occurrence is often, in the context of art criticism, the occasion of trying to locate their causes. Now in the *Treatise*, Hume contended:

> To have the sense of virtue, is nothing but to *feel* a satisfaction of a particular kind from the contemplation of a character. The very *feeling* constitutes our praise or admiration. We go no farther; nor do we enquire into the cause of the satisfaction. We do not infer a character to be virtuous, because it pleases: But in feeling that it pleases after such a particular manner, we in effect feel that it is virtuous. The case is the same as in our judgments concerning all kinds of beauty, and tastes, and sensations. Our approbation is imply'd in the immediate pleasure they convey to us. (T.471)[34]

Hume immediately admits that "under the term *pleasure*, we comprehend sensations, which are very different from each other", as is evident in the examples of a good piece of music and a good bottle of wine; moreover, only some of our pleasurable sentiments are of the relevant kind to make us "praise or condemn". It is only when we set aside "our particular interest" and consider a thing "in general", that our judgment "can separate" pleasurable feelings having different sources (T.472); he later says it is the imagination which picks out the special feelings produced under "the *general* views of things" (T.587). He explicitly states that "no passion of another discovers itself immediately to the mind. We are only sensible of its causes and effects. From *these* we infer the passion" (T.576). The mind is clearly involved, not only in achieving the general point of view, but in separating the relevant from the irrelevant pleasures in terms of their sources (cp. T.141). Moreover, the remark that "the very *feeling* constitutes our praise" implies an intimate link between the pleasure and the perception or view of the object; and supports the interpretation of his position in the essay on taste as holding that a response constitutes an appraisal.

Returning directly to that essay, the second point to notice is that the procedures for articulating the relevant viewpoints have to be learned; hence Hume's remark that by comparison we "learn how to" assign the epithets of praise and blame (G.1.275). Even the pretender, at the outset of his career, must learn the same conventions as his peers, whether the conventions cover physical viewpoints or linguistic behaviour, in order to be able to communicate with them at all. Hume maintained that "in changing the point of view, tho' the object may remain the same, its proportion to ourselves entirely alters" (T.390); and "a very small variation of the object, even where the same qualities are preserved, will destroy a sentiment" (M.41n). Disagreement in judgments may have their sources in variations in the observer, in the object observed, in the relations between observer and object; the first set of variations includes internal differences, as well as behavioural differences such as those in linguistic competence. Hume never doubts the possibility of reaching agreement on descriptions of states of affairs, although it is an empirical fact whether a given community possesses the conventions to achieve them. Hume asserts that a calm passion "marks a certain conformity or relation between the object and the organs or faculties of the mind; and if that conformity did not really exist, the sentiment could never possibly have being" (G.1.268); such assertions, which authorise inferences from sentiments to their constant correlates, Hume quietly amends so that the sentiment is internal to the perception of the object, and no such inference is required.

What sort of person, then, is the pretender ? If the presence of a certain inner sentiment plays no role in discussions of the publicly discernible objects we call works of art, a pretender must be one who wishes to be esteemed for judgments on those works, even though he lacks, and knows he lacks, the normal pleasurable sentiments derived from attending to them. He may have different motives for intending to deceive others about his sentiments. In Hume's view, the most general reason why people want to agree is that they are social beings; because of the power of sympathy between social beings it is almost impossible to hold out against the general opinion of others (T.592; G.1.131; G.11.152; cp. T.316). Moreover, as social beings we begin by learning what to say, and only subsequently discover any internal accompaniments to our utterances. Someone thrust into a new culture and society, as Shaftesbury recognised,[35] would not know what judgments it was appropriate to make, and at first would not even know what descriptions to offer of the phenomena at issue. Of course, education can lead to purely mechanical reactions (M.43, 33) which, in this case, might mean judgments made in the absence of the inner sentiments which are their ground. A man can become a pretender only when he discovers that his internal life differs from those of his peers, but by then he may well have established alternative associations which act as cues, in much the same way as a colour-blind man does. Hume's pretender, indeed, has much in common with a colour-blind man. Both, for the most part, can get by with their learned responses; both, in his view, suffer from a defect in their mental constitution, as a result of which they are lacking in certain basically natural reactions (G.1.198).

Even at the conclusion of 'Of the Standard of Taste', Hume follows Dubos. Psychological facts about individuals, and social facts about communities explain variations within otherwise agreed overall evalua-

tions. Thus, Ovid, Horace and Tacitus are all worthy of esteem, although
at different times of his life a man may prefer one above another (G.I.281;
M.49 credits the example to "a French poet"); Dubos's authors had been
La Fontaine, Racine, and Molière (*Réflexions*, I.xlix). Hume's view is
that such preferences are "innocent" and "can never reasonably be the
object of dispute", since "it is almost impossible not to feel a predilection
for that which suits our particular turn and disposition". Dubos held that
the predilection we have in favour of one work above another depends
upon the organisation of our mind, but that our preferences do not prevent us from doing justice to others (I.xlix). Like Dubos, Hume argues
that, even if it requires "some effort", we should not judge the repre-
sentations of other ages and cultures as deformities; adverse judgment of
alien and unfamiliar works should be restricted to those which confound
the boundaries of vice and virtue. This is a point about which we have
been given no advanced warning. Having conceded that "we are not so
sensibly touched" by works from another age or tradition, he nevertheless
thinks that "a man of learning and reflection can make allowance for these
peculiarities of manners", since any history of works reveals "continual
revolutions of manners and customs" (G.I.282). It is not proper that I
should enter into the sentiments of any author, or any work, however,
where "the ideas of morality" are confused. "Where a man is confident
of the rectitude of that moral standard, by which he judges" he will not
properly change his "judgment of manners, and excite sentiments of
approbation and blame, love or hatred, different from those to which the
mind from long custom has been familiarized" (G.I.283). Just as thought
is involved in determining the proper viewpoint of a work, and in comparing it with works of a like kind, so thought must be involved in grasping
the moral content or stance. We learn how to praise and blame, as we have
seen, by implicit comparison of each case with "the highest excellence of
the kind" known to us (G.I.276), that is, with the empirically established
models; such comparison is a public, corporate effort, influenced by the
procedures and traditions of the community. Presumably a man discovers what are called his personal idiosyncrasies in his failure to respond
as his peers apparently respond; that is, he either fails to feel what they
claim to feel, or to perceive what they claim to perceive. Such a person,
no doubt, could become a pretender. But it seems likely that Hume
intended to mark a moral distinction between a bad critic and a pretender.
A bad critic dogmatically insists on his sentiment, despite his failure to
convince others, and the counter-evidence. A pretender sets out to
deceive, knowing what means might achieve his ends; in the worst cases,
he elicits moral approval of what is really reprehensible, and this is an
extreme case of claiming to perceive what is not there. For Hume it
matters morally which works people spend their time on.

When people in a given community differ in their judgments "from prejudice, from want of practice, or want of delicacy", "there is just reason for approving one taste, and condemning another" (G.1.280). The notions of mistake, error, falsity, although Hume does not discuss them directly, are associated with a critic's failure to convince a suitable peer group, over a suitable period of time, about the alleged facts; the possibility of mistake entails the possibility of correction, and a bad critic is one who persists in his mistakes. It is an empirical question, Hume insists, who the arbiters of taste are at a particular time, and how they achieve recognition. In fact, Hume believes that most men "are apt to receive a man for whatever he has a mind to put himself off for" (G.11.380), and he could argue, with plausibility, that critics are usually self-proclaimed people, with special contextual interests and goals. Hume declares that "few are qualified to give judgment on any work of art, or establish their own sentiment as the standard of beauty", because "the joint verdict" of "strong sense, united to delicate sentiment, improved by practice, perfected by comparison, and cleared of all prejudice" (G.1.278) is rarely found. These conditions for being a qualified judge are satisfied in various degrees, of course, but they do not make the notion of an expert impossible. Hume can maintain that when practices are already going concerns, we learn who the acknowledged experts are while learning those practices ourselves; for in learning established conventions we normally learn what count as the best examples, and who count as the master practitioners of our time. What he is less clear about is how the first experts in a given field gain recognition, and how established judgments are modified or, exceptionally, overturned. He cannot appeal solely to the passing of time since, by itself, that does nothing to establish either correctness or appropriateness, and is useless as a criterion in the present. Hume admits that eighteenth-century responses to "Homer and the Greek tragedians" (G.1.282) differ from those of their own time, at least in respect of the moral content, and that there are "continual revolutions of manners and customs". On the other hand, he holds that once factors such as prejudice are removed, along with other obstacles to accurate perception, "the beauties, which are naturally fitted to excite agreeable sentiments, immediately display their energy; and while the world endures, they maintain their authority over the minds of men" (G.1.271). The removal of obstacles will, indeed, take time, but that does not disbar contemporaries from proper response; and once the properties of a work are truly discerned it is hard to see why the endorsement of later times does much more than clarify which works should function as models, at different stages in a tradition. "Speculative opinions . . . are in continual flux and revolution", Hume concedes; but any works which "alter the natural boundaries of vice and virtue" suffer from "eternal blemishes . . . nor are the prejudices and false opinions of the age sufficient to justify them" (G.1.284). The fact that the works of Homer have been admired for two thousand years can count for little if the majority of admirers over that time subscribed to mistaken moral principles. Hume did not raise the question of whether long admired works are either in fact, or necessarily, understood in the same ways at different times, once prejudices have been removed; or whether some works admit of significantly varying inter-pretations. Each individual is presumably constrained by the judgments established in his tradition by his forbears, but he is unlikely to witness the vindication of any re-assessment he might attempt. In the light of his allegiance in other essays to a cyclical view of the progress of the arts, it is surprising that Hume did not consider more carefully changes of fashions in taste. And since he categorically states that whatever pleases cannot be condemned as a fault (G.1.270), we should wonder whether someone might not derive greater pleasure from a work which, in the view of experts, he has misunderstood or misperceived; is this not what a bad critic might do?

In the major part of the essay Hume is concerned with the conditions for determining what a particular work is. Traces of admirable qualities need acute perception, and merit according to species calls for com-parative judgment. A proper sentiment is a response to a work as thought of in certain ways. The ineradicable exercise of the mind at once brings any critic into communion with his peers, who then act as a jury upon his verdicts, and his capacity to communicate. At the end of the essay, Hume suddenly introduces a moral criterion: the overall merit of a work stands or falls on an estimate of its moral stance, if there is one. In addition, he concedes that expressions of personal likes and dislikes, if they amount to no more than that, are not open to worthwhile discussion, although they can be morally praiseworthy. There seem to be at least three kinds of observation that a critic can make, therefore: 'I like the work', 'The work is good of its kind', and 'The work is morally praiseworthy'. Reference to 'the standard of taste' covers the conditions for establishing what some-thing is, the models against which particular works are measured, and the true standards. Even if pleasure is the occasion of more carefully attending to a work, an account of that work must be separated from an account of the pleasures a percipient may experience; and Hume is quite clear that a critic should concentrate on the work, not on himself.

Like Dubos, Hume distinguishes expressions of preference from the objective judgments he has been discussing, but there is no absolute dis-tinction between them. Hume says that "our approbation is imply'd in the immediate pleasure" (T.471) a work causes in us; in this sense, a man himself needs no justification for the pleasure he experiences. But as a social being he wishes to communicate his pleasure, and to seek re-assurance that he does not deviate markedly from his peers; these aims can be achieved only by reference to the putative causes of his experience, and if no one endorses his causal claims he has grounds for anxiety. Hume himself, for example, admits distress at being unable to change his senti-ments to accord with those of men he respects; he hopes that the long-term verdict of posterity will vindicate him (L.11.133). In another letter he remarked that we often conceal our dislike of something because of our inability to give reasons for our verdict (L.1.30). To express our dislike is often to publicise our deviation from the accepted evaluation and, as such, our judgment calls for explanation. We can retreat, of course, in the direction of our psychological idiosyncrasies, but in so doing we with-draw our original verdict from public discussion; if we advance towards a viewpoint available to others, however, we proceed towards objective verdicts. Likes are always personal, though they may be shared. It is a social fact, and Hume was well aware of it, that we all like to like what we know is good; and some of us claim to. The old pretender lurks in us all.

As we saw in the previous chapter, Hume was familiar with the long-standing disputes over the nature of the interpretation and meaning of biblical, and other historical, texts. Shaftesbury had extended the context explicitly from sacred to secular texts, and Dubos had called for the study of art by scholars and fellow artists, notwithstanding the sometimes bad consequences of their doing so. But Hume nowhere discusses the special issues of meaning in art, separate from the requirement that understand-ing a work in some way is a precondition of deriving pleasure from it. In his essay 'Of the Authenticity of Ossian's Poems', he gives reasons for the inappropriateness of admiring the poems, but there is no question of what anything in the poems *means* (G.11.415ff.).[36] A letter of 1747 expresses surprise that commentators have mistaken the "sense" of a verse in Horace,[37] and Hume never raises the possibility that complexity of mean-ing and studied ambiguities may be essential features, indeed the special merit, of some literature – although he does concede that "many of the beauties of poetry" "are founded on falsehood and fiction, on hyperboles, metaphors, and an abuse or perversion of terms from their natural meaning" (G.1.269). One reason for Hume's silence on these matters is to be found in his view that in the general context of communication, any distortion of the "natural meaning" of terms is socially irresponsible. Finally, it should be recorded that, compared with the absolute necessities of life, art is one of life's "superfluities" (G.1.302); in this sense it is "gratuitous" (D.198). Nevertheless, Hume holds that the habit of con-versing together, and of contributing to each other's pleasures, increases the level of both knowledge and humanity (G.1.302). Art is an important factor in these matters, because it is a human practice whose principal goal is the provision of pleasure, unlike all those other phenomena whose aesthetic dimension is, so to say, inessential and accidental.[38]

It is unfortunate, perhaps, that in the absence of alternative texts, a single, condensed, derivative essay of under twenty pages should be taken as representative of Hume's considered views on art and criticism. More-over, it may be urged that my constructive interpretation of the essay on taste is unduly sympathetic, even anachronistic. Rather than argue that Hume's opening statements about the causal relations between a work and our sentiments are either blatantly contradicted later in the essay or quite unable to sustain the subsequent weight of his views, I have argued as follows: like his predecessors, Hume trades on the ambiguity of the term 'sentiment', and self-consciously builds judgmental elements into the notion; that shift itself alters the nature of the causal relation, because the work of art is no longer merely the stimulus to a passive mind, but is itself only characterised by means of an active and attentive mind; the causal story is then supplemented by a broader conception of the con-ditions necessary for a proper critical judgment, and pleasure is treated as integral to the perception of the work, rather than an effect of that percep-tion. Certainly, the judgmental element becomes so dominant in the essay on taste, that it is hard, at times, to draw a clear distinction between 'sentiment', 'taste', 'good sense'; and that is not because Hume sometimes seems to echo the old distinction between faculties, and the judgments uniquely associated with each faculty. A modern philosopher is likely to demand a sharper distinction between causes and logical conditions on the one hand, and between causes and justifying reasons on the other, than Hume openly admits; and a fuller analysis of the nature of pleasure than he offers. In the last chapter we met Hume's view that the meaning of a text would become ever less clear with the passage of time; he never mentions this when discussing art, and indeed holds, as we have seen, that the passage of time reveals the true merit of a work. But he does not discuss what limits might be placed on the future, when the reputation of a work has yet to be established;[39] nor does he indicate what should be done if we do not know what counts as an appropriate general point of view. It should be noticed, however, that freedom from prejudice does not mean freedom from all beliefs, but only freedom from the wrong beliefs, especially about the kind, and aims, of the work.

Hume's overall view can now be characterised: a man becomes con-scious of his pleasure in a certain object; he needs only a vague awareness of its properties to be able to pick it out for further attention, although we ought always to beware of the inaccuracies of first appearances (T.47, 132,446; M.67; G.1.275). The aim is to make the "obscure and confused" sentiment "clear and distinct" (G.1.274–5; T.441) but, as it turns out, it is not strictly the same sentiment that becomes clear. Attention requires all the man's perceptual and intellectual faculties, which themselves naturally seek a state of rest, equilibrium, balance, consistency – a point further elaborated in the final chapter of this book: Hume most often uses the terms *consistency* and *unity*. If the observer can make sense, in some way, of what he perceives, he will experience new sentiments, which are related to his first response at least via temporal succession, and which may be loosely described as an enhancement of it. To determine the focus of his pleasures he must appeal to publicly discernible phenomena, using the conventions of his community, and these conventions secure all the objectivity we need in our judgments and verdicts. Moreover, as a social being, he wishes to check that his responses are similar to those of his neighbours, and to share the pleasures he experiences; he can achieve these ends by making known the circumstances of his pleasure.

Hume did not ask, and would have regarded the question as outside the province of a philosopher, why certain forms or structures in fact cause the pleasure they do, but the search for intelligibility in a work of art, usually triggered off by an initial pleasurable response to it, rests on assumptions about the purposiveness of human actions. But while Hume sees all artists as potential purveyors of pleasure, his views about the need for pleasure and the nature of responsible communication, imply that artists occupy a relatively low social status, and also that there is a hierarchy of arts, with literature placed above painting and music.

Beauty and Judgments of Beauty

I have argued that a proper response to works of art, in Hume's view, requires the active participation of our minds. Hume prepared the ground for such a view in the *Treatise*, where, although he mentions art hardly at all, he attempts to mark out the domain of reason and sentiment in matters of beauty. In the first half of the eighteenth century, at least, beauty was still taken to be the central notion in the field we now call 'aesthetics'. Hume's remarks on beauty are strictly subordinate to his other concerns, usually moral concepts, but a brief study of them helps us to augment the interpretation in the previous section.

An advance summary will be helpful here and will show how Hume qualifies his causal claims. His view is that, provided they are perceived in special and definable ways, certain sorts of objects cause normal people to have certain sorts of sentiments. As a particular kind of inner feeling, the sentiment of beauty is a calm passion or secondary impression, pleasurable but otherwise indefinable; beauty itself is not a sentiment, nor the name of a strictly perceived (seen or heard) property, but rather a "power" (cp. E.75, 79) in objects whose presence is *felt*. No argument can change the physiological mechanisms which enable a man to feel the sentiments he does (T.211), but discussion can focus on the causes of his feelings, and by altering a man's perceptions of the world it can set off a new causal chain, which results in new sentiments. Perceptual judgments can thus be said to be *mediate* causes of our sentiments (T.462), in contrast to perceptions themselves, which Hume treats as *immediate* causes. Although detected by a sentiment, beauty is as "real" as colour and other allegedly secondary qualities, and discussion of it is objective, however difficult. Three factors, at least, are necessary to the objectivity of judgments of beauty: the conventions of language, the universal psychological make-up of men, and the possibility of publicly attainable and discernible viewpoints. Strictly, shared viewpoints enable us in the first place to correct what we say, rather than what we feel; but it is important to recognise that reasoning always grounds, and may often precede, the proper sentiment. Moreover, Hume holds that one can neither make a judgment of beauty without some concept of the object to which beauty is ascribed, nor justify such a judgment without appeal to the type of beauty in question. Apart from the rare cases of natural beauty which "command" (M.6; cp. Kant) our approbation, we have to learn what objects can cause pleasure; our verdicts on the mere form of something are relatively uninteresting, precisely because reasoned discussion seems out of place. Because pleasure and pain are the principal motives to action, all men share a ready, even a natural, interest in anything that is found to please (M.112; cp. T.574), and thus in the search for shareable viewpoints of whatever can give pleasure.

In the first *Enquiry* Hume declares that "the mind of man is so formed by nature that, upon the appearance of certain characters, dispositions, and actions, it immediately feels the sentiment of approbation or blame"; such "natural sentiments of the human mind", which arise from "the natural and immediate view of the objects", cannot "be controlled or altered by any philosophical theory or speculation whatsoever" (E.110–111). Such a view about natural and immediate responses separates Hume from his main British influence, Shaftesbury,[40] who tended to merge beauty and truth, and from Shaftesbury's explicit defender, Hutcheson, whose aim was to resolve "the Constitution of our present Sense of Beauty into the divine Goodness".[41] One French writer inspired by Shaftesbury should be mentioned again here, J-P. de Crousaz, whose *Traité du Beau* was published in Amsterdam in 1714. Hume would have encountered Crousaz's views in Dubos, even if he had not read the original work. Crousaz held that beauty was not an absolute, but expressed "le rapport des objets, que nous appellons *Beaux* avec nos idées, ou avec nos sentimens".[42] There are two kinds of perceptions, according to Crousaz, ideas and sentiments, the latter being associated with the heart rather than the mind; judgment of beauty requires both: "on donne le nom de Beau aux objets dont les diversitez se rassemblent sous quelque unité".[43] He insists, moreover, that "La Beauté d'un Poême excellent se fait sentir à ceux même qui n'en voyent point les raisons, et n'en découvrent point les causes: Mais ces causes sont très-réelles et leur rapport avec les dispositions de notre coeur ne l'est pas moins".[44] Crousaz lists the real and natural features of beauty as: variety, unity, regularity, order and proportion. Versions of this popular view, which appear in both Shaftesbury and Hutcheson of course, recur until the notion of beauty drops out of aesthetic discussion later in the century. It is time to turn directly to Hume.

Hume distinguishes between beauty, perception of beauty, and judgments of beauty. Beauty "is not, properly speaking, a quality in any object, but merely a passion or impression in the soul"; as such, it "cannot be defin'd" (T.301). In a passage which he uses twice, and which was certainly understood to be Hutchesonian in spirit by later writers such as Diderot,[45] Hume asserts:

> Beauty is not a quality in the circle. It lies not in any part of the line *whose* parts are all equally distant from a common center. It is only the effect, which that figure produces upon a mind, whose particular fabric or structure renders it susceptible of such sentiments. In vain would you look for it in the circle, or seek it, either by your senses, or by mathematical reasonings, in all the properties of that figure. (G.1.219; repeated M.110)

On the previous page occurs a passage of equal importance in this context:

> the case is not the same with the qualities of *beautiful and deformed, desirable and odious*, as with truth and falsehood. In the former case, the mind is not content with merely surveying its objects, as they stand in themselves: It also feels a sentiment of delight or uneasiness, approbation or blame, consequent to that survey; and this sentiment determines it to affix the epithet *beautiful or deformed, desirable or odious*. Now, it is evident, that this sentiment must depend upon the particular fabric or structure of the mind, which enables such particular forms to operate in such a particular manner, and produces a sympathy or conformity between the mind and its objects. Vary the structure of the mind or inward organs, the sentiment no longer follows, though the form remains the same. The sentiment being different from the object, and arising from its operations upon the organs of the mind, an alteration upon the latter must vary the effect, nor can the same object, presented to a mind totally different, produce the same sentiment. (G.1.218)

The distinction between beauty and perception of beauty comes out in a further passage:

> It is on the proportion, relation, and position of parts that all natural beauty depends, but it would be absurd to infer that the perception of beauty, like that of truth in geometrical problems, consists wholly in the perception of relations and was performed entirely by the understanding or intellectual faculties. (M.109)

There can be public discussion, of course, over the properties or relations constitutive of the beauty which causes the sentiment by which it is principally detected. Hume is also anxious to stress that the "reality" of beauty is in no way diminished as a result of his claim that beauty lies not

in bodies "but merely in the senses", and that critics and moralists need
be no more worried by such claims than are natural philosophers by
parallel claims about colours (G.1.219n): "the appearance of objects in
day-light, to the eye of a man in health, is denominated their true and
real colour, even while colour is allowed to be merely a phantasm of the
senses" (G.1.272).

Hume claims that "the beauty of all visible objects causes a pleasure
pretty much the same, tho' it be sometimes deriv'd from the mere *species*
and appearance of the objects; sometimes from sympathy, and an idea
of their utility" (T.617); "both these causes", as he earlier insisted, "are
intermix'd in our judgments" (T.589). The claims imply that the species
of pleasure we experience depends on some conceptual judgment, but
before this point is developed, we need to take note of an earlier passage.
Since beauty "is discern'd only by a taste or sensation", Hume claims
that "the power of producing pain and pleasure make in this manner the
essence of beauty and deformity" (T.299); the essence of beauty is a
"power" precisely because the occurrence of a sentiment (and a proper
viewpoint, as we shall see) is necessary to its detection. Similarly, to speak
of beauty as the "effect" of the interaction of an object with certain
properties, and a properly tuned mind, is only to emphasise his view that
powers are detectable only in their exercise, that is, in this case, by means
of the sentiment of beauty. Hume does not further explain "the sense of
beauty" (T.118), any more than does Hutcheson who says little more
than that it "determines us to approve and delight in Uniformity amidst
Variety, wherever we observe it".[46]

Shaftesbury had claimed that "there is a beauty of each kind", and that
the simplest kind was that of "mere figure".[47] In line with such remarks,
Hume distinguishes different "kinds" (T.298) of beauty: beauty of
"form", which would contribute to the "intrinsic worth and value" of
something (T.593); beauty of "interest"; beauty according to "species".
By means of such distinctions Hume aims to show that variations in our
sentiments of pleasure can be traced to discernible variations in the perceptions and perceptual judgments that function as their immediate and
mediate causes, respectively.

Hume gives two closely related examples of intrinsic beauty, perception of which is mediated by conceptual judgment only minimally, if at
all. First, he says that we might attend to the beauty of "form" of "some
senseless inanimate piece of matter" (T.363–4). Second, in a passage
very close to Shaftesbury, he claims that "some species of beauty,
especially the natural kinds, on their first appearance command our
affection and approbation; and where they fail of this effect, it is impossible for any reasoning to redress their influence or adapt them to our
taste and sentiment" (M.6).[48] The references here to nature and natural
kinds are echoed later, of course, in Kant; he maintained that "the

empirical interest in the beautiful exists only in *society*", and that interest can combine with a judgment of taste "after it has once been posited as a pure aesthetic judgment".[49] Hume would probably reply that his own agreement with the former point was part of his attempt to avoid anything like the latter.

Excluding intrinsic beauty, Hume asserts that two important "principles" operate in judgments of beauty. The first, comparison, functions in our classification of objects into kinds: "we judge more of objects by comparison, than by their intrinsic worth and merit; and regard every thing as mean, when set in opposition to what is superior of the same kind" (T.593; 372; cp. T.375, 534, 538, 557; G.1.152). The second (which Hume, in fact, treats as "the *first*" principle: T.592), is sympathy (T.576, 618): "tho' our first object be some senseless inanimate piece of matter, 'tis seldom we rest there, and carry not our view to its influence on sensible and rational creatures" (T.363). "Most of the works of art are esteem'd beautiful, in proportion to their fitness for the use of man, and even many of the productions of nature derive their beauty from that source" (T.577). Our sympathy with the owner of a house enables *us* to derive pleasure from the "convenience" of *his* house; his own pleasurable sentiment, however, is a mixture of beauty of utility and "beauty of interest, not of form" (T.364; cp. 330). In this same passage, Hume claims that pleasure derived from the utility of objects concerns "only the owner, nor is there any thing but sympathy, which can interest the spectator". The beauty of "tables, chairs, scritoires, chimneys, coaches, sadles, ploughs, and indeed" "every work of art" is "chiefly deriv'd from their utility" (ibid.). It should be added that Shaftesbury first, and then Hutcheson with increasing emphasis, argued that, in the latter's phrase, "the sense and Desire of Beauty of several kinds is entirely abstracted from Possession or Property".[50]

It was evident to everyone that reference to utility required the exercise of judgment, as Berkeley pointed out,[51] and we may now begin to see how, for Hume, the justifications appropriate to judgments of beauty depend both on the kind of beauty in question, and on the concept of the object to which beauty is ascribed. If "nothing renders a field more agreeable than its fertility, and . . . scarce any advantages of ornament or situation will be able to equal this beauty" (T.364), it is clear that to describe a stretch of land as a 'field' is *ipso facto* to limit what can be beautiful about it. Hume holds that in any social community there are agreed descriptions of the phenomena that most concern the community; any deviation from the conventions governing such descriptions requires explanation, but no special mystery surrounds the conventions themselves, although philosophers of the science of man may seek for their historical and psychological origins. One cannot predicate beauty of something already described as an overgrown plain because of the conventions governing the denotation of 'overgrown' and 'plain'; what counts as a beautiful plain depends on a given community's concept of a plain. Hence, "a plain, overgrown with furze and broom, may be, in itself, as beautiful as a hill cover'd with vines or olive-trees; tho' it will never appear so to one, who is acquainted with the value of each. But this is a beauty merely of imagination, and has no foundation in what appears to the senses" (T.364). Two points can be separated here. An overgrown plain may be beautiful "in itself" if, eschewing any comparative judgments, we respond to some aspect of its form, say its colour, or alternatively, using comparison, we judge it to be a good example of overgrown plains; in addition, by thinking of the plain under another description, that is, one "merely of the imagination", one might be able to *think* of it as beautiful, but not, perhaps, *feel* it to be so. There are other cases, however, in which the imagination operates and yet it is justifiable to predicate beauty of the phenomena in question. An empty but well-designed house, an un-inhabited but fertile land, an imprisoned athlete, may be justifiably judged to be beautiful, because "where any object, in all its parts, is fitted to attain any agreeable end, it naturally gives us pleasure". In these cases, "the imagination adheres to the *general* views of things", so that "the *seeming tendencies* of objects affect the mind" (T.584–7). We are entitled to call these things beautiful "even tho' some external circumstances be wanting to render it altogether effectual" (T.584). In other words, the house is well designed and ready for use, and is therefore beautiful; the plain is overgrown, not ready for use, and is therefore not beautiful. Hume often treats utility as a potential or power, as here (T.299, 311).

Beauty of utility is always relative to species, whether the utility benefits the animal itself, or the owner of an object (T.299, 483, 615).[52] The conventions which govern the attribution of beauty of utility differ between cultures: "in countries where men's bodies are apt to exceed in corpulency, personal beauty is placed in a much greater degree of slender-ness than in countries where that is the most usual defect" (M.86).[53] Hume is at pains to insist that "the more we converse with mankind, and the greater social intercourse we maintain, the more shall we be familiar-ised to these general preferences and distinctions without which our conversation and discourse could scarcely be rendered intelligible to each other" (M.55).

The importance of the descriptions under which we see something becomes perfectly clear in Hume's account of beauty in art and of criticism in general, with his special emphasis on appropriate viewpoints as a con-dition of proper response. Central factors in such viewpoints are the beliefs and attendant attitudes that we have towards the phenomena in question. More than this, however, the special viewpoints function three times over as necessary conditions: for the appropriate causal relations to obtain between the phenomena and an observer; for the objectivity of our judgments; and for social communication (T.581–3).

Hume writes: "'tis only when a character is considered in general, without reference to our particular interest, that it causes such a feeling or sentiment, as denominates it morally good or evil" (T.472). Of course, not "every sentiment of pleasure or pain, which arises from characters and actions, [is] of that *peculiar* kind, which makes us praise or condemn" (ibid.); but after practice, a man "who has command of himself, can separate these feelings, and give praise to what deserves it". Such skills, as we saw earlier (p.116), explain how he is able to praise wine for its flavour and music for its harmony, even when both "equally produce pleasure" (ibid.); no account is offered of the mechanisms involved in such detection. Although "the approbation of moral qualities most certainly is not deriv'd from reason, or any comparison of ideas; but proceeds entirely from a moral taste, and from certain sentiments of pleasure or disgust, which arise upon the contemplation and view of particular qualities or characters", and although these sentiments "must vary according to the distance or contiguity of the objects", we can, nevertheless, "arrive at a more *stable* judgment of things" by trying to "fix on some *steady* and *general* points of view; and always, in our thoughts, place ourselves in them, whatever may be our present situation" (T.581). Hume insists that "'twere impossible we cou'd ever make use of language, or communicate our sentiments to one another, did we not correct the momentary appearances of things, and overlook our present situation" (T.582). Strictly speaking, the adoption of a "general" viewpoint enables us to correct our language (T.583, 582; also 348, 375, 594), rather than our sentiments. This is because firstly, "our passions do not readily follow the determination of our judgment" (T.583), and change more slowly than the operations of the imagination as it functions in the general viewpoint (T.441); secondly, our sentiments are caused by the interaction of properties in the perceived object and the particular physiological constitution of the brain and, as such, are not influenced immediately, but only mediately, by judgments. The complexity of the issue is evident if we consider a particular case:

> though the value of every object can be determined only by the sentiment or passion of every individual, we may observe, that the passion, in pronouncing its verdict, considers not the object simply, as it is in itself, but surveys it with all the circumstances, which attend it. A man transported with joy, on account of his possessing a diamond, confines not his view to the glistening stone before him: He also considers its rarity, and thence chiefly arises his pleasure and exultation. Here therefore a philosopher may step in, and suggest particular views, and considerations, and circumstances, which otherwise would have escaped us; and, by that means, he may either moderate or excite any particular passion. (G.1.224)[54]

Two important points in this loosely worded passage become clearer if we first juxtapose it with another quotation: "in many orders of beauty, particularly those of the finer arts, it is requisite to employ much reasoning in order to feel the proper sentiment; and a false relish may frequently be corrected by argument and reflection"; "in order to pave the way for such a sentiment and give a proper discernment of its object, it is often necessary, we find, that much reasoning should precede, that nice distinctions be made, just conclusions drawn, distant comparisons formed, complicated relations examined, and general facts fixed and ascertained" (M.6). The two points are these. First, the proper sentiment depends on the proper discernment, and the latter may involve many complex factors, the particulars of which, presumably, have to be learned. Second, discussion can bring about a different survey of an object, and thus a different causal sequence, and thus a different sentiment, and thus a different verdict.

Hume states that "'tis impossible men cou'd ever agree in their sentiments and judgments, unless they chose some common point of view, from which they might survey their object, and which might cause it to appear the same to all of them" (T.591). The general viewpoint is the source of the "general inalterable standard, by which we may approve or disapprove of characters and manners. And tho' the *heart* does not always take part with those general notions, or regulate its love and hatred by them, yet are they sufficient for discourse, and serve all our purposes in company, in the pulpit, on the theatre, and in the schools" (T.603). Such standards are revisable, of course, since they serve the needs of a community, and those needs may change (M.56, 56n); furthermore, "*general rules* are often extended beyond the principle whence they first arise" (M.37; T.362), and only a sharp historical sense will enable us to distinguish between the origins of a principle and its present foundations (G.1.446). It must be emphasised, however, that although it is contingent which standards are judged sufficient in a given context, since the judgment is made on grounds of utility, it is necessary that there are some standards, as we saw in the last section.

It is important to ask what a general viewpoint is supposed to be, and how we know, in a given case, what it is. Hume uses both a literal and a metaphorical notion of "point of view", as we detected in the essay on taste; in the former, he often seems to be concerned with the optimum distance for perceiving certain features, such as the beauty of a face (T.582); in the latter, reference is to beliefs, attitudes, interests. A general point of view is something we adopt "in our thoughts", and which requires us to "over-look our own interest" (T.582; 472). "Every particular person's pleasure and interest being different", agreement in sentiments and judgments can be reached only if those involved perceive specifiable phenomena under agreed descriptions (T.591). We learn those descriptions, and what constitutes a general viewpoint in representative cases, when learning the language of our own social community. Speaking of cultural differences in the assessment of personal beauty, Hutcheson observes that it is crucial to know "from themselves under what Idea such Features are admir'd".[55] Hume remarks that "if one person sits down to read a book as a romance, and another as a true history" they receive the same ideas, and put "the very same sense upon their author", but the former has a fainter conception of the incidents and derives less entertainment from them (T.97–8; cp. 121–2, 626). In general, men "proportion their affections more to the light, under which any object appears to them, than to its real and intrinsic value" (T.534; cp. 348). By the time of his essay on taste, twenty years later, Hume no longer separates the "real" value of a work of art from the various ways it appears to people, but ties the real value intimately to particular ways of perceiving the work. Nor, in the later essay, does he continue to countenance the possibility of "a certain sense, which acts without reflexion" with regard to "a certain *je-ne-sçai-quoi* of agreeable and handsome" and also "that of wit and eloquence" (T.612).

Hume contends that although "precept and education" have some influence, our most general sentiments of "approbation and dislike" (M.42) have a natural foundation; that explains why any tolerable representation of a passion arouses a sympathetic response, since there are no passions "of which every man has not within him at least the seeds and first principles" (M.50). In addition, Hume claims that certain fundamental "rules of art are founded on the qualities of human nature; and the quality of human nature, which requires a consistency in every performance, is that which renders the mind incapable of passing in a moment from one passion and disposition to a quite different one" (T.379; cp. 441). In the final chapter we shall see that this observation is related to his emphasis on moderation, but here it suffices to notice that the requirement for consistency is said to have its foundations in nature, understood in this case to be certain capacities of the mind. Hume gives another example: "an heroic and burlesque design, united in one picture, wou'd be monstrous; tho' we place two pictures of so opposite a character in the same chamber, and even close by each other, without any scruple or difficulty" (T.380). Hume's point is that because a spectator can consider the two pictures *as* two, "this break in the ideas, breaks the progress of the affections"; furthermore, "the want of relation in the objects or ideas hinders the natural contrariety of the passions" (ibid.). The example of the two pictures shows the importance of descriptions under which something is viewed; since, by design or accident, we may establish a relation between two items "which may cause an easy transition of the ideas, and consequently of the emotions or impressions, attending the ideas" (ibid.). Different emotions may be experienced as a result of thinking of a lake, for

example, as small in relation to a sea, or huge in relation to a pond
(T.373); such considerations are important in Hume's passing observations on the sublime (T.432ff.; 436), which we must otherwise leave
aside. We have seen that, according to Hume, many of our responses have
a natural foundation; our descriptions of them and of their putative
causes, are governed by the linguistic conventions that operate in our
particular community, and those have to be learned. Complex conventions
also govern our criteria for determining whether we have given one
description of two pictures or two descriptions of one picture. Hume
suggests that if we think of a work as a forgery we may discern no merit in
it at all (L.I.399), as indeed happened in connection with the so-called
Ossian poems (G.II.415):

> A tiresome, insipid performance; which, if it had been presented in
> its real form, as the work of a contemporary, an obscure Highlander,
> no man could ever have had the patience to have once perused, has,
> by passing for the poetry of a royal bard, who flourished fifteen
> centuries ago, been universally read, has been pretty generally
> admired, and has been translated, in prose and verse, into several
> languages of Europe.

Moreover, if our descriptions arouse unfulfilled expectations, our con-
sequent disappointment may be disproportionate to the facts (M.77n);
this point is also related to the fact that surprise can be effective as a device
only once (G.I.243). Our aversion to a city may change into "the opposite
passion" (T.354) when familiarity provides us with more accurate
descriptions of the city than those based on the uncertainties of our "first
perusal" (cp. T.446). To the extent that the sentiments of beauty are
natural responses to certain situations, they can be called "involuntary"
(T.608); and Hume remarks that the reasoning posited as the associative
link between the attendant ideas can be called "implicit" (T.553). He
suggests that our displeasure at a figure that seems off-balance, is caused
by our sympathy for something that we think will fall and suffer pain
(T.364); he concedes that discussion might persuade us that our relatively
immediate interpretation of the situation is mistaken, although he adds,
as we have seen, that sometimes the verdicts of our heart may outlive the
judgments of the head, as when we say 'I know it is (meant to be) a man
just beginning to move forward, but it still looks to me like a man falling
over' (cp. T.586).

Although Hume allows beauty of utility to offset any "disproportion or
seeming deformity" (M.41, 11), he does not think that failure in utility
can be offset either by beauty of form, or by claiming that even greater
failure has been avoided; from the fact that it could have been worse, it
does not follow that it could not and should not have been better (D.204;
T.586; M.41).[56] The reason is that beauty of utility is parasitic upon
beauty according to species.

Summary. A summary of the last two sections can now be provided.

1. 'Of the Standard of Taste' sets out to establish that not all tastes are equal, but recognises that whoever introduces sentiment into an analysis must resist claims that everyone is right in matters of sentiment. In effect, Hume extends his reflections from the second *Enquiry* on the respective roles of reason and sentiment in the realm of values. He argues that if judgments are to be possible, there must be some 'standards' or agreed procedures and criteria, and he urges that in the present context they have a natural foundation, and are to be discovered empirically.

2. The relevant causal relation between a work, or its parts, and the appropriate calm passions requires a finely tuned mind. Three causes of failure to feel the proper sentiment are listed: lack of delicacy, lack of good sense, and prejudice. All these derive from Dubos, and all involve judgment of some kind. Practice and comparison are needed to improve our perception; both notions entail conscious acts of mind.

3. Every work of art presupposes a certain point of view from which it is to be assessed; 'point of view' is to be understood both literally and metaphorically to cover attitudes and beliefs. 'Good sense' amounts to interpretation, which must consider the ends of the work, the relations of its parts, and its overall intelligibility, in order to understand it. The principles which inform human agency are carried across into the products of agency; thus, because art is a human activity, a requirement of intelligibility arises, which is satisfied by investigations into the relations between the work and the artist, audience, morality, etc., and into the internal structure and content of the work itself. Our affections for our fellows are aroused only if their actions and products possess a certain transparency; works of art must have "sufficient unity to make them be comprehended", although that unity may be created by a critic (E.39).

4. The "proper sentiment" is a complex response involving causal relations between objects and minds which have picked them out in identifiable ways, and a critic's task includes specification of the viewpoint he has adopted; he justifies his verdict by bringing others to perceive the work in the way he has. (In the literal sense, one sees things *from* a viewpoint; in the metaphorical sense, one perceives them *through* one's beliefs.) In the second *Enquiry* Hume refers to "the judgment" which "corrects the inequalities of our internal emotions and perceptions", and he contrasts "general judgments" with "our real feeling or sentiment" (M.54 and 54n).

5. A man of taste must have an internal sentiment, because that is the pleasurable experience whose sources and justification he seeks to locate in the work itself. The way to silence a bad critic who insists on

his own sentiment in the face of counter-evidence to his causal claims, is to present him with parallel cases whose relevance he acknowledges. Hume's question about pretenders is a legacy of a search for a criterion of knowledge, and of debates about genuine faith in religion. If, as is possible, a pretender's judgments eventually gain acceptance, they do so in the absence of sentiments in him similar to those felt by other people. What matters to those others is the identification of the viewpoints from which and through which properties of the work are discernible. We all begin by learning what to say from others; a man cannot begin by being a pretender. Pretenders have much in common with the colour-blind who, for the most part, can get by on alternative cues, but who suffer from a basic physiological defect, as a result of which they lack the capacity for certain natural responses. Only when a man discovers this lack, can he pretend not to have it.

6. Hume's reliance on longevity to establish proper verdicts is required by his account of causal relations, which are discernible only by repeated experience of them or relevantly analogous cases; but he also uses the view, in combination with the fact that we still admire the classics, to maintain the unverifiable contention that genius, like truth, always triumphs in the end. Hume allows as unavoidable two sources of variation in our verdicts: psychological facts about individuals, such as age, and social facts about communities; but he urges that one should sharply separate judgment of the author, from judgment of his work (G.1.282). Moreover, he distinguishes expressions of preference from objective critical judgments, and holds that the arbiters of taste are often self-proclaimed people with special interests in the context. As a social being, a man wishes to communicate his pleasure, and to seek re-assurance that his experience does not deviate radically from that of his peers.

7. 'Of the Standard of Taste' is heavily indebted to Dubos, and the notion of judgment is integral to all the central concepts Hume borrows from Dubos, such as 'good sense'; even the notion of 'sentiment' which is initially used to denote some kind of 'mental' feeling, is largely absorbed into the notion of judgment. Hume's overtly causal account is also subtly transformed in order to incorporate the activities of the mind, and the unanalysed concept of pleasure is treated as integral (cp. T.121) to the perception of the work, rather than a mere effect of that perception.

8. In his early work, during which the topic is never of central concern, Hume treats beauty as a 'power' in objects which causes a pleasurable sentiment; beauty is not itself a sentiment, nor a property discernible by the five senses, but rather a property whose presence is *felt* only when objects with certain perceptible properties interact, under certain conditions, with minds having certain properties. Discussion

can focus upon the object in which a man takes delight, and by altering his perceptions of it, can set off a new causal chain resulting in a new sentiment.

10. Although Hume distinguishes beauty, perception of beauty, and judgments of beauty, he concentrates on the last, further distinguishing between beauty of form, of interest, and of species. Two principles operate in judgments of beauty: sympathy, comparison. Justification of judgments of beauty depends on the species and nature of the object to which it is attributed; beauty of utility is relative to species. Three factors are necessary to the objectivity of judgments of beauty: the conventions of language, the universal psychological make-up, and the possibility of publicly shareable viewpoints, a notion which includes beliefs.

11. Strictly speaking, a general viewpoint secures agreement in language, rather than immediate change in passions; the general viewpoint is a condition of general standards or criteria, and we learn about it in learning the language of our community. Hume recognises the central importance of the descriptions under which we view things, and that is why he holds that reasoning is often necessary to elicit the proper sentiment. In spite of this, our sentiments, to an extent, can be said to be natural or involuntary; this feature carries over into the general standards and rules of art, which can also be said to have a natural foundation, notwithstanding the special requirements of different genres.

12. Hume's requirement of consistency in works of art suggests a basic search for intelligibility, and his emphasis on reasoning the ubiquity of interpretation. Hume's account of criticism places man in a social context where, alone, reasoning is possible.

13. Hume wants the authority of critical judgments to rest on their truth, not on the accident that they may, for other reasons, last a long time, and thereby encourage certain habits of response. Agreement about what count as the facts can be reached only on the assumption of shareable viewpoints, language, and psychological states. A discovery of the facts is necessary for a proper estimate of a work. The celebration of false moral values within a work can never be condoned, and ultimately, therefore, the value of art is subordinate to moral considerations.

FOUR

Medium and Message

According to some interpretations of his views about knowledge and ideas, Hume is logically committed to certain assumptions about language and meaning. There is little textual evidence, however, for a claim that he self-consciously held such assumptions, and much against it. In particular, he did not slavishly echo Locke's discussion. Since no one has yet attempted to gather together Hume's remarks on language, it is proper in this prelude to Humean studies to do so here. Moreover, the task is best separated from other issues, including those in aesthetics with which it might readily be associated. One aim of the present brief discussion is to alert readers to another dimension of Hume's writing that has received no serious attention: his views on rhetoric, and the rhetoric of presentation in his various works. These issues will not be taken up in this book, and it must suffice to record that they are not merely questions of literary appreciation. Hume's conceptions of philosophy, and of the ways in which it might best be practised and promoted, differed widely from those of modern philosophers who write almost exclusively for fellow specialists, and who make little effort to be interesting or intelligible to anyone outside that group. Hume said that "love of literary fame" had been his "ruling passion" (D.239). Hostile critics have taken this remark in 'My Own Life' to indicate an improper goal for a philosopher, and a partial explanation (although in no way a justification) of his philosophical failings. It is an unhappy accident that in avoiding pedantry himself, Hume only generated it in his commentators.

Hume on Language

Hume propounded no theory of language; such a task belonged to grammarians, in his view, and philosophical enquiries ought not to be confused with grammatical. Nevertheless, Hume was familiar with much of the seventeenth- and eighteenth-century speculation on language, particularly by French writers.[1] He refers to the views of Vaugelas, the Port-Royal writers, Vossius, Ménage, Lamy, Pufendorf, Perrault, Boileau, Malebranche, Fénelon, Rapin, Rollin, Dubos, Girard; and among later British writers refers to Harris, Priestley and Monboddo in letters. Reflection on language was likely to occur, of course, in several contexts: when discussing the social nature of man, for example, or the relative merits of the ancients and moderns, or Biblical texts, or the principles of rhetoric, or the communication of ideas, or the nature of knowledge. A brief consideration of remarks made in such varied contexts will help to show the nature of Hume's interest in language, and why that interest cannot be fully understood against the background of the famous discussions on language by Locke and Berkeley.

Remarques sur la Langue Françoise, by Claude Favre de Vaugelas, was published in Paris in 1647, and went through twenty, posthumous, editions before the end of the century.[2] Hume refers to Vaugelas in a letter of 1742 (L.1.42), although it is likely that he read the work while in France, or even earlier; further references occur in 1753 and 1775, when Hume describes Vaugelas as "the first great grammarian of France" (L.1.182; 11.298). The aim of Vaugelas, like that of Malherbe before him, was to purify the French language. He propagated no theory, but insisted that usage must prevail over rules, which themselves can only be grounded on usage: "L'usage est comme l'ame et la vie des mots".[3] We can best find out the proper usage by consulting those who speak well – detectable how? – but who have not self-consciously studied language; the best candidates are the women of the court.[4] This suggestion, for various reasons, including those of rhetoric and social theory, was extremely popular, and a host of writers refer to it, including Hume (L.1.182) and Adam Smith.[5] Vaugelas insists that any living language slowly, yet constantly, changes, and his frequent references to what it is necessary, proper, best, to say are more concerned with clarity of *signification* than with propriety.[6] Hume wrote:

> Of all the vices of language, the least excusable is the want of perspicuity; for, as words were instituted by men, merely for conveying their ideas to each other, the employing of words without meaning is a palpable abuse, which departs from the very original purpose and intention of language. It is also to be observed, that any ambiguity in expression is next to the having no meaning at all; and is indeed a species of it; for while the hearer or reader is perplexed between different meanings, he can assign no determinate idea to the speaker or writer. . . . Vaugelas, the first great grammarian of France, will not permit, that any one have recourse to the sense, in order to explain the meaning of the words; because, says he, it is the business of the words to explain the sense – not of the sense to give a determinate meaning to the words; and this practice is reversing the order of nature. (L.11.298)

Hume refers to this "essential rule" as one "of grammar and rhetoric" (ibid.). One reason for associating perspicuity and usage is the view, held by Vaugelas and Hume, that "whenever any Expression or Action becomes customary it can deceive no body" (L.1.20). Hume himself was anxious to "follow the common Use of Language", because it was a condition of being "intelligible", a prior requirement to that of truth (L.I.33, 29).[7] He held that "in a living Language the continual Application of the Words and Phrazes teaches at the same time the Sense of the Words and their Reference to each other" (L.II.157).

Vaugelas's views provided a focus of discussion for almost a century, and in the Preface to the Port-Royal *Grammaire Generale et Raisonnée*, 1660, Lancelot and Arnauld declare that they wish to go beyond usage or custom, in order to discover the systematic reasons beneath language. Their opening statement is well known:

> La grammaire est l'Art de parler. Parler, est expliquer ses pensées par des signes, que les hommes ont inventez à ce dessein.[8]

Almost all subsequent writers agreed with the view, not original to the Port-Royal, that language was the invention of man, and that we must understand what passes in the mind in order to understand different sorts of signification. The Port-Royal *Logic* begins with the declaration:

> La Logique est l'art de bien conduire sa raison dans la connoissance des choses, tant pour s'en instruire soi-même, que pour en instruire les autres.
>
> Cet art consiste dans les reflexions que les hommes ont faites sur les quatre principales operations de leur esprit, *concevoir, juger, raisonner, & ordonner*.[9]

In Chapter I we saw that Arnauld and Nicole assert that "we can express nothing by our words, when we understand what we say, without having an idea of the thing which we signify by our words", and that "we are not able to express our thoughts to each other, unless they are accompanied with outward signs".[10] Grammarians list the ideas which men have agreed to connect with certain sounds, and are concerned with the arbitrary definitions of names. Philosophers or logicians, on the other hand, are concerned with the real definitions of things in terms of their essential attributes, or failing this, with descriptions of a thing's accidents.[11] Words, understood in the definition of the Port-Royal *Grammar* as distinct and articulate sounds used to signify thoughts,[12] succeed in signifying only if they "excite an idea connected with that sound in our mind".[13] Strictly speaking, the principal ideas excited by words, not the accessory ideas, constitute the signification of a word.[14] Fifty years later, as we also saw in the first chapter, Crousaz claimed that "most words, used by Men, express their Sentiments and Passions rather than their Ideas";[15] words such as *chance* "signify nothing", whereas words such as *nothing* signify the absence of an idea; "sacred Words" are "at most attended with some Sensations", and words such as *substance, number* "express only Ideas, without any actual objects answering those words".[16] It would be admissible to restrict attention to the use of language, Crousaz argued, only if that use were exact and constant; but the signification of words changes over time, and men differ greatly over the accessory ideas they take words to express.[17] What Crousaz means is that general statements of use are often inadequate; it is often necessary to examine the precise use of expressions in order to understand them, by studying custom, context, personal idiosyncrasies and so on.

However much the writers of the Port-Royal were endebted to predecessors such as Campanella, Ramus and Vossius on the one hand, and Descartes on the other, the topics and contentions of the *Grammar* and *Logic* dominated European thought for almost a century. In 1672, Samuel Pufendorf,[18] developing hints in Hobbes and the Port-Royal (as his learned editor Barbeyrac pointed out crossly), considered the role of intentions in communication, and argued that it was a duty according the law of nature that "no man deceive another either by discourse, or any other signs which customarily are accepted to express an inward meaning".[19] Pufendorf claims that there are two obligations concerning "discourse": first, by virtue of a

> *tacit Compact* every man is bound in his common *Discourse* to apply his Words to *that Sense*, which agrees with the *receiv'd Signification* thereof in that Language: from whence also it follows, that albeit a man's *Sentiments* may differ from what he expresses in Words, yet in the Affairs of Human Life he must be look'd upon as *intending* what he *says*, though as was said, perhaps his inward Meaning be the clear contrary. For since we cannot be inform'd of *another's Mind* otherwise than by *outward* Signs, all use of Discourse would be to no purpose, if by *mental Reservations*, which any man may form as he lists, it might be in his power to elude what he had declared by Signs usually accepted to that end.
>
> The other obligation which concerns *Discourse*, consists in this, that every man ought by his *Words* so to express to another his *Meaning*, that he may be plainly *understood*.[20]

Hutcheson explicitly refers to these claims,[21] but of greater importance for us is the fact that Hume's account of promising in *Treatise* Book III, where his own views on language are expressed, reveals agreement with Pufendorf. Hume writes:

> to distinguish those two different sorts of commerce, the interested and the disinterested, there is a *certain form of words* invented for the former, by which we bind ourselves to the performance of any action. This form of words constitutes what we call a *promise*, which is the sanction of the interested commerce of mankind. When a man say *he promises any thing*, he in effect expresses a *resolution* of performing it; and along with that, by making use of this *form of words*, subjects himself to the penalty of never being trusted again in case of failure. A resolution is the natural act of the mind, which promises express: But were there no more than a resolution in the case, promises wou'd only declare our former motives, and wou'd not

create any new motive or obligation. They are the conventions of men, which create a new motive, when experience has taught us, that human affairs wou'd be conducted much more for mutual advantage, were there certain *symbols* or *signs* instituted, by which we might give each other security of our conduct in any particular incident. After these signs are instituted, whoever uses them is immediately bound by his interest to execute his engagements, and must never expect to be trusted any more, if he refuse to perform what he promis'd. (T.521–2)

Hume claims that there is nothing "requisite to form this concert or convention, but that every one have a sense of interest in the faithful fulfilling of engagements, and express that sense to other members of the society" (ibid.).

the will alone is never suppos'd to cause the obligation, but must be express'd by words or signs, in order to impose a tye upon any man. The expression being once brought in as subservient to the will, soon becomes the principal part of the promise; nor will a man be less bound by his word, tho' he secretly give a different direction to his intention, and with-hold himself both from a resolution, and from willing an obligation. (T.523)

There are, however, some exceptions. We absolve from such responsibilities a speaker who jests, or who is ignorant of the conventions. Unfortunately, "as the obligation of promises is an invention for the interest of society, 'tis warp'd into as many different forms as that interest requires, and even runs into direct contradictions, rather than lose sight of its object" (T.524). Theologians, for example, recognised "the obvious truth, that empty words alone, without any meaning or intention in the speaker, can never be attended with any effect" (M.31n, re-phrasing T.525), and "they have commonly determin'd, that the intention of the priest makes the sacrament" (T.525); "the terrible consequences of this doctrine were not able to hinder its taking place; as the inconvenience of a similar doctrine, with regard to promises, have prevented that doctrine from establishing itself" (ibid.).[22] Promises "arise from human conventions" and conventions themselves are not to be understood in terms of private intentions – or 'promises' in the rejected sense (T.490) – although we may talk of "agreement" when a "common sense of interest is mutually express'd, and is known to both" parties, and "produces a suitable resolution and behaviour" (ibid.). "Two men, who pull the oars of a boat, do it by an agreement or convention, tho' they have never given promises to each other" (ibid.). This good example draws attention to the need for the two oarsmen to assume that they share common goals. Indeed, Hume holds that languages are "gradually establish'd by human conventions" (T.490), where a convention is taken to be a set of shared attitudes and procedures, not necessarily articulated or formalised, which enable members of a community to achieve common, determinate goals (see M.122).

Shortly after Pufendorf, other writers turned to different issues raised in the Port-Royal *Grammar* and *Logic*. Several, including Lamy, writing in 1675, agreed that there are not enough terms for all the ideas we have and addressed themselves to the problem of abbreviation or metaphor. Lamy[23] claimed that all subsequent languages derive from the first language given by God to Adam, and he also held that the criteria of good custom were to be found in the experience, reason or analogies of certain qualified judges. The chief interest of du Tremblay's *A Treatise of Language*, 1700, is that he begins to urge some philosophical difficulties, although he resorts to God at the crucial moment. Du Tremblay argues that we can teach children languages because we already possess language, but that men who could not speak could not determine what sorts of sounds to employ; in brief, without words men could not agree on words.[24] He surmises, in ways later developed by writers such as Vico and Condillac, that the first men communicated by natural signs which, as a result of slowly developing agreement, later functioned as arbitrary signs. Du Tremblay insists that as a condition of effective communication God needed to ensure that the first speaker and listener both had the same speech dispositions, the same brain images, and the same ideas in the mind.[25] It is possible that Hume read a popular work by César Chesneau du Marsais, *Des Tropes ou des Diférens Sens*, published in 1730. Following the Port-Royal writers, du Marsais argues that abstract terms do not represent real things, since there is no such thing as substance or whiteness; everything around us is particular, and abstract ideas serve as exemplars.[26] He also distinguishes between *le sens litéral*, for understanding which a knowledge of the language is sufficient, and *le sens abstrait*, for understanding which it is necessary to have particular impressions.[27] Adam Smith greatly admired Girard's *Synonymes François*, 1736,[28] which at times reads like a work in linguistic philosophy, and we know that Hume was familiar with the book.[29]

Insistence on effective communication as a bond of society, and on the conventional nature of language were two of the most important views which Hume adopted from the French writers he studied, although the former view had also been a central doctrine in Cicero, and Plato, of course, had canvassed the latter.[30] Stress on the conventional is important for Hume, because a reasonable man, in his eyes, is not one who merely performs some formal moves, but is to be defined, rather, in terms of what he has learned to do in particular social contexts. "Men cannot live without society" (T.402, 493, 363; M.35): this view, as prominent among French as among British philosophers after the middle of the seventeenth century, led to Hume's emphasis of the social nature of language, and underlay his recognition of the social nature of knowledge.

What we learn and how we learn it, is governed by the particular society in which we live, and what counts as acceptable behaviour is determined by the conventions of society. Learned conformity, we might say, is a condition of social being. An hypothetical being who lived cut off from all others – Adam, in fact, as characterised by Pufendorf, Malebranche, Shaftesbury, Butler, Hume and a host of other writers – would be "incapable" of "social discourse and conversation" (M.22). These tenets explain the tone of censure whenever Hume detects a "dispute of words" (G.1.154), because it is socially and morally reprehensible that such misunderstandings should arise; men are failing to be responsible communicators. If we suspect that confusion rests on "some ambiguity in the expression" (G.1.151) we want to find out what the speaker or writer is trying to say. Sometimes, we find that a man "abuses terms" because he "confounds the ideas of things" (G.1.154); sometimes, especially in questions of comparative merit, that the disputants are not comparing the same things, but "talk of things that are widely different" (G.1.152); sometimes, we find that it is genuinely difficult "to find *words*" to mark the precise distinction or point on a scale (G.1.121; 113n). But language is a tool for our own use, and the needs of various societies differ; by reflecting on the fact that "languages differ very much with regard to the particular words" by means of which a given distinction is made, we can make "very strong inferences concerning the manners and customs of different nations" (L.1.389n; see also 392n).

Emphasis on the public dimension of language leads Hume to talk of general language and general viewpoints. General language "being formed for general use, must be molded on some more general views and must affix epithets of praise or blame in conformity to sentiments which arise from the general interests of the community" (M.55); that is, language "must invent a peculiar set of terms in order to express those universal sentiments of censure or approbation which arise from humanity, or from views of the general usefulness and its contrary" (M.95). Earlier in this book (p.129) we saw the importance in Hume's system of "general" viewpoints, and of learning what constitutes a general viewpoint in representative cases when learning the language itself. Although there are occasions when it matters to the agent himself, it does not matter to others what a man feels in his heart when he makes judgments according to the general standards of his society (T.603). As social beings we have to learn what to say, and the conventions may vary between communities; but what matters for the purposes of communication is the articulation of publicly available viewpoints from which objective properties of phenomena can be discerned.

If one enters a foreign country, it is necessary "first, to learn the meaning of the terms in their language, and, then, to know the import of those terms and the praise or blame attached to them" (M.141: *A Dialogue*), since "every tongue possesses one set of words which are taken in a good sense, and another in the opposite" (M.8; G.I.266). Empirical study will be needed to determine what these terms are, in a given community, and their conditions of application. For example, confusion sometimes arises when the French "express self-love as well as vanity by the same term" (M.130n); we have already seen that writers from the Port-Royal period onwards deplored the ambiguity in such terms as *sentiment* and *sens*. Again, we might be misled by the evaluative terms in the Koran; examination of the text reveals, however, that the prophet "bestows praise on such instances of treachery, inhumanity, cruelty, revenge, bigotry, as are utterly incompatible with civilized society" (G.I.268). Language is full of clues about evaluations (M.8, 67), some of which are clearly expressions of self-interest (M.93); mastery of a language includes the ability to detect and respond appropriately to such features. In our own community, for example, Hume claims that we reserve the term 'beautiful' for exceptional cases determined by comparative judgment (G.I.154).

Brief consideration must now be given to the opening of the *Treatise*, where some readers have claimed to find a modern interest in, but a mistaken view of, language.[31] The aim of *Treatise* Book I, as both the Introduction and the *Abstract* make clear, is to explain the principles and operations of our reasoning faculty, and the nature of our ideas (cp. T.263). Versed as he was in the principles of classical rhetoric, it is unlikely that Hume intended his opening sections to be startling, or to be anything other than comfortably familiar. Book I Part I reverberates with allusions to Locke and Berkeley, to Hobbes and the Port-Royal *Logic*, and to Malebranche; Hume says in the *Abstract*, quite openly, that "this book seems to be written upon the same plan with several other works that have had a great vogue of late years in England" (A.183). In the same place he characterises the method used at the beginning of the *Treatise* ('he' is Hume himself):

> wherever any idea is ambiguous he has always recourse to the impression which must render it clear and precise. And when he suspects that any philosophical term has no idea annexed to it (as is too common), he always asks "from what impression that idea is derived?" And if no impression can be produced, he concludes that the term is altogether insignificant. It is after this manner that he examines our idea of *substance* and *essence*. (A.186; cp. T.65)

As should now be clear, Hume is adopting the Port-Royal method and terminology, and no doubt expects his readers to recognise that fact because one of his aims is to use their methods to discount some of their philosophical conclusions. Hume wants to know which ideas are *annexed* to certain philosophical terms, granting that words or sounds causally excite ideas, that the same idea may be annexed to different terms, and that "we do not annex distinct and compleat ideas to every term we make use of" (T.22–3; cp. T.93; E.166n); Hume further grants that we can properly use words for "unknown qualities" (T.168). He describes his enquiry into abstract ideas as one concerning "mental actions" (T.22), and a later passage helps us to understand his position:

'Tis impossible to reason justly, without understanding perfectly the idea concerning which we reason; and 'tis impossible perfectly to understand any idea, without tracing it up to its origin, and examining that primary impression from which it arises. The examination of the impression bestows a clearness on the idea; and the examination of the idea bestows a like clearness on all our reasoning. (T.74)

Only causation renders one thing intelligible in terms of another, because causation is the only "relation" "that can be trac'd beyond our senses, and informs us of existences and objects, which we do not see or feel" (ibid.). For Hume, as for the writers of the Port-Royal *Logic*, signification and annexation are partly causal notions; but it is unclear whether words are supposed to excite ideas in the way that impressions do. Hume at times seems to be undecided on the nature and extent of his enquiry into "the foundation of our reasoning" (T.97). In Book I he is often concerned to clarify what certain ideas are *of* (T.113), as when he talks about extension or vacuum (T.32, 62); at the beginning of Book II he says that it is no part of his present subject to enquire into the "natural and physical causes" of impressions (T.275).

Hume agrees with the Port-Royal writers that we cannot "by a multitude of words" "give a just definition" of simple impressions such as "*pride* and *humility*"; in the absence of definition, however, we can offer *descriptions* which may help us towards "explication" of the phenomena: "provided we agree about the thing, it is needless to dispute about the terms" (T.277; E.62). In philosophical contexts, prolonged controversy is often a sign of "some ambiguity in the expression" and a sign that "the disputants affix different ideas to the terms employed", although some words, such as *force, power, energy* "have very loose meanings annexed to them" (E.90, 88n). Verbal disputes in philosophy can be avoided by means of "clear definitions", "precision of those ideas which enter into any argument", and "strict and uniform use of those terms which are employed" (D.217). However, "controversies concerning the degrees of any quality or circumstance" are subject to "perpetual ambiguity", "from the very nature of language and of human ideas"; disputants "may here agree in their sense and differ in the terms, or *vice-versa*; yet never be able to define their terms, so as to enter into each other's meaning" (D.217). It may need philosophical reflection and analysis to reveal that a dispute is merely verbal; Hume's discussions of liberty and necessity, innate ideas, scepticism, theism, and personal identity, for example, are all philosophical, even though he reaches a point in each case where what remains can be set aside as merely verbal disagreement. The distinction between a "real" and a "verbal" dispute, in which Hume follows Arnauld and Nicole, is a distinction between the thoughts it is appropriate or justifiable to have in certain conditions, and what it is proper to say – which is a matter of linguistic conventions, the nature of which can be explained by competent grammarians (see G.1.151). The extended sense in which 'what it is proper to say' is synonymous with 'what it is justifiable to think' must be separated from grammatical discussions of usage (see G.1.451: "Can we seriously say.... We may as well assert ..."). Hume frequently insists on sharply distinguishing philosophers from grammarians (e.g. T.610), not because grammarians have characteristically encroached on the philosopher's territory, but *vice-versa*: "nothing is more usual than for philosophers to encroach upon the province of grammarians and to engage in disputes of words" (M.127). It should be mentioned that Hume talks of words, expressions, propositions and terms as having meaning or lacking it; but even though such items sometimes fail to express ideas, language, in its many forms, is the only medium available for the expression of ideas. Ideally, in Hume's view as in that of many other philosophers, language should be *transparent*, enabling us to concentrate upon the ideas the words mediate.

How do Hume's views compare with those of Locke ? Locke's interest in language was subordinate to his analysis of knowledge and the understanding; his discussions of abstraction and general names, of the relations between ideas, words and things, of the use and abuse of language and the way in which language can provide clues to problems about knowledge, are all to be understood against that background. We know from his private notes and public references that he had read much of the contemporary writing on language, including the Port-Royal *Grammar* and *Logic*, and works by Ménage, Lamy, Pufendorf, Malebranche and others, and he seemed content to use their views where appropriate; few of his comments on language were original, or intended to be. He adopts the Port-Royal terms 'idea' and 'signification', and constantly re-iterates their views that "the meaning of words" consists in "the ideas they are made to stand for by him that has them",[32] and that "the only sure way of making known the signification of the name of any simple idea is by presenting to his senses that subject, which may produce it in his mind, and make him actually have the idea that word stands for".[33] Locke also agrees with Arnauld and Nicole that there is no natural connection between words and ideas, that many things are called by the same name which differ internally, and that words are "no man's private possession", although we should make every effort to understand a speaker's intentions.[34] For Locke, as for his predecessors and his successors, the main functions of language are the recording and communication of thought;[35] Hume took little notice of Berkeley's objections to this simplified view, precisely

because his own interest was not in *language,* as such. In line with essentially practical, rather than metaphysical aims of the *Essay,* we could say
that Locke's concern in Book III is not primarily about the nature of
language, but about how mistakes are made in the acquisition of knowledge.[36] It is true that contemporaries such as William Wotton, in 1694,
and later writers such as Horne Tooke, in 1786, failed to read the discussion in that way, partly because of their own preconceptions;[37] but
there is reason to think that Hume was not misled, if only because he saw
no need for any overt discussion of language in Book I of the *Treatise.*[38]

In a letter of 1754 Hume contrasts associations "of the intellectual
kind" with other species: "in much of our own thinking, there will be
found some species of association. 'Tis certain we always think in some
language, viz. in that which is most familiar to us; and 'tis but too frequent
to substitute words instead of ideas" (L.1.201).[39] Unfortunately, the view
that we think in language is left unsupported; unless he means by it that
the *expression* of thought requires language, Hume did not mention any
such view in his earlier philosophical work, and it may reflect his reading
subsequent to it. No matter how many problems Hume leaves unexplored,
his own position is moderately clear: talking is distinct from thinking, and
most talk expresses thought; when confused by talk, we have to struggle
to identify the thought behind it, and in the rarified regions of philosophy
we often find that such thought is itself confused or incoherent.

The upshot of this discussion can be stated briefly. The beginning of
the *Treatise* is about the nature and relation of our ideas, and Hume's
remarks are heavily derivative. Hume nowhere addresses himself to the
nature of language *per se,* and nowhere propounds a theory of language.
Influenced by his extensive French reading, he locates language in its
social dimension, and considers some aspects of that dimension in *Treatise*
Books II and III; incidental remarks in Book I are subordinate to the
central concern with ideas, and the aim of establishing that none are
innate. In order to get at a man's ideas one requirement is *transparency* in
the medium, language; Hume offers no sustained reflection on the conditions of transparency (see p.112 above). Like Bacon and Locke, Hume
did not speculate on the origins of language; in this, he differed from many
of the French writers, almost all of whom, it is true, resorted to a Divine
act.

A study of Hume's views on language can be usefully supplemented by
a study of his own use of language. Among the many terms which he left
undefined, some, no doubt, were used in a semi-technical way no longer
familiar to us (e.g. *idea, signification*), some (e.g. *meaning*) carried less
weight than they would today, and others (e.g. *argument*) ranged over
most of the entries recorded by the *Oxford English Dictionary* (e.g. discussion; middle term; conclusion; proof; evidence; consideration).
Although frequently discussed in the past, there is still need for a balanced

judgment on the meaning and roles Hume assigned to his doctrine concerning impressions and ideas. Hume did not strenuously pursue the questions about meaning, truth and justification which unavoidably arise in a comprehensive discussion of knowledge, and which he only occasionally mentions.[40] Careful analysis is required of his notion of abstract ideas, and of the scope of grammar; in addition, because we know that Hume aligned himself with Cicero on such matters, attention should be given to his views on rhetoric, and to the influence of those views on the overall presentation of his own works. I shall contribute to analyses of these issues on another occasion.

Summary. In this section we have seen that:

1. Hume refers to most of the prominent writers on language of his time, but particularly to seventeenth-century French writers on grammar and rhetoric. Among these, Vaugelas is significant, for emphasising that language constantly changes, and therefore that usage rather than rules should be studied in order to determine and clarify signification.

2. Almost all writers agreed that language was the invention of man, and thus a convention-governed phenomenon. The Port-Royal *Logic* proclaimed the standard view that language expresses thought, and that whereas grammarians might profitably list the ideas men have agreed to connect with certain sounds, philosophers should concern themselves with real definitions of things, in terms of their essential attributes.

3. Under the influence of the Port-Royal, other writers took up issues such as metaphor, and the origins of language. Hume's account of promising owes much to Pufendorf's discussion, of 1672, of the roles of intention and convention in communication. Hume developed the view that languages are slowly established by human conventions, and endorsed Cicero's contention, widely adopted in the seventeenth and eighteenth centuries, that effective communication is a necessary bond of society; as a result, Hume tends to treat what he regards as verbal disputes as morally irresponsible.

4. Hume accepts that language is a tool for our use, and that the needs of various societies differ. The conventions which govern language are essentially shared procedures, often unformulated, for attaining common goals, and they presuppose the recognition and adoption of general viewpoints; these are learned in the process of learning the language itself, as are the evaluative overtones, and associations of the vocabulary. Foreigners always need to know such facts about language in order to understand the values of a society.

5. *Treatise* Book I is about the principles and operations of our reasoning faculty, and the nature of our ideas. The opening sections were not intended to be strikingly original. Under the influence of the Port-Royal writers, Hume asks what ideas are annexed to certain philo-

sophical terms. Annexation and signification are at least partly causal notions; sounds causally excite ideas, and the same idea may be annexed to different terms. Hume also follows the Port-Royal view that simple impressions cannot be defined, but only 'described'. It is often a philosophical discovery, however, that some disputes are only 'verbal', concerning propriety of usage, and not a 'real' dispute over the conditions for making claims of the kind in question.

6. Locke's interest in language was subordinate to his analysis of knowledge and understanding, and many of his comments were derivative, especially from the Port-Royal writers.

   Hume did not directly address himself to the nature of language, and did not propound a theory; moreover, he did not recognise the need for a theory of meaning, and one should beware of anachronistic interpretations of his aims.

Hume's views about usage and convention are mentioned casually, not least because it was no part of his scheme to discuss them, and because he shared those views with many of his contemporaries. There is no case for ascribing to him a crude positivist view of meaning, and none for assuming that the sometimes complex claims made about ideas, by him and his predecessors, can be readily translated into alternative twentieth-century terms.

FIVE

Hume's Ends

Nature and Moderation

The point of this study has been to establish sources of Hume's views as a means to determining his ends, and the reasons for his route to them. One of his major tasks was to provide a theoretical support for predetermined conclusions; but his goal was to offer a secular philosophy of man, for man. The goal itself involved an attitude towards the practice of philosophy, and the aim of the present chapter is to characterise that attitude. In order to do this, it is necessary to comment on his views about moderation and scepticism; we shall find that there are significant parallels between some of his views and those of his predecessors such as Cicero on the one hand, and those of modern philosophers such as Wittgenstein on the other.[1]

We saw in the first chapter that Cicero expressed many of the basic tenets Hume wished to support. In arguing that man should live in harmony with nature, Cicero recognised that the term 'nature' can be taken in different senses: as a non-rational cause of motion, as a rational force, as the whole of existence, as order or design of the kind displayed in organic matter. Moreover, the view that all animals have the common end of living according to nature, although their own natures differ, reveals a further sense of 'nature', synonymous with 'essence'.[2] A philosopher's task, according to Cicero, is thus to establish the nature of man, in this last sense, and to set out what is involved in living according to that nature. Man differs from the lower animals chiefly in his superior capacity for thought, which enables him to trace causal connections, to link the future with the present, and to develop language, which is necessary for communication and which also functions as a social bond. All animals, however, share common instincts, such as those of self-preservation and propagation. Cicero contends that man is designed by nature for activity, and that one can consider the virtues as implanted by nature, but developed by reason. In the absence of certainty, probability must be the guide to life; in any case, practical life and extreme scepticism are incompatible. The influence of habit is great but, Cicero insists, nature itself, in the end, is always too strong for any habit. Self-knowledge is achieved by determining the character and extent of our mental and

physical powers, and a wise man gains peace of mind through restraint
and consistency. Moreover, stability in the political realm requires man
to overcome his egoism, to affirm his social nature and recognise its
implications; in brief, to live in harmony with one's own nature entails
living in harmony with others, and such a life is governed by *moderatio*
and *honestum*.

In *Meditation* VI Descartes distinguished between 'nature', taken as
the sum of all things, and a limited sense in which it is taken as what is
given to man, understood as a finite composition of mind and body. In
this latter sense, we can be misled by nature, and we should not regard its
promptings as "règles très certaines"[3] for determining the essence of
things outside us. We saw in the first chapter how Malebranche extended
such reflections, and claimed that natural judgments are essential to life,
although they can indeed mislead us, as when we hold that what we sense
is outside us; such natural judgments are like sensations in their immedi-
acy and ubiquity, and "sans eux on ne peut rendre raison de nos diverses
sensations". Malebranche also agreed with his predecessors that in all
practical sciences, including the science of man, we must judge by
probabilities. It was left to Bayle to underline the link between what he
called 'naturalism' and atheism:

> on peut réduire l'Athéisme à ce dogme général, que la Nature est la
> cause de toutes choses, qu'elle existe éternellement, & d'elle-même,
> & qu'elle agit toûjours selon toute l'etenduë de ses forces, & selon les
> loix immuables qu'elle ne connoit point.[4]

Notoriously, the term 'nature' was used in both allegedly neutral and
overtly normative ways by almost every thinker of the seventeenth and
eighteenth centuries, to cover a diverse range of phenomena and to mark
a large range of distinctions. Sometimes it denoted what was universal,
simple, original and prior to reason; sometimes it was deemed to be everywhere the same, and to be understood to function mechanically; at other
times an organic view of nature was canvassed. Shaftesbury, like
Berkeley[5] and a host of other writers, deplored the fact that philosophers
talk "of nature with so little meaning" (*Characteristics*, 1.74). His own
view was that "nature may be known from what we see of the natural state
of creatures, and of man himself, when unprejudiced by vicious education" (1.325). He argues that "the social or natural affections" are
"essential to the health, wholeness, or integrity of the particular creature"
and "the welfare and prosperity of that whole or species, to which he is by
Nature joined" (II.293). Shaftesbury holds that only "contrary habit
and custom (a second nature)" – Cicero's phrase – can displace what is
"of original and pure nature" (1.260); and if the word 'innate' is objection-
able in this context, he suggests we "call instinct that which Nature
teaches, exclusive of art, culture, or discipline" (II.135). Apart from
conspicuous references to *honestum* (e.g. 1.92; II.268n to *De Finibus*),

Shaftesbury constantly argues for "the principles of moderation" (11.224), observing that "all affections have their excess, and require judgment and discretion to moderate and govern them" (11.178). In his view, there is a close relation between what is natural and what is moderate (see e.g. 1.325). We shall see that when Hume himself argues for this last point, the ambiguities in the two terms cause him difficulty.

When writing to Hutcheson, Hume significantly observed: "I cannot agree to your Sense of *Natural*. 'Tis founded on final Causes" (L.1.33; cp. LG.31). In the same letter Hume confesses his own allegiance to Cicero, and Cicero is the most general influence on Hume in this context, with Shaftesbury and, in certain respects, Malebranche providing additional inspiration. One warning, however, succinctly expressed by Bayle, went unheeded in almost all the discussions; it does not follow that because "*cela vient de la nature, donc cela est bon et juste*".[6]

Hume ascribes various achievements to nature, and refers to principles and laws of nature, natural propensities, propensions and sentiments, for example. Remarking that "the word, Nature" is "ambiguous and equivocal", he contrasts the term with five senses in which 'unnatural' can be taken: miraculous, unusual, artificial, civil, moral (T.474); the last two are omitted when he repeats his distinction in later works (E.30n; M.124n), but he has meanwhile added a further sense of 'natural' in which it can be taken as 'essential' or 'necessary' (T.484); he also associates the term with "constancy and steadiness", and contrasts it with "original" (T.280–1). To declare that "nature, by an absolute and un-controllable necessity has determin'd us to judge as well as to breathe and feel" (T.183; cp. 269; D.134) is not to revert to a rationalist definition of man; it is to make an empirical claim about his characteristics which sub-sequently serves to define normality. Hume insists that, likewise, the two operations of the "principle, which makes us reason from causes and effects", and "which convinces us of the continu'd existence of external objects, when absent from the senses", are "equally natural and necessary in the human mind" (T.266). We should not be surprised, therefore, by Hume's references to "what is natural and essential to anything" (T.258); the emphasis is on the pre-reflective, and in that sense 'animal', and the non-supernatural; man is an integral part of nature, and nature, although often unexplained, is in principle explicable. It might be thought that Hume's remarks in the first *Enquiry* contradict such a view. "Nature has kept us at a great distance from all her secrets", he declares, and "no philosopher who is rational and modest has ever pretended to assign the ultimate cause of any natural operation" (E.47, 44). Belief that the future will resemble the past is a "necessary" "operation of the soul", and "all these operations are a species of natural instinct, which no reasoning or process of thought and understanding is able either to produce or prevent" (E.60; cp. 111); moreover, it is

conformable to the ordinary wisdom of nature to secure so necessary
an act of the mind by some instinct or mechanical tendency which
may be infallible in its operations, may discover itself at the first
appearance of life and thought, and may be independent of all the
laboured deductions of the understanding. (E.68)

Many of Hume's references to natural principles, operations, beliefs, are
intended to provide "foundation" to our enquiries: "at this point it
would be very allowable for us to stop our philosophical researches"
(E.60). That is, they are cited as terminal notions which mark problems
for future reflection, but which serve at present to increase our understanding. As the last quotation shows, however, their status is unclear:
Hume needs them as elements or principles in his methodology, and he
also wishes to claim that we experience them as basic, unanalysable facts;
a similar ambivalence attends his familiar contention that there can be no
ideas without impressions. The notion of nature as a problem-marker
is clearly seen when it is used to denote whatever prevents the triumph of
sceptical reasoning (see e.g. T.269); and the empirical dimension of the
move is affirmed in the second *Enquiry*: "it is no just reason for rejecting
any principle confirmed by experience that we cannot give a satisfactory
account of its origin, nor are able to resolve it into other, more general
principles" (M.42).

One further expression requires brief comment, because it is associated
with various senses of nature, and was widely used by Cicero and by
Hume's French predecessors: "custom and habit". Fontenelle remarked
that "la coûtume a sur les hommes une force qui n'a nullement besoin
d'être appuyée de la raison". Hume associated the notion of custom with
undesigned, pre-reflective, repetitive behaviour: "we call every thing
CUSTOM, which proceeds from a past repetition, without any new reasoning or conclusion"; "the far greatest part of our reasonings, with all our
actions and passions, can be deriv'd from nothing but custom and habit"
(T.102, 118). He claims that

> Custom has two *original* effects upon the mind, in bestowing a
> *facility* in the performance of any action or the conception of any
> object; and afterwards a *tendency or inclination* towards it; and from
> these we may account for all its other effects, however extraordinary.
> (T.422)

In the first *Enquiry* Hume repeats his view that "all inferences from
experience . . . are effects of custom, not of reasoning" – deductive
reasoning, that is – but he tries to clarify the character and explanatory
force of the claim:

> wherever the repetition of any particular act or operation produces a
> propensity to renew the same act or operation without being impelled
> by any reasoning or process of the understanding, we always say that
> this propensity is the effect of *custom*. By employing that word we

pretend not to have given the ultimate reason of such a propensity. We only point out a principle of human nature which is universally acknowledged, and which is well known by its effects. Perhaps we can push our inquiries no further or pretend to give the cause of this cause, but must rest contented with it as the ultimate principle we can assign of all our conclusions from experience. (E.57)

These remarks occur, of course, during Hume's "sceptical" attack on the alleged domain of reason, where that faculty is restricted to the apprehension of necessary truths and deductive relations. To say that "habit is nothing but one of the principles of nature" (T.179) is to say that certain repetitions of behaviour occur; but some habits are learned or even consciously acquired (cp. T.140) and many can be consciously acknowledged and subsequently modified by the agent himself. Above all, however, neither natural nor artificial habits are necessarily good or beneficial; even the custom or instinct to suppose that the future will resemble the past, "like other instincts, may be fallacious and deceitful" (E.167), in the sense that any empirical prediction may remain unfulfilled, and there is no (demonstrative) necessity that a particular description, applicable in this instant, should be instantiated on some other occasion. Moreover, the possibility of mistake is a necessary condition for classifying a claim as empirical, not a sufficient condition for judging such a claim to be false; no intellectual recognition of this truth is required, however, to enable animals to go on living, because the conditions of life are satisfied outside the reflective consciousness and control of the animal itself.

One other point should be mentioned. Artificial habits can conflict with natural habits. For Hume, "education is an artificial and not a natural cause . . . built almost on the same foundation of custom and repetition as our reasonings from causes and effects" (T.117). Its artificial character can be seen most clearly in "the effects of discipline and education on animals, who by the proper application of rewards and punishments may be taught any course of action the most contrary to their natural instincts and propensities" (E.113). The combination, therefore, of natural and artificial "custom and education" "mold the human mind from its infancy and form it into a fixed and established character" (E.95). It is important to recognise that responses that are 'natural' in one of its senses, may need to be self-consciously curbed and subsequently constrained by artificial habits, in order to bring about responses that are 'natural' in another sense; thus, the commonplace passions and fears which result from ignorance of causes and lead to religious superstitions and practices, *ought* to be curbed by the defining characteristics of a proper human being, in the normative sense: the desire to search for causes, the recognition of our limited knowledge and capacities, and the acceptance of our place as part of nature. The nature of man, in brief, requires that nature, in some aspects, be improved, and this view is nowhere more apparent than in Hume's observations on moderation, to which we must now turn. In the *Treatise* they are not prominent. He maintains that "our moderation and abstinence are founded" on the supposition of shared interests and regular conduct among our fellows (T.490), and that philosophy "if just, can present us only with mild and moderate sentiments" (T.272); but there is no association of 'natural' and 'moderate', and no indication of the central place accorded to the notion of moderation in the *Essays* of 1741–2.

In the original preface to the 1741 volume, Hume declared that most of the essays "were wrote with a view of being published as WEEKLY-PAPERS, and were intended to comprehend the Designs both of the SPECTATORS & CRAFTSMEN", and he expressed the hope that readers would "approve of my Moderation and Impartiality in my Method of Handling POLITICAL SUBJECTS" (G.I.41). Clearly, sympathisers with Bolingbroke were thus expected to find their 'moderate' political views displayed with suitable Addisonian 'moderation'. The dominant aspect of the essays is political or, in a wider sense, moral, many of the discussions being focussed on the nature of the public good, and methods of its attainment. Almost no attention is given to the strictly epistemological issues canvassed in *Treatise* Book I, but on the other hand there is a good deal of comment on the roles of philosophy in society.

Hume's views on moderation can be considered, conveniently but artificially, under four aspects. Behind most of his claims there lies an assumption that the health of an organism, and the efficiency of a machine, both require the proper functioning of all their constituent elements. Sometimes he implies that not all our faculties can operate at once or in harmony, and on these occasions it is presumably a man's duty to restrain the more powerful faculties with the aim of a democratic representation for them all: "When the affections are moved, there is no place for the imagination. The mind of man being naturally limited, it is impossible that all its faculties can operate at once: And the more any one predominates, the less room is there for the others to exert their vigour" (G.I.242).

Firstly, Hume regards an attitude of moderation as a condition of understanding. Philosophers sometimes overwork a favourite explanation, reducing the dissimilar to the similar, or conflating causes and collateral effects (G.I.214, 320, 328); on other occasions they rely on a single source of evidence or fail to see that the evidence is incomplete or inconclusive ((G.I.229n, 351n, 400). "Impartiality" (G.I.414n) is one quality needed, parallel to disinterestedness in the realm of morals and criticism, and the criteria, as we shall see, are precisely those adumbrated for mitigated scepticism, when that is properly understood.

Secondly, Hume consciously adopts an attitude of moderation as a rhetorical means to secure communication and conviction. Expressions such as "perhaps I have gone too far in saying . . ." (G.1.93; cp. 259n) reveal a move akin to artillery bracketing, where the proper range is determined by shots both beyond and short of the target. Rhetorically, this allows the audience an opportunity to think through their own position and prepare their defences before encountering the full attack. In partial contrast to this device, however, is another whereby moderation is recommended as a means to elicit moderation in response (G.1.117n; cp. M.84–5). Newtonian considerations lie behind several of Hume's remarks here, with frequent allusions to equal and opposite forces and to inertia: thus "one extreme produces another" (G.1.409; cp. 462), a claim that Hume is willing to treat as "necessary" (G.1.355).

> All water, wherever it communicates, remains always at a level. Ask naturalists the reason; they tell you, that, were it to be raised in any one place, the superior gravity of that part not being balanced, must depress it, till it meet a counterpoise; and that the same cause, which redresses the inequality when it happens, must for ever prevent it, without some violent external operation. (G.1.333)

Hume considers the proper or natural condition of most bodies to be a state of equilibrium or balance, and such a condition is alterable only by some force. In an essay of 1758, significantly entitled 'Of the Coalition of Parties', he declares: "moderation is of advantage to every establishment: Nothing but zeal can overturn a settled power: And an over-active zeal in friends is apt to beget a like spirit in antagonists" (G.1.469). The same model of opposing forces lies behind his pendulum metaphors, and the claim that "violent Things have not commonly so long a Duration as moderate" (G.1.144n); Hume apparently puts this forward as an empirical claim, although it sounds like a definitional truth. As a result of his historical analyses, however, he came to see that what is judged, initially, as an excessive deviation from a given condition, may acquire, merely because of duration, the status of a new condition with its own centre of gravity and balance; thus, "Time, by degrees . . . accustoms the nation to regard, as their lawful or native princes, that family, which, at first, they considered as usurpers or foreign conquerors" (G.1.451; cp. T.557, 566). Moderation is relative to a reference point, and changes in that reference point bring changes in what counts as moderation. One other feature should be noted in connection with the rhetorical aspect of moderation. A moderate attitude enables one more easily to acknowledge mistakes and change one's mind (G.1.141n), without causing discomfort to oneself or confusion to others. Hume had already, in the *Treatise*, remarked that even if the opinions of philosophy are false, they are, unlike those of enthusiasts and fanatics, "merely the objects of a cold and general speculation, and seldom go so far as to interrupt the course of our natural propensities" (T.272). The best way to secure peace between opponents is "to prevent all unreasonable insult and triumph of the one party over the other, to encourage moderate opinions, to find the proper medium in all disputes, to persuade each that its antagonist may possibly be sometimes in the right, and to keep a balance in the praise and blame, which we bestow on either side" (G.1.464). Rhetorically, then, moderation requires careful assessment of a speaker's needs as well as of the audience's condition and commitments, together with the skilful adaptation of available means towards the desired ends: "there is not a more effectual method of betraying a cause, than to lay the stress of the argument on a wrong place" (G.1.470). Such considerations, it should be emphasised, were present to Hume in the writing of all his works, and receive their final, dramatic, embodiment in the *Dialogues*.

The third and fourth aspects of moderation are the concern of morality and politics. In *De Officiis* (I.xl.142) Cicero said that everything in the conduct of our life should "balance and harmonize, as in a finished speech", and that moderation was, above all, "the art of doing the right thing at the right time". Under the influence of Cicero Hume maintains that moderation is an essential constituent of genuine humanity (G.1.162, 274n, 408), and reveals itself in balanced judgments. Any "original inclination . . . or instinct" that a man has towards exclusive self-concern, must be "checked and restrained by a subsequent judgment or observation. . . . [I]t is reflection only, which engages us to sacrifice such strong passions to the interests of peace and public order" (G.1.455; this remark dates from 1748). It is as important, of course, to moderate the strength of our passions as it is to broaden their scope (G.1.206, 222, 281; 214) but this does not mean that we should adopt an attitude of "provoking coolness and indifference" (G.1.408). Hume nowhere states or implies that it is a proper act of moderation to mediate between, or compromise with, both of two adversaries who are equally wrong or immoral, or to "balance between the virtuous and the vicious course of life" (E.149); moderation, for him, involves neither taking the half-way position between any two views, whatever they are, nor seeking peace at any price. He fully agrees with Aristotle's opinion that it is often difficult to discern which actions and passions admit of a mean, and where it is to be found.[7] The procedures appropriate to enquiry and judgment may not be the same as and need to be distinguished from those appropriate to action based on such judgment; one can act with passion, after assessing the situation calmly. Sometimes there is a special task for a philosopher

> who is of neither party, to put all the circumstances in the scale, and assign each of them its proper poise and influence. Such a one will readily, at first, acknowledge that all political questions are infinitely complicated, and that there scarcely ever occurs, in any deliberation, a choice, which is either purely good, or purely ill. Consequences, mixed and varied, may be foreseen to flow from every measure: And many consequences, unforseen, do always, in fact, result from every

one. Hesitation, and reserve, and suspense, are, therefore, the only
sentiments he brings to this essay or trial. (G.I.475–1752)
We have already learned from the *Treatise* that to achieve a balanced view,
to arrive at a "*stable* judgment of things, we fix on some *steady* and *general*
points of view", because "'tis impossible we cou'd ever converse together
on any reasonable terms, were each of us to consider characters and
persons, only as they appear from his peculiar point of view" (T.581).
The common point of view, understood in both the literal and metaphorical senses we discussed, will constitute the standard, or norm, or
mean, or measure, or *modus* against which deviations will be measured;
Cicero himself observed that one aspect of moderation was associated
with *modus* (*De Officiis* I.xl.142). It is easy to see how, for Hume, a
common point of reference which acts as a condition of intelligibility and
communication, acquires a normative dimension, because the adoption
of a shared viewpoint helps to secure social cohesion and stability. Ideally,
a stable and moderate judgment leads to understanding, which in turn
leads to appropriate action when the passions provide the motive force.

Politically, Hume maintains that moderation is integral to peace,
stability, law and order, and like Shaftesbury, as we have seen, is ready
to inveigh against enthusiasm and superstition, faction, fanaticism and
zeal, wherever they appear – in politics, morality or religion (see G.I.149).
Consistent with such views, Hume holds that "violent innovations no
individual is entitled to make" (G.I.452; cp. T.552, 563), even though
the consequences be desirable and beneficial. He maintains that "factions
subvert government, render laws impotent, and beget the fiercest
animosities among men of the same nation, who ought to give mutual
assistance and protection to each other" (G.I.127). Man is an essentially
social being, and "the chief source of moral ideas is the reflection on the
interests of human society" (G.II.403); chaos results from a total
opposition between those engaged in such reflection, and that is why "the
only dangerous parties are such as entertain opposite views with regard
to the essentials of government" (G.I.464–1758). Where customs had
failed to establish moderation in a society, good laws could do so, but such
laws must be concerned with establishing or preserving liberty and serving the public good, ends worthy of the most strenuous pursuit (G.I.106,
107, 98). Although his own ideal was a commonwealth (see G.I.480ff.),
Hume believed it necessary to defend the "regular system of *mixed* government" (G.I.119) of his time, largely because of his view that excess
engenders excess.[8]

Hume fully admits that "all questions concerning the proper medium
between extremes are difficult to decide; both because it is not easy to find
words proper to fix this medium, and because the good and ill, in such
cases, run so gradually into each other, as even to render our *sentiments*
doubtful and uncertain" (G.I.121). This difficulty, combined with our

ignorance of the future (see G.1.475), leads to reliance on the past and on what is established, and therefore known; that is largely why "antiquity always begets the opinion of right" (G.1.110). Moreover, "human society is in perpetual flux, one man every hour going out of the world, another coming into it" (G.1.452; cp. 465), and stability can be maintained only by gradual innovations. It should be emphasised that Hume does not use the notions of inertia and equilibrium to argue for a static and unchanging society; rather, he subscribes to a dynamic model of a complex machine which can easily go wrong, needs the most tender care and maintenance, but which certainly needs to be kept moving: "rust may grow to the springs of the most accurate political machine, and disorder its motions" (G.1.493–1752).

It is here appropriate to return to the quartet of essays in which Hume began to experiment with the dialogue form, and in which, following the Ciceronian model, he briefly outlines elements of Epicureanism, Stoicism and Platonism, before characterising, in very much greater detail, a sceptical position. In 'The Epicurean' we read that although "the health of my body consists in the facility, with which all its operations are performed" (G.1.198), my will has little power over its internal condition. Worthwhile and lasting pleasure cannot result from self-absorption, because pleasure depends on both internal and external factors over which we have little control. Pride can beget only *"artificial happiness"* (ibid.). In the next essay, the stoic underlines the implication of this remark by stressing that man is a social being, but he denies the epicurean's claim that we can justifiably ignore the past and the future while enjoying the present (G.1.200). On the contrary, we can attain happiness only if we are historically conscious, noting our mistakes, and seeking their causes and their remedies (G.1.205). The stoic follows Cicero's comparison between man and other animals, and observes that chance can be combatted only by a knowledge of causes, wherein man differs from other animals; such knowledge is a necessary condition for attaining sustained happiness: "happiness cannot possibly exist, where there is no security; and security can have no place, where fortune has any dominion" (G.1.207). The epicurean failed to see that a social environment itself requires the exercise of social virtues, for these alone are sustaining: "as sorrow cannot overcome them, so neither can sensual pleasure obscure them" (G.1.208). The stoic asserts that a mind properly sensitive to social virtues will view "liberty and laws as the source of human happiness" and devote itself "to their guardianship and protection" (G.1.209). In effect, the stoic articulates a secular morality rooted in social virtues, as distinct from the egotistical, sensual indulgence and "lethargic indolence" (G.1.206) of the epicurean.

In "their reasonings concerning human life, and the methods of attaining happiness" (G.1.213) – the topic of the preceding essays –

philosophers, the sceptic insists, commonly overwork or mis-apply their favourite principles. People are governed by the narrowness not only of their understanding, but of their passions, and most of us are influenced by "a predominant inclination" to which our other desires submit (G.1.214). Once we realise that there is a "vast variety of inclinations and pursuits among our species", we may discern that one man "may employ surer means for succeeding than another", by "employing his reason to inform him what road is preferable" (G.1.215). To the objection that this is no more than "common prudence, and discretion", and that a philosopher might be expected to advise on ends rather than means, the sceptic replies that such a request rests on two confusions. First, "objects have absolutely no worth or value in themselves" (G.1.219), such as could be discerned by reason; we discussed the view in Chapter 3. Secondly, it is a mistake to think of a philosopher as being in possession of special knowledge, as if he were an expert in "magic or witchcraft"; he is not, in this sense, "a cunning man" (G.1.215) – Shaftesbury's phrase.[9] There is a third point. Because taste is subject not only to custom, prejudice and humour, but also to "education" (G.1.217), one can make some general observations about reliable grounds for happiness. "To be happy, the *passion* must be" moderate, social, cheerful and, in order to sustain it over any length of time, appropriate to the situation (G.1.220); and to achieve such appropriateness, historical reflection is necessary. A mind possessing these traits is not said to be a properly *rational* mind, as a reader might expect, but a *virtuous* mind. The two notions, however, are no longer separable, as the summary of the sceptic's argument at this stage of the essay shows: a virtuous mind is

> that which leads to action and employment, renders us sensible to the social passions, steels the heart against the assaults of fortune, reduces the affections to a just moderation, makes our own thoughts an entertainment to us, and inclines us rather to the pleasures of society and conversation, than to those of the senses. (G.1.221)

The sceptic adds that because "nature has a prodigious influence" over all men, rules of morality, and philosophical reflections generally, can aid only those who already have a "lively sense of honour and virtue" (G.1.222); philosophy can be no *"medicine of the mind"* – Cicero's phrase – to the perverse. What philosophy, broadly conceived, can do is to harness antecedent dispositions, and inculcate habits: "it is certain, that a serious attention to the sciences and liberal arts softens and humanizes the temper, and cherishes those finer emotions, in which true virtue and honour consists" (G.1.223). The *"artificial* arguments" of philosophy, however, "will never produce those genuine and durable movements of passion, which are the result of nature and the constitution of the mind"; indeed, there is a danger that "refined reflections", if they influence the passions at all, will entirely extinguish them, "rendering the mind totally indifferent and unactive" (G.I.225; cp. 456). A "disdain towards human affairs", found so often among philosophers, lasts only "as long as nothing disturbs him or rouses his affections" (G.I.227).

There are two major reasons why the fourth essay of the quartet is entitled 'The Sceptic', apart from its obvious debts to Cicero, and to Shaftesbury. Any challenge to an orthodox religious view, or to an alleged consequence of such a view, was commonly branded as 'sceptical' or even 'atheistic'; and since moral and epistemological enquiries were taken to be dependent upon religious views, any challenge to an established doctrine in these fields was also taken to be evidence of scepticism. In 'The Sceptic' the role of reason in the realm of value has been diminished, and an apparently unpretentious task assigned to philosophy: "It insensibly refines the temper, and it points out to us those dispositions which we should endeavour to attain, by a constant *bent* of mind, and by repeated *habit*"; "the reflections of philosophy are too subtle and distant to take place in common life, or eradicate any affection" (G.I.224–5). The second reason, closely related to the downgrading of reason, displays itself in the positive attitude to life advocated by the sceptic: moderation. All the aspects we have so far mentioned are discernible in the essay, and we can summarise them before concluding this part of the discussion.

Firstly, moderation is a condition of understanding, requiring disinterestedness; secondly, moderation is a rhetorical device for securing communication and conviction, since moderation breeds moderation; thirdly and fourthly, moderation is a condition of political peace and moral and social stability, but in these contexts, no less than the others, it does not amount merely to compromise, it can be established by law, and it requires shared points of view and controlled passions. To these points we can now add three observations made earlier in this book. In our discussion of Hume's views on religion, we saw that he agreed with Cicero, and Malebranche too, in holding that in practical life we must be governed by probabilities and certain natural judgments; thereby we could achieve *moderatio*, but only if, in addition, we adopted a properly sceptical attitude towards religious claims. In our discussion of Hume's views on art, we saw that he held that a moderate amount of pleasure was necessary to the physical well-being of an individual, and the political well-being of society. During our discussion of art, we saw that not only does art arise under conditions of moderation, but that the criteria of its merit are also to be found in moderation; the mind's fundamental requirement of intelligibility in what it confronts, is grounded in our natural incapacity to change, instantly, from one passion or disposition to another; in this sense, some degree of consistency or uniformity in experience is necessary to the proper functioning of the mind.

Like several of Hume's favourite notions, including that of nature, *moderation* suffers from over-use, and among the puzzles to which it gives rise, two should be emphasised. Firstly, in view of his assertion that "all causes are of the same kind" (T.171), we might expect Hume to deny a distinction between causes and logical conditions, or at least to reduce the latter to the former. The cases we have discussed, however, show that he used the notion of moderation as both a causal and a logical condition, and it is unclear how he took them to be related. Secondly, as either a goal or an achievement, the criteria of moderation can be specified only in relation to existing contextual conditions and accepted standards; effective action pre-supposes knowledge of those criteria. It is unclear, however, how we could expect to learn from history or from cultures whose notions of moderation are defined in relation to contexts other than our own; and if an attitude of moderation must be self-adjusting to changing circumstances, it is unclear what other principles function as checks. Above all, on Hume's account, acts of moderation could not be due to original principles of nature, and could not become habitual in any strong sense entailing the absence of conscious thought; this point will be of great importance in our consideration of mitigated scepticism, and its place in philosophy, to which we must now turn. Moderation, like mitigated scepticism, can only be 'natural' in one of its normative senses; that is, in the sense in which a properly developed and balanced human being will display it.

Knowledge and Scepticism

In the 'Author's Letter' to the translator of the *Principles of Philosophy*, Descartes listed four principal means by which a man may obtain knowledge: the possession of clear notions, our own sensory experience, the sensory experience of others which we hear about in conversation, books; the fifth means, revelation, produces infallible belief.[10] Hume also discusses four sources of knowledge: instinct, education, experience, abstract reasoning. He formally defines none of these notions, and like Hume himself I shall say nothing about abstract reasoning.

Hume frequently compares man's capacities and instincts with those of other animals and, like Cicero, he claims that men differ from other animals in "the superiority of their reason" (T.610). Man "traces causes and effects to a great length and intricacy; extracts general principles from particular appearances; improves upon his discoveries; corrects his mistakes; and makes his very errors profitable" (G.1.153). Moreover, other "animals are but little susceptible either of the pleasures or pains of the imagination" (T.397). All animals, however, including man, derive "many parts" of their knowledge "from the original hand of nature"; "these we denominate 'instincts', and are so apt to admire as something very extraordinary and inexplicable by all the disquisitions of human understanding" (E.115). Some instincts strike us as more extraordinary than others; for example, we find a dog's avoidance of fire or precipices less remarkable than a bird's "art of incubation" (T.177; E.116). But the dog's behaviour proceeds "from a reasoning, that is not in itself different, nor founded on different principles, from that which appears in human nature" (T.177). Indeed,

> the experimental reasoning itself, which we possess in common with beasts, and on which the whole conduct of life depends, is nothing but a species of instinct or mechanical power that acts in us unknown to ourselves, and in its chief operations is not directed by any such relations or comparisons of ideas as are proper objects of our intellectual faculties. (E.115)

Hume is referring to this latter type of comparative reasoning of ideas when he denies that any animal is guided by "any process of argument or reasoning" in its conclusions that "like events must follow like objects, and that the course of nature will always be regular in its operations" (E.113). Hume's claim is intended to be universal: no brute, child, philosopher, nor "the generality of mankind in their ordinary actions and conclusions" (E.114) engages in self-conscious deductive reasoning on these occasions. They do not, because they could not. The assumption of the uniformity of nature *is* just an assumption, and cannot be 'demonstratively' proved, and the beliefs which impel to action are immediate sentiments of certain kinds.

We have already seen, in the previous section, that for Hume the philosophical analysis of the nature of man ends, in one direction, with descriptions of the unanalysed 'instincts' or 'principles of nature' he exhibits: "we must stop somewhere in our examination of causes" (M.47n). Instincts are not ultimate explanations in the rationalists' sense which Hume so vehemently repudiates, but terminal notions which ground our current explanations in the light of our present knowledge, interests and methods. At least some instincts "may be fallacious and deceitful" (E.167), and some natural habits can be associated with instincts.

But if our basic life-sustaining actions are informed by instincts, "more than one half of those opinions, that prevail among mankind" are due to education, and "the principles, which are thus implicitly embrac'd, over-ballance those, which are owing either to abstract reasoning or experience" (T.117). We know that Hume regards education as an artificial cause, and as essentially the inculcation of artificial habits, sometimes within man-made institutions (T.353; G.1.164, 178; E.95). In Chapter 2 we saw that discussion of education and testimony go together, because "the experience of others" can become ours only by "the credit" we give to "their testimony" (L.1.349). "There is no species of reasoning more common, more useful, and even necessary to human life than that which is derived from the testimony of men and the reports of eye-witnesses and spectators" (E.119), but testimony "is not altogether infallible, but in some cases is apt to lead us into errors" (E.118). For important reasons associated with the fact that man is a social being, not all testimony can be false, but we shall return to this point shortly. Firstly, it needs to be emphasised that if the earliest stages of education are conceived as habit training, then a passive element is central:

> as to the youthful propensity to believe, which is corrected by experience; it seems obvious, that children adopt blindfold all the opinions, principles, sentiments, and passions, of their elders, as well as credit their testimony; nor is this more strange, than that a hammer should make an impression on clay. (L.I.349)

Hume holds, then, that only after I have accepted certain things am I in a position to reflect on the nature of the testimony and to question it. A parallel remark by Wittgenstein should be quoted here: "The child begins by believing the adult. Doubt comes *after* belief. I learned an enormous amount and accepted it on human authority, and then I found some things confirmed or disconfirmed by my own experience" (*On Certainty*, §§160–1).[11] And alongside Hume's views on instincts, we should place Wittgenstein's claim that in the earliest learning processes, man can be regarded as "a primitive being to which one grants instinct but not ratiocination" (OC.475): "the squirrel does not infer by induction that it is going to need stores next winter as well. And no more do we need a law of induction to justify our actions or our predictions" (OC.287).

Without overt discussion, Hume implicitly assigns to memory a central role in the acquisition of knowledge, since we must remember what happens to us as well as what we are told; 'experience', indeed, involves 'memory' in his scheme. "Animals, as well as men, learn many things from experience"; "The ignorance and inexperience of the young are here plainly distinguishable from the cunning and sagacity of the old, who have learned, by long observation, to avoid what hurt them and to pursue what gave ease or pleasure" (E.112–13). Although Hume refers here also to the "conjectures" of a greyhound, his main emphasis is on the passive element in learning, with particular stress on conditioning.

Hume devotes little attention to what we can learn by ourselves because he wishes to stress the social dimension of knowledge. The four most important tenets concern: the social nature of man, the public nature of discourse, the requirement of truth or at least trust in communication, the nature of language. Although all these points are evident in the first *Enquiry*, and, indeed, in the 1741–2 *Essays*, they make their first appearance only in *Treatise* Books II and III, not in *Treatise* Book I. All readers notice that in Book I man is treated as an apparently isolated being, whereas he is subsequently treated in his social relations with others. Hume's decision may have been influenced by a remark in Shaftesbury: "to understand the manners and constitutions of men in common, 'tis necessary to study man in particular, and know the creature as he is in himself, before we consider him in company, as he is interested in the State, or joined to any city or community" (*Characteristics*, 11.5).

Brief comment on the four tenets is here appropriate. Firstly, "men cannot live without society, and cannot be associated without government" (T.402, 485, 494; M.35); man can alleviate his necessitous condition only, if at all, by associating with others: "man is altogether insufficient to support himself; and . . . when you loosen all the holds, which he has of external objects, he immediately drops down into the deepest melancholy and despair" (T.352). An hypothetical self-sufficient being who had lived entirely alone and apart from all others, "would be as much incapable of justice as of social discourse and conversation" (M.22); and no men who "give free course to their appetites" can maintain society (T.568). The former point is important, because it alludes to one of Hume's favourite arguments, the Adam-argument, which was extremely popular among writers on the nature of man, and which appears in Pufendorf, Filmer, Locke, Butler, Hutcheson (to name only a few); the ancient model had been revived as a result of Hobbes and Milton and, by the time of Hume, Defoe's *Robinson Crusoe* had aroused additional interest in the argument. Two formulations will suffice to show its characteristic form. Pufendorf writes:[12]

> Let us suppose a man come to his full strength without any *over-sight* or *instruction* from *other* men; suppose him to have no manner of *knowledge* but what springs of itself from his *own natural wit*; and thus to be plac'd in some *Solitude*, destitute of any *Help* or *Society* of all Mankind beside. Certainly a more miserable Creature cannot be imagin'd. . . . It must then follow, that whatsoever Advantages accompany Human Life, are all owing to that *mutual help* men afford one another.

The main difference between this and Butler's version, which appeared while Hume was writing the *Treatise*, is that Butler focussed on the epistemological issues:

> if we suppose a person brought into the world with both these [powers of body and mind] in maturity, as far as this is conceivable; he would plainly at first be as unqualified for the human life of mature age, as an idiot. He would be in a manner distracted, with astonishment, and apprehension, and curiosity, and suspense: nor can one guess, how long it would be, before he would be familiarized to himself and the objects about him enough, even to set himself to any thing. It may be questioned too, whether the natural information of his sight and hearing would be of any manner of use at all to him in acting, before experience. . . . In these respects, and probably in many more, of which we have no particular notion, mankind is left, by nature, an unformed, unfinished creature; utterly deficient and unqualified, before the acquirement of knowledge, experience, and

habits, for that mature state of life, which was the end of his creation, considering him as related only to this world.[13]

Hume's frequent thought-experiments based on this example (see e.g. T.293; A.187; E.42, 56; M.23; N.24; D.196, 203) receive their subtlest expression in the *Dialogues*:

> Were a man to abstract from every thing which he knows or has seen, he would be altogether incapable, merely from his own ideas, to determine what kind of scene the universe must be, or to give the preference to one state or situation of things above another. For as nothing, which he clearly conceives, could be esteemed impossible or implying a contradiction, every chimera of his fancy would be upon an equal footing; nor could he assign any just reason, why he adheres to one idea or system, and rejects the others, which are equally possible.
>
> Again; after he opens his eyes, and contemplates the world, as it really is, it would be impossible for him, at first, to assign the cause of any one event; much less, of the whole of things or of the universe. He might set his fancy a rambling; and she might bring him in an infinite variety of reports and representations. These would all be possible; but being all equally possible, he would never, of himself, give a satisfactory account of his preferring one of them to the rest. Experience alone can point out to him the true cause of any phenomenon. (D.145)

Hume is here repeating his fundamental view that, considered singly and discreetly, no item of experience points to its causal relations with any other item; so that "*reason* . . . by considering *a priori* the nature of things" (E.57n) can give no guidance, and imagination cannot alone determine which of its images has external reference or represents actuality. Only "*experience*", understood as repeated "sense and observation" (ibid.) establishes the customary inferences and expectations.[14] In the *Dialogues*, Hume moves overtly towards a Kantian view that brute experience is insufficient for understanding, and mere thought is insufficient for knowledge of the world.[15] But can Hume intelligibly formulate such a view, in the light of his insistence that there can be no ideas without impressions, and notwithstanding his early recognition of the need for rules (see e.g. T.110, 141, 146, 149)? It is not enough to reply that many thought-experiments require some relaxation in the normal criteria of intelligibility, and that Hume allows varying latitude to his doctrine of ideas.

Hume's remarks about what seems to be man's purely contingent need of society to ease his otherwise necessitous circumstances, are supplemented by tenets which function as logical conditions; he holds that there could be little knowledge without others on whom to rely for testimony about events we have not experienced ourselves, and there is no case for restricting the concept of knowledge to only *a priori* reasoning, or to individual experience. Hume's use of the term "necessity" is therefore not accidental:

> Man, born in a family, is compelled to maintain society, from necessity, from natural inclination, and from habit. The same creature, in his farther progress, is engaged to establish political society, in order to administer justice; without which there can be no peace among them, nor safety, nor mutual intercourse. (G.1.113, published only in 1777)[16]

The first point in Hume's attempt to establish the social aspect of knowledge is thus that man is born into a group, which trains him in its ways, and inculcates its rules "of conduct and behaviour" (M.21). The second point is that most of our claims must be open to public assessment. When someone talks about the world "the course of nature lies open to my contemplation as well as theirs" (E.151), and "it is almost impossible for us to support any principle or sentiment against the universal consent of every one" (G.11.152). In spite of the necessity for mutual checks and independent referents, general agreement, on occasion, might be mistaken, as over the disposition of the planets, or in the way the East Indian prince was mistaken about ice (G.1.218; E.121). The third point is that man exhibits "an inclination to truth and a principle of probity"; in due course we discover these qualities to be "inherent in human nature", but initially we simply assume it (E.119; T.405) because it is, indeed, a condition of the possibility of communication. The fourth point also concerns communication. In the last chapter we saw that, according to Hume, languages are "gradually establish'd by human conventions" (T.490), where conventions are taken as shared procedures, not necessarily rule-bound in any strict sense, for achieving common goals. Many activities are intelligible only on assumptions about social groups and conventions; thus, "a promise is not intelligible naturally, nor antecedent to human conventions" (T.516). Conventions are important factors in that "uniformity in human actions" without which "it were impossible to collect any general observations concerning mankind" (E.95). Indeed, "the mutual dependence of men is so great in all societies that scarce any human action is entirely complete in itself or is performed without some reference to the actions of others, which are requisite to make it answer fully the intention of the agent" (E.98). It follows that the "science of man" must take proper account of the social nature and context of man; it also follows that no account of knowledge can be adequate which restricts itself to what an individual can do by himself, by concentrating on himself, or "by study and reflexion alone" (T.486).

Hume's attitudes towards scepticism in particular, and philosophy in general, are governed by his views on the social nature of man and man's knowledge. There are differences, however, between what he says in the

Treatise and what he says in later works. In the *Treatise* he claims that:

> the study of history confirms the reasonings of true philosophy; which, shewing us the original qualities of human nature, teaches us to regard the controversies in politics as incapable of any decision in most cases, and as entirely subordinate to the interests of peace and liberty. (T.562; cp. 531)

This remark refers only to "controversies in politics", and it needs to be juxtaposed with earlier observations:

> many philosophers have consum'd their time, have destroy'd their health, and neglected their fortune in the search of such truths, as they esteem'd important and useful to the world, tho' it appear'd from their whole conduct and behaviour, that they were not endow'd with any share of public spirit, nor had any concern for the interests of mankind. (T.450)

This remark refers to the social negligence of some philosophers, who have ruined their health and benefited no one in the process. A Ciceronian model of philosophy in the service of man is here evident, but we are no wiser about scepticism. *Treatise* Book I, however, as we know, was accused of espousing "universal scepticism" (L G.17), and there, Hume constantly contrasts sceptical arguments with the "unavoidable" judgments nature "determines" (T.183) us to make. It is fortunate that man is saved by his natural judgments and responses, because his own sanity would be at risk were he to await the "self-destruction" of sceptical arguments (T.187). In all "abstruser subjects" "the attention is on the stretch: The posture of the mind is uneasy", the "effort of thought disturbs the operation of our sentiments", and "the straining of the imagination always hinders the regular flowing of the passions and sentiments"; under these conditions there can be no unhesitating belief, because belief "can never be entire, where it is not founded on something natural and easy" (T.185–6). Hume holds that minds, or the spirits in the minds, naturally follow the path of least resistance, although various factors, including the associative forces and the intensity of the original impressions, determine the ease with which a particular idea makes its way in the mind. "Such opinions as we form after a calm and profound reflection" require sustained and continuous attention, "but the moment we relax our thoughts, nature will display herself, and draw us back to our former opinion" (T.214). Hume insists, however, that although "very refin'd reflections have little or no influence upon us", it does not follow that "they ought not to have any influence"; indeed, it would be "a manifest contradiction" to "establish it for a rule" that they ought not (T.268) because, apart from prejudging the issue, it would result in the substitution of one dogma for another: the dogma, not that man ought to be governed entirely by his reasoning faculty, but that man ought not to be governed at all by his reasoning faculty. The detection of causal sequences and the interpretation of resembling but changing experiences require reflective thought; nature cures man of the "philosophical melancholy" induced by the second-order question of when and how to follow reason, "either by relaxing this bent of mind, or by some avocation". It is necessary to "live, and talk, and act like other people in the common affairs of life", but "in this blind submission" "to the current of nature" Hume declares that he shows "most perfectly" his "sceptical disposition and principles" (T.269). "Indolent belief in the general maxims of the world" displays scepticism because it is a belief caused by nature, without the intercession of reasoning, and because no formal argument for it is given or needed. Hume confesses, of course, that he feels himself "naturally *inclin'd*" towards philosophical speculation, that he is "concern'd for the condition of the learned world", and that he has an ambition to contribute "to the instruction of mankind"; "pleasure" in such endeavours is "the origin" of his philosophy. Nevertheless, "if we are philosophers, it ought only to be upon sceptical principles, and from an inclination, which we feel to the employing ourselves after that manner. Where reason is lively, and mixes itself with some propensity, it ought to be assented to" (T.270-1).

In their studies of human nature, philosophers discover the "contradictions, and absurdities, which seem to attend every explication, that human reason can give of the material world", and this is a "sufficient" reason, even if it "be not a good *general* reason for scepticism" (T.633). They also discover the force of nature, and the extent of its principles which sustain life in almost complete independence from conclusions of reason. But the universal natural beliefs, that is, the 'assumptions' we ascribe to man in order to make sense of what he does, can conflict with the consciously achieved results of an individual's, equally natural, inclination to pursue philosophy. Whatever doubts *he* has, however, presuppose that he is a living being, and a normal human being is defined in terms of someone over whom the universal 'beliefs' maintain dominance. In order to combat "superstition of every kind", philosophers should search for principles "which will suit with common practice and experience", and undertake this task with "an easy disposition", grounded in recognition of the apparent limits of reason: "a true sceptic will be diffident of his philosophical doubts, as well as of his philosophical conviction" (T.271-3). Such a view lies behind the justification of sceptical reasoning as a device for instilling "Modesty . . . and Humility, with regard to the Operations of our natural Faculties"; "a Kind of *Jeux d'esprit*" (LG.19).

At the very end of the *Treatise* Hume asserts that a man's "peace and inward satisfaction entirely depend upon his strict observance" of "the *social* virtues", and that "the most abstract speculations concerning human nature, however cold and unentertaining, become subservient to *practical morality*" (T.620–1; cp. 450). This view, coupled with the emphasis on moderation in the *Essays* of 1741–2, leads to a slightly different attitude towards scepticism in the first *Enquiry*. There, he argues that *a priori* we cannot determine "the proper criteria of truth and falsehood" for every "sphere" of inquiry (E.160); experience alone can teach us the criteria. That is why an exclusive attitude of doubt, before and during every investigation, and towards every conclusion we reach, is radically misconceived; the exclusive use of reason is typical of philosophers who "confine too much their principles" (G.1.213). Hume argues that *mitigated* scepticism is both more "durable and useful" than *excessive* scepticism, although it may result from it when the latter's "undistinguished doubts are, in some measure, corrected by common sense and reflection". Firstly, it is a useful check against dogmatism, and helps to instil a proper "degree of doubt and caution and modesty" (E.169–70). Secondly, it may succeed in "the limitation of our inquiries to such subjects as are best adapted to the narrow capacity of human understanding"; and we "find what are the proper subjects of science and inquiry" by "examination into the natural powers of the human mind" (E.170–1). Hume's view, not paralleled in Cicero, is that we might best appreciate the proper scope of an attitude or method, by experiencing the attitude or indulging the method to their limits, however painful that might be; it is as if succumbing to a disease protects one against further extreme attacks. Such a thought occurs in Wittgenstein: "In philosophizing we may not *terminate* a disease of thought. It must run its natural course, and *slow* cure is all important" (Z.382).[17] For his part, Hume declares that "to bring us to so salutary a determination, nothing can be more serviceable than to be once thoroughly convinced of the force of the Pyrrhonian doubt and of the impossibility that anything but the strong power of natural instinct could free us from it" (E.170); then we shall recognise that "philosophical decisions are nothing but the reflections of common life, methodized and corrected" (ibid.). It need be added only that Hume valued the dialogue form partly because it allowed the full expression of rival views.

Hume's attitude towards scepticism in the first *Enquiry* differs from that in the *Treatise* mainly in the "narrow limitation" of our inquiries. But although we become convinced of the need to limit our speculations by experiencing the bewilderment of excessive scepticism, each individual must discover for himself the limits within which he can comfortably move. More insistently than in the *Treatise*, Hume asserts that "nature has pointed out a mixed kind of life as most suitable to the human race"; "man is a reasonable being", but also "a sociable" and "an active being" (E.18). "Inward search or inquiry" "becomes in some measure requisite to those who would describe with success the obvious and outward appearances of life and manners" (E.19), but we have to recognise that man is a social animal, whose complex mechanisms are inexplicable by reference to reason alone. In Hume's view a properly functioning machine is one in which none of the constituent parts malfunction, idle, or run out of control; man functions as a balanced *organism* when his reasoning, social and active sides act as mutual checks.

It is because "difficulties, which seem unsurmountable in theory, are easily got over in practice" (T.572) that we deem only moderate scepticism to be compatible with ordinary life. But how, in advance, can an individual know what counts as moderation in his context, and where not to extend his inquiries? It will not suffice to rely on his teachers or his peers; on that score, Hume himself had no right to challenge what he took to be the prevalent superstitions and dogmas of his day. We must already know the boundaries if we are to keep within them; but while some areas of thought might be morally proscribed, however ineffectively, it is unclear how logical and psychological proscriptions would work. At the outset of investigation one can only be sceptical; if nature checks an indefinite extension of scepticism, then one can discover, in *retrospect*, the achievements of moderate scepticism. That is, one discovers the issues over which one did, and did not, withhold a decision.

The "moderate scepticism" (T.224) of philosophers also denotes the particular doctrine that man is a social animal, in which natural instinctive behaviour predominates, but over which education has some influence. This doctrine underlies Hume's assertion that no one ever sincerely held "that all is uncertain" (T.183), and it is allegedly supported by two reasons he cites against the possibility of "universal Doubt" (LG.19). Firstly, Pyrrhonist scepticism is "founded on this erroneous maxim, that what a man can perform sometimes, in some dispositions, he can perform always, and in every disposition" (D.133), a criticism parallel to Wittgenstein's attack on the proposition that "What sometimes happens might always happen" (*Philosophical Investigations*, §345).[18] Hume always acknowledged that the "authority" (T.143) depends on the circumstances of an argument, and with the further recognition of the importance of literal and metaphorical viewpoints (see e.g. T.537, 581, 625), it became clear that our knowledge-claims and beliefs are relative to context; since what counts or is to be accepted as 'knowledge' changes, one cannot lay down immutable foundations or criteria of knowledge, and it is significant that Hume gradually abandons his yearning for "clear and distinct" ideas and principles, and settles for the richer, if less determinate, method of varied and overlapping interpretations of nature. The second reason for rejecting the possibility of universal doubt concerns the nature of evidence and certainty. Hume had drawn a double distinction between kinds of evidence and kinds of certainty, on the one hand, and between degrees of certainty within each kind of evidence, on the other (see e.g. T.131; E.118): "there are many different kinds of

Certainty; and some of them as satisfactory to the Mind, tho' perhaps not so regular, as the demonstrative" (L.1.187). "The only objects of the abstract sciences, or of demonstration, are quantity and number" (E.171), but it is not demonstrative reasoning, but "other measures of evidence on which life and action entirely depend, and which are our guides even in most of our philosophical speculations" (A.184). In Hume's view and that of many of his predecessors, reasoning about matters of fact is, strictly, probable reasoning; causal relations are not logical relations, and causal inferences have no deductive certainty. Because, as we have seen, belief is more *"an act of the sensitive than of the cogitative part of our natures"*, we can say that "all probable reasoning is nothing but a species of sensation" (T.183, 103). This strictly formal distinction between knowledge and probability, however, will mislead us if it is allowed to infect our understanding of everyday language, and our confidence in experience. Hence Hume insists, as had the writers of the Port-Royal *Logic* and a host of other writers, that it is not "only probable the sun will rise tomorrow, or that all men must dye" (T.124; E.122); it is not only probable that my friend will refrain from holding his hand in the fire "till it be consumed"; "I know with certainty" these things, and "no suspicion of an unknown frenzy can give the least possibility" to such events (E.100). Hume claims that "extravagant sceptics" maintain their "opinion in words only" (T.214). Merely saying that one doubts, however, does not alone amount to doubting, as Wittgenstein also insists (*On Certainty*, §§10–12, 208–9); on the contrary, an identifiable context of a certain kind is a necessary condition of an utterance having a meaning, *a fortiori* of being an expression of doubt or knowledge. Hume contends that the test of whether a man "really" doubts what he claims to doubt is that he can "make it appear in his conduct for a few hours"; but it is "impossible" (D.132) for an extreme sceptic to pass this test, because he will either be dead ("If they be thoroughly in earnest, they will not long trouble the world with their doubts" (ibid.)), or no longer human, since his scepticism will "have totally destroy'd human reason" (T.187) and he will be deprived of the capacity for normal social intercourse.

Because he has already identified 'real belief' and 'causally efficacious belief', he feels entitled to argue that the "intense reflection" (D.132; T.268) of a total sceptic does not result in "real" doubt since natural constraints and propensities forestall any efforts he may make to conduct his life in accordance with those doubts. But a man might have some beliefs and doubts only under limited conditions or for a limited period, as Hume himself argued of some sceptical beliefs. A critic might describe such doubts as transient, ineffective, pointless, unreasonable, impracticable, or theoretical; but to do so is not to question the existence or reality of such doubts, and nowhere else does Hume cite the transience of a state as a reason for questioning its existence. In the context of scepticism, as in that of religion, Hume dismisses beliefs which he finds unjustified as unreal.

Aside from this objection, Hume himself endorses the doubts of the moderate sceptic, and claims a number of positive discoveries on his behalf. For example, one proper task for philosophy is the detection and prevention of various illusions from which all of us suffer at some time. At least five sources of illusion are identified: illusions caused by imagination (T.267), which become evident when we mis-represent similarities (T.551) (assuming, for example, that unknown causes are all "of the same kind or species" (N.30)) or when we make illicit comparisons (G.1.152); illusions caused by our passions (G.1.230n); or by "our partiality in our own favour" (D.148); or by scepticism (E.168); or by "religious superstition or philosophical enthusiasm" (M.158; G.1.414n). There are also illusions due to habit and custom (G.11.155). To avoid such illusions, we should search for "a natural, unforced interpretation of the phenomena of life" (M.68). This will help us achieve "an easy sympathy" with others, and our own "peace and inward satisfaction" (T.354, 620; M.103); at that stage, philosophy will pose no threat, since "every thing remains as before" (T.251). The unforced interpretations will match the mind's propensity to follow the easiest path, and since human nature is everywhere basically the same the interpretations offered will be found to gain general acceptance.

Such optimism should not be taken to imply that, in practice, and in every context, a philosopher's task is simple. Hume is clear that the appropriate method for dispelling a particular illusion will depend on its source and on the context; there is no single procedure, and some methods, even those established within a tradition, might be misguided. For example, introspection might be the wrong way to grapple with "questions concerning liberty and necessity" (E.102); a demand for simplicity might be misplaced, as we can see in some physical explanations, where it is the "source of much false reasoning" (M.116). It is not the task of moral philosophy to engage in "the examination of our sensations" (T.8), because the procedures in moral philosophy are "not the same" "as in physics" (M.116). A useful task for philosophers in these, as in other, cases, is to point out the use of misleading analogies; for although "all our reasonings concerning matter of fact are founded on a species of *analogy*" (E.112), nevertheless, suppositions of resemblance are "the most fertile source of error" (T.61, 551). Philosophers, like other people, are likely to misconceive the nature of their own activities. While it is their task to point out where "subtle and ingenious" "hypotheses and systems" in natural philosophy and ethics rest on mishandling language (M.8), it is not "for philosophers to encroach upon the province of grammarians and to engage in disputes of words" (M.127, 130). As we saw in the previous chapter, it is "worth while to consider what is real,

and what is only verbal" (G.1.151) in a dispute, but no special philosophical knowledge or acumen is needed to realise, for example, that
"a moral reflection cannot be plac'd on the right or on the left hand of a
passion" (T.236); although it may need one philosopher to persuade
another that the criteria for speaking of the "same" church differ from
those for speaking of the "same" sound and "same" river (T.258).
Philosophers may also be needed to persuade their peers that philosophy
properly begins and ends with what actually happens and what we in fact
do; philosophical reflection of the kind Hume pursues is abnormal and
unnatural, he admits, in the sense that the bulk of mankind survives
without it, and feels no need for it. In any community there are agreed
descriptions, however indeterminate or provisional, of what men characteristically do; it is Hume's view that philosophical explanations of
human nature, of the kind and level in which he is interested, are properly
tested by their compatibility with the original descriptions of the
behaviour at issue (cp. T.272). Philosophers generally resort to "obscure
and uncertain principles" when they fail to find "such as are clear and
intelligible" (T.158); but, Hume contends, to the extent that they are
concerned with beliefs and assumptions, and even processes, of which
men could be conscious, they invariably move in the wrong direction.

Several of Hume's immediate predecessors argued that man should not
be regarded as an exclusively rational being. Montesquieu wrote: "Il vaut
bien mieux enlever l'esprit hors de ses réflexions, et traiter l'homme
sensible, au lieu de le traiter comme raisonnable";[19] and Voltaire insisted:
"L'homme est né pour l'action, comme le feu tend en haut & la pierre en
bas. N'être point occupé & n'exister pas est la même chose pour
l'homme".[20] But it was Cicero's insistence, notably in *De Finibus* and
De Officiis, on man as an active, social being, that governed Hume's
account of human nature, and his attitude towards philosophy; especially
the subservience of abstract speculation to "*practical morality*" (T.621).
Summary. The last two sections can now be summarised.

1. Many of Hume's aims and conclusions were stated for him by Cicero;
   of particular importance is the view that man should strive to live in
   harmony with nature, and that such a life should be governed by
   moderatio.
2. Most writers, including both Cicero and Hume, acknowledged
   different senses of the term 'nature', but frequently traded on
   normative uses of it. Hume's 'natural' principles and operations of
   the mind are cited as terminal notions or problem-markers in his
   explanations of human nature; he tends to take them as both basic
   facts of experience, and elements in his methodology.
3. Neither natural habits, nor artificial habits mainly brought about by
   education, are necessarily good or beneficial; and they can conflict.
   For these reasons not everything can be left to nature, and some

control or mediation is required; 'nature', in some aspects, needs improvement.

4. The dominant notion of moderation in the 1741–2 *Essays* is not prominent in the *Treatise*, but is absorbed into the revised account of the understanding in the first *Enquiry*. Hume treats moderation as a condition of understanding, as a rhetorical device for securing effective communication, as an essential moral constituent of humanity, and as an essential element in political and social stability (there are also economic implications). In practical life, moderation can be achieved by relying on appropriate probability judgments, and by withholding assent from uncheckable dogmas. A moderate amount of pleasure is necessary to the well-being of both the individual and the state, and it is characteristically provided by art, the merit of which is assessed in terms of harmony, consistency and moderation. Moderation must not be confused with compromise. It should be added that although the notion is presupposed in his discussion of the virtues, Hume does not discuss moderation as a separate virtue.[21]

5. In the 1741 quartet of essays, the epicurean argues that worthwhile pleasure cannot result from self-absorption, and the stoic expounds a secular moral outlook rooted in the social virtues. The sceptic insists that man is governed by certain dominant inclinations, and that a man who achieves a balance between his passions is truly virtuous. In this context, 'virtuous' and 'rational' are treated as synonymous. The sceptic claims that abstract philosophy cannot affect ordinary life, but that what philosophy, broadly understood, can do is to harness man's dispositions, and inculcate habits which harmonise with them.

6. Hume's notion of moderation is overworked, and seems to function both as a cause and logical condition of states of affairs. The criteria of moderation are specifiable only in relation to existing limits, and knowledge of the limits and criteria is necessary before moderation can be achieved. Moreover, the criteria of moderation can change. In this sense, at least, moderation cannot function as a regulative principle guiding a man at the outset of his endeavours. In addition, the self-consciousness required prevents it from becoming a strictly habitual attitude, and it cannot be described as a natural propensity or principle.

7. Hume discusses four sources of knowledge: instinct, education, experience, abstract reasoning. He agrees with Cicero that man differs from other animals in his use of reason, especially to discover causes; this humanist view, along with the fact that he never renounces and generally presupposes, dualism, was enough to enable Hume to resist the materialist views of La Mettrie and others. Nevertheless, Hume insists that man derives much of his knowledge

from nature, in the form of 'instincts'; factual reasoning is itself such an instinct. 'Instincts' are among the natural data which function as terminal notions in Hume's analyses. Hume treats education as the inculcation of habits, re-inforced by rewards and punishments, and displaceable only in the same manner.

8. For Hume, knowledge has an essential social dimension; four related arguments contribute to that conclusion: those concerning the social nature of man, the public nature of discourse, the requirement of trust in communication, the conventional nature of language. While arguing that man cannot live without society, Hume uses the popular Adam-argument, in his final formulation of which he moves towards a Kantian position, according to which neither mere thought nor mere experience is alone sufficient for understanding. Hume treats man's need of others, not merely as a contingent means to alleviate his own situation, but as a logical condition of humanity.

9. In the *Treatise* Hume argues that man is fortunately saved by natural judgments and responses from the self-destructive consequences of excessive scepticism. When the mind is uneasy or strained, it cannot sustain belief or doubt; it is proper for philosophers to strive for ease of mind, especially since abstract speculation is one cause of unease. "Indolent belief in the general maxims of the world" is indicative of scepticism because neither the maxims nor belief in them is the result of conscious reasoning. Some individuals, however, experience a natural propensity towards sceptical enquiry, and this propensity leads to conflict with the universal natural propensities all men inherit.

10. At the end of the *Treatise* Hume advocates the Ciceronian view that abstract speculation ought to be subservient to practical morality. This view, supplemented by emphasis on moderation, leads to a different account of scepticism in the first *Enquiry*. There, scepticism is defined as properly applicable only to certain topics. The main contention of the resulting moderate scepticism is that our "self-command" "is circumscribed within very narrow boundaries" (E.80), because we are so much governed by our natural instincts. Hume claims that the transient beliefs of an extreme sceptic are not real because life cannot be conducted for any length of time in accordance with them; but he does not elsewhere take duration as a criterion of existence, least of all in the case of sensations and sensory states.

11. Hume uses the notion of 'moderate scepticism' to cover the manner, degree and scope of inquiry, and seems to concede that since the proper limits of scepticism are unknown to us in advance, we can only determine those limits by transgressing them.

12. Among the proper tasks for philosophy are the detection and pre-

vention of illusions which have their sources in our imagination, and passions, for example. But there is no single procedure which can dispel all illusions. It is, moreover, a philosophical discovery that nature has established a mixed life as best for man; a life which harmonises his capacities for action, social communion and reasoning.

Parallels with the Later Work of Wittgenstein

The aim of this section is to reveal some of the striking parallels, and contrasts, between Wittgenstein's later views about philosophy and scepticism, and the conclusions we ascribed to Hume in the previous section.

An initial outline will show the kind of similarities in question. Wittgenstein holds that if we recognise the fundamental role of training in the acquisition of beliefs and capacities, we shall see that such education presupposes ranges of natural and instinctive behaviour which, as it were, it sometimes codifies, sometimes extends. Training is a social activity, requiring the acquiescence of the participants; that is one reason why a different education may lead to the acquisition of different concepts. Many philosophical muddles can be traced to misconceptions about the nature of the behaviour that education codifies, or to mishandling the codification. In Wittgenstein's view, philosophical problems are not empirical, but what he calls 'conceptual', and in many cases the proper philosophical method is 'description' not explanation. Our linguistic behaviour has roots in primitive behavioural activities, and changes in our linguistic performances entail changes in our concepts, and thus in the meanings of the words we use. Scepticism of a Cartesian variety is ultimately incoherent, not just mistaken, because it fails to take account of how man, as a social animal, acquires cognitive attitudes. The anxieties felt by post-Cartesian empiricists over their failure to 'justify' inductive arguments, rested on misconceptions about the nature and varieties of justification. Wittgenstein claims that philosophers should examine the grounds of beliefs, not their causes; and the ultimate ground is what a man does.

We can now turn to the detailed expression of these views. Wittgenstein declares: "I really want to say that scruples in thinking begin with (have their roots in) instinct. Or again: a language-game does not have its origin in *consideration*. Consideration is part of a language-game. And that is why a concept is in its element within the language-game" (*Zettel*, §391). Many language-games are extensions of primitive behaviour (see Z.545), and it is often misleading to apply to primitive reactions terms which imply the learning and application of rules; it might be wrong, for example, to speak of 'understanding' in connection with a particular "primitive language-game" (P I.146). In Wittgenstein's view, "any explanation has its foundation in training. (Educators ought to remember this.)" (Z.419); very often what we teach is a "capacity" (Z.421). In teaching a child to talk, for example, "the teaching of language is not explanation, but training" (PI.5), and during the process the child "learns to react in such-and-such a way; and in so reacting it doesn't so far know anything. Knowing only begins at a later level" (OC.538). The following paragraphs, also from *On Certainty*, are important:

472. When a child learns language it learns at the same time what is to be investigated and what not. When it learns that there is a cupboard in the room, it isn't taught to doubt whether what it sees later on is still a cupboard or only a kind of stage set.

473. Just as in writing we learn a particular basic form of letters and then vary it later, so we learn first the stability of things as the norm, which is then subject to alterations.

474. This game proves its worth. That may be the cause of its being played, but it is not the ground.

475. I want to regard man here as an animal; as a primitive being to which one grants instinct but not ratiocination. As a creature in a primitive state. Any logic good enough for a primitive means of communication needs no apology from us. Language did not emerge from some kind of ratiocination.

Three points in these passages are important to our enquiry: emphasis on the context for doubt, reference to "the ground" of an activity, and reference to instincts. To the first two points we shall return. Firstly, however, we should observe that, at the outset of his learning, man should not be credited with ratiocination, because that is precisely one of the capacities to be taught and developed. Initially, animals learn, and are taught, what to *do*; children, for example, "do not learn that books exist, that armchairs exist, etc. etc., – they learn to fetch books, sit in armchairs, etc. etc." (OC.476). If it is inappropriate, at this stage of their learning, to ascribe to children theories and presuppositions about what they are doing, or knowledge of rules which could codify their activities, there may be ranges of adult behaviour which would be better understood if described as 'primitive' or 'natural' or 'instinctive'. Wittgenstein remarks that "our naïve, normal way of expressing ourselves, does not contain any theory of seeing – does not show you a *theory* but only a *concept* of seeing" (Z.223); or, to take another example:

Being sure that someone is in pain, doubting whether he is, and so on, are so many natural, instinctive, kinds of behaviour towards other human beings, and our language is merely an auxiliary to, and further extension of, this relation. Our language-game is an extension of primitive behaviour. (For our *language-game* is behaviour.) (Instinct.) (Z.545)

By emphasising the central place of *doing* in the acquisition of knowledge, at least in the early stages, Wittgenstein shows the degree of acquiescence, if not pure passivity, that must prevail:

> We do not learn the practice of making empirical judgments by learn-
> ing rules: we are taught *judgments* and their connexion with other
> judgments. *A totality* of judgments is made plausible to us. When
> we first begin to *believe* anything, what we believe is not a single
> proposition, it is a whole system of propositions. (Light dawns
> gradually over the whole.) (OC.140–1)

Although "what we believe depends on what we learn", and although
"bit by bit there forms a system of what is believed", Wittgenstein holds
that the system itself "is something that a human being acquires by means
of observation and instruction. I intentionally do not say 'learns'"
(OC.286, 144, 279). Sometimes the conditions required for conveying
and acquiring a particular capacity are complex; for example, to grasp
what "expressive playing" in music is, a pupil may need knowledge and
experience of a whole culture (Z.164). But even here, perhaps, as in the
case of judgments of colour, and also in mathematics, "if there were not
complete agreement, then neither would human beings be learning the
techniques which we learn. It would be more or less different from ours
up to the point of unrecognizability" (PI.p.226). That is why "an
education quite different from ours might also be the foundation for quite
different concepts" (Z.387).

If our grasp of concepts has its roots in what we learn and are taught to
do, it is clearly important to understand the methods appropriate for
characterising what we do:

> How could human behaviour be described? Surely only by sketching
> the actions of a variety of humans, as they are all mixed up together.
> What determines our judgment, our concepts and reactions, is not
> what *one* man is doing *now*, an individual action, but the whole hurly-
> burly of human actions, the background against which we see any
> action. Seeing life as a weave, this pattern (pretence, say) is not
> always complete and is varied in a multiplicity of ways. But we, in our
> conceptual world, keep on seeing the same, recurring with variations.
> That is how our concepts take it. For concepts are not for use on a
> single occasion. (Z.567–8)

Wittgenstein would agree with Hume that assumptions of resemblance are "the most fertile source of error" (T.61). Because of their
re-applicability, concepts may over-emphasise similarities, and blind us
to the nature of the particular case. Wittgenstein remarks that some of
our misunderstandings over "the use of words" are caused by "certain
analogies between the forms of expression in different regions of
language"; sometimes these misunderstandings "can be removed by
substituting one form of expression for another" (PI.90). Sometimes,
he claims, when we are "impressed by the possibility of a comparison,
we think we are perceiving a state of affairs of the highest generality"

(PI.104). We must always ask ourselves whether a putative similarity is *important* for our purposes (Z.380); and this may help us see that we do not always have "a single concept everywhere where there is a similarity" (ibid.). Furthermore, we cannot justifiably assume that the recurrence of a proposition ensures that it is being used in the same way or for the same purposes. On the contrary, "the same proposition may get treated at one time as something to test by experience, at another as a rule of testing" (OC.98); "our empirical propositions do not all have the same status, since one can lay down such a proposition and turn it from an empirical proposition into a norm of description" (OC.167, qualified in OC.321). A good example of a proposition treated in quite different ways is Hume's "first proposition" (A.185) that there are no ideas without impressions. This is sometimes treated as a testable empirical claim, sometimes as a methodological device for establishing the meaning of puzzling expressions, and sometimes as an unquestioned "general maxim" (see e.g. T.5; A.186; T.6). The proper way to take Hume's proposition depends on the particular context and the stage reached in the overall argument.

What consequences do Wittgenstein's remarks have for the characterisation of his own philosophy? Although, in one place, he says that "what we are supplying are really remarks on the natural history of human beings" (PI.415), this is clearly not his view of philosophy. On the contrary, when pointing out that his interest is not in the causal explanation of the formation of concepts, he writes:

> Our interest certainly includes the correspondence between concepts and very general facts of nature. (Such facts as mostly do not strike us because of their generality.) But our interest does not fall back upon these possible causes of the formation of concepts; we are not doing natural science; nor yet natural history – since we can also invent fictitious natural history for our purposes. (PI.p.230)

Philosophical investigations, in Wittgenstein's view, are not factual or causal but "conceptual investigations" (Z.458). Dismissal of causal enquiry is crucial in his account of the limits of philosophy, as is evident in his discussion of the justification and grounds of belief. "The causes of our belief in a proposition are indeed irrelevant to the question what we believe. Not so the grounds, which are grammatically related to the proposition, and tell us what proposition it is" (Z.437): "Giving grounds, however, justifying the evidence, comes to an end; – but the end is not certain propositions' striking us immediately as true, i.e. it is not a kind of *seeing* on our part; it is our *acting*, which lies at the bottom of the language-game" (OC.204). It is of the utmost importance to realise that even the notion of justification has boundaries; indeed, "justification by experience comes to an end. If it did not it would not be justification" (PI.485). "At the end of reasons comes *persuasion*" (OC.612); "if I have exhausted the justifications I have reached bedrock, and my spade is turned. Then I am inclined to say: 'This is simply what I do.'" (PI.217). In so far as philosophical problems are concerned with those human activities which form the bedrock of our language-games, "problems arising through a misinterpretation of our forms of language", and whose "roots are as deep in us as the forms of our language" (PI.111), the proper philosophical method is 'description':

> we may not advance any kind of theory. There must not be anything hypothetical in our considerations. We must do away with all *explanation*, and description alone must take its place. And this description gets its light, that is to say its purpose, from the philosophical problems. These are, of course, not empirical problems; they are solved, rather, by looking into the workings of our language, and that in such a way as to make us recognize those workings: *in despite of* an urge to misunderstand them. The problems are solved, not by giving new information, but by arranging what we have always known. (PI.109)

Although it is perfectly possible to reform language "for particular purposes" (PI.132), that is not a task for philosophers; their work "consists in assembling reminders for a particular purpose" (PI.127). "Philosophy may in no way interfere with the actual use of language; it can in the end only describe it. For it cannot give it any foundation either. It leaves everything as it is" (PI.124). Much of what we say will then have the form "This is how things are" or "*this language-game is played*" (PI.134, 654). Wittgenstein emphasises that "there is not *a* philosophical method, though there are indeed methods, like different therapies" (PI.133) – although most fall under the general classification of 'description' – and this is connected with the fact that, because of the inter-connection of human activities, it will not be "a *single* problem" that is solved, but rather "problems" (PI.133). In Wittgenstein's view, "the confusions which occupy us arise when language is like an engine idling, not when it is doing work" (PI.132); by reminding ourselves of its essential roles in human activities, in what we do, we can set it back to work. This is one consideration behind the remark that "the real discovery is the one that makes me capable of stopping doing philosophy when I want to. – The one that gives philosophy peace, so that it is no longer tormented by questions which bring *itself* in question" (PI.133).

Once we begin to grasp the connections between "the concept of teaching and the concept of meaning" (Z.412), and realise that "a great deal of stage-setting in the language is presupposed" (PI.257) in our linguistic activities, many issues come into focus, but none more clearly than traditional philosophical speculations about doubt. Wittgenstein holds that "a person can doubt only if he has learnt certain things; as he can miscalculate only if he has learnt to calculate. In that case it is indeed involuntary" (Z.410). Thus, "if you tried to doubt everything you would not get as far as doubting anything. The game of doubting itself presupposes certainty" (OC.115); this means that, *pace* Descartes, our "first attitude of all" could no more be one of doubting than it could "be directed towards a possible disillusion" (Z.415). It is easy to misrepresent the case here, so that doubt is dismissed merely on pragmatic grounds: "But it isn't that the situation is like this: We just *can't* investigate everything, and for that reason we are forced to rest content with assumption" (OC.343). On the contrary: "the *questions* that we raise and our *doubts* depend on the fact that some propositions are exempt from doubt, are as it were like hinges on which those turn"; "That is to say, it belongs to the logic of our scientific investigations that certain things are *in deed* not doubted" (OC.341-2). We must recognise that "about certain empirical propositions no doubt can exist if making judgments is to be possible at all" (OC.308). A child, for example, "learns by believing the adult. Doubt comes *after* belief" (OC.160); and a teacher would be quite right to reprimand a pupil who "continually interrupts with doubts", because at that stage his "doubts don't make sense at all" (OC.310). Thus, a pupil who "cast doubt on the uniformity of nature, that is to say on the justification of inductive arguments . . . has not learned how to ask questions. He has not learned *the* game that we are trying to teach him" (OC.315). Some putative expressions of doubt simply would not be understood, such as a doubt "whether the earth had existed a hundred years ago" (OC.231). "I shall get burnt if I put my hand in the fire: that is certainty. That is to say: here we see the meaning of certainty. (What it amounts to, not just the meaning of the word 'certainty'.)" (PI.474); someone who argued that "it is *only in the past* that I have burnt myself" has failed to grasp "the character of the belief in the uniformity of nature" (PI.472). Philosophical sceptics, of a Cartesian variety, say, subscribe to "a false picture of *doubt*" (OC.249); they assume, falsely, that "we are in doubt because it is possible for us to *imagine* a doubt" (PI.84), and fail to see that they "have no system at all within which" their "doubt might exist" (OC.247). The trouble is that "it may easily look as if every doubt merely *revealed* an existing gap in the foundations; so that secure understanding is only possible if we first doubt everything that *can* be doubted, and then remove all these doubts" (PI.87). Such a view ignores the crucial fact that doubting is a practice we are taught; and we are also taught the places, within the system of beliefs we acquire, where the exercise of doubting is proper. We learn that "a doubt without an end is not even doubt" (OC.625), that "at the foundation of well-founded belief lies belief that is not founded" (OC.253).

Wittgenstein emphasises the inter-connection of our beliefs. Our convictions, doubts, knowledge, methods of verification are all said to form systems (OC.102, 126, 410, 279): "all testing, all confirmation and disconfirmation of a hypothesis takes place already within a system. . . . The system is not so much the point of departure, as the element in which arguments have their life" (OC.105). It is essential, in each case, to ask how doubt is "introduced into the language-game" we are examining (OC.458), because "doubting has certain characteristic manifestations, but they are only characteristic of it in particular circumstances" (OC.255). One problem is that there exists "no clear boundary" between "cases where doubt is unreasonable" and "others where it seems logically impossible" (OC.454). Of course, where "a doubt would be unreasonable, that cannot be seen from what *I* hold" (OC.452), since it is not "just *my* experience, but other people's, that I get knowledge from" (OC.275). We must examine the system of beliefs in which the doubt is supposed to occur; it might then turn out that a doubt is possible only if a proposition is isolated from its natural surroundings (see OC.274). Eventually we must recognise that "the reasonable man does *not have* certain doubts" (OC.220), that "rational suspicion must have grounds" (OC.323), and that most enquiries properly end with the observation: "any 'reasonable' person behaves like *this*" (OC.254; see also OC.39, 47, 620).

We must also recognise that "my picture of the world . . . is the inherited background against which I distinguish between true and false" (OC.94). My world-picture is, so to say, "the substratum of all my enquiry and asserting" (OC.162); hence one can say that at the end of grounds is "not an ungrounded presupposition: it is an ungrounded way of acting" (OC.110). If we want to speak of certain propositions which "seem to underlie all questions and all thinking" (OC.415), propositions which "form the foundation of all operating with thoughts (with language)" (OC.401), then we might well come to "speak of fundamental principles of human enquiry" (OC.670). We should observe that although most of my convictions are "anchored in all my *questions and answers*" (OC.103), they have not been "consciously arrived at". "I do not explicitly learn the propositions that stand fast for me" (OC.152); they are acquired in acquiring the whole system of beliefs. It would be quite appropriate, to take an example from this book, for Hume to regard or describe the law of induction as a 'natural' belief, since it is generally "not an item in our considerations" (OC.135). Wittgenstein claims that we can discover the nature and scope of our most basic convictions only when the whole system in which they function is challenged. That is why something like "conversion" (OC.92, 612) may be necessary to overthrow my beliefs, to change my *"way of looking* at things" (PI.144).

Wittgenstein held that "if language is to be a means of communication, there must be agreement . . . in judgments" (PI.242). Since "we belong to a community which is bound together by science and education" (OC.298), we can even say that "knowledge is in the end based on acknowledgement" (OC.378). This means that "in order to make a mistake, a man must already judge in conformity with mankind" (OC.156). "Sure evidence is what we *accept* as sure, it is evidence that we go by in *acting* surely, acting without any doubt. What we call 'a mistake' plays a quite special part in our language games, and so too does what we regard as certain evidence" (OC.196). To survive as social animals we have to do what we have been taught to do; the non-conformist always risks being branded as insane. Thus, where we cannot fit a man's strange utterances into a framework of what we think he knows, such that we can say he is merely mistaken, we may doubt his sanity (OC.74, 465–469). This is another place where the philosophical sceptic goes wrong. Most of our remarks will not bear the weight of what we might call "metaphysical emphasis" (OC.482); the fact that I use all "the words in my sentence without a second thought, indeed that I should stand before the abyss if I wanted so much as to try doubting their meanings – shows that absence of doubt belongs to the essence of the language-game" (OC.370). Our ordinary certainty is "something that lies beyond being justified or unjustified"; rather, it is "something animal" (OC.359).

Wittgenstein offered no clear criteria of individuation and identity for his strange notion of a language-game, but he conceded that a language-game changes with time, that what counts as reasonable alters, and that some systems of beliefs are better than others (OC.256, 336, 286). It needs to be asked, therefore, who judges the efficacy of a language-game or its need for revision. Although Wittgenstein gives no explicit reply to the question (OC.326), it seems as if the judges would have to be the qualified practitioners in the particular field. Other practitioners learn who these are in learning the practice in question. We have already seen that Hume appeals to the notion of qualified practitioners (pp.64, 119), and also that he emphasises the dominance of instinct and education over the formation of our beliefs; by means of the latter move, he sought to establish the limited influence over our lives of rational thought and enquiry. But in stressing the extent of the relatively unconscious adoption of habits, attitudes and beliefs from our environment, both Hume and Wittgenstein face the problem of explaining the possibility of revision, extension and overthrow of our position. Their fundamental views are essentially conservative, grounded in the past and preservation of its traditions. Wittgenstein claims that, in the end, we must resort to persuasion or conversion in order to change a person's views, and these are devices as devoid of rationality, in the narrow sense, as the means by which our basic convictions were themselves acquired; it is as if only retraining can modify in any radical degree what we have been originally trained to do. Hume, on the other hand, sees reasoning as having its proper place in the social context, and one of its tasks as being the determination of the grounds of intelligibility of what we say. Every individual is taught and learns within a tradition, and although the conventions which operate within it are neither absolute nor sacrosanct, their authority suffices to restrain deviations until they can be absorbed within, or survive alongside, the tradition itself. To this extent, Hume gives to conventions, in terms of which all social phenomena are defined, a status which might be called that of the 'secular *a priori*'. Any general discussion of such matters would need to consider whether passivity must play a central role in any account of knowledge as a social phenomenon, and also what social consequences follow from a refusal to ground epistemology, and centre education, on the traditions of the community.

One reason for Wittgenstein's insistence on description, not explanation, as the proper philosophical method – granting that what we call 'description' may serve different functions (see PI.291, 304) – is that there is nothing in terms of which the fundamental principles and elements of thought could be explained; hence the characteristic remark at the end of philosophical investigation: 'This is so'. Moreover, he wants to avoid an impression of giving essentially causal accounts of human practices. By means of his emphasis on the fact that much early learning is and must be the acquisition of habit, often re-inforced by rewards and punishments, Wittgenstein is able to assert that subsequent following of rules also becomes habitual and unselfconscious; and since people are largely unaware of the rules they follow, he can view his own task as conceptual analysis of the conditions that must be fulfilled for them to perform as they do. His interest in such conditions explains why he never considers the detailed contexts of actual linguistic utterances – the precise words used; in this sense he does not discuss linguistic problems, and it does not matter to him what people say. However, if philosophy describes the conditions under which thought in its various forms is possible, it is not clear why there is no empirical aspect to the descriptions. Wittgenstein holds that the "everyday use" of language, when working properly, is generally clear (OC.347; cp.388), and that what we call 'philosophical' problems occur when the machinery of thought is idling; this is one reason behind the inconsequentiality of scepticism. On such a view it might seem as if philosophical problems are un-natural, and that one goal of philosophers should be to rectify the machinery of thought so that such puzzles no longer occur. This feature of Wittgenstein's position has its parallel in Hume's attitude towards excessive scepticism. It would be a question of fact, of course, to determine whether equilibrium had been restored and no philosophical tasks remained, and it might be a philosopher's responsibility to ensure that social practices did not generate new puzzles which could hamper people's lives. It is unlikely that Wittgenstein would have agreed with this last suggestion, because he assigned no preventive, as opposed to therapeutic, task to philosophy (see PI.255; Z.382).

Summary.

1. Wittgenstein holds that 'consideration' is a relatively sophisticated form of thought, and has its roots in instinct. At the earliest stages of learning, man is essentially an animal. Initially, we teach children to do things; they learn what to investigate and what not to, and they gradually acquire, unselfconsciously, whole systems of beliefs.

2. Training a child involves an element of passivity on his part, and this needs to be remembered when descriptions are offered of the complex weave of human behaviour. Accounts in terms of concepts are likely to mislead us about particular cases.

3. For Wittgenstein, philosophical investigations are not causal, but conceptual; they seek to establish the grounds of our various judgments. But the giving of grounds ends in our just doing certain things; it does not end, as Descartes held, in our seeing certain truths with peculiar clarity. By comparison, Hume's position is here ambivalent since he talks both of basic natural responses and propensities, and of the need to establish clear and distinct impressions as the ground of our beliefs.

4. If the end of justification is persuasion, the proper philosophical method, according to Wittgenstein, consists in description; to this end, however, there are many routes, although in each case the appropriate way is likely to illuminate a set of inter-related issues. Because philosophical problems characteristically occur when the machinery of thought is idling, setting it back to work should produce peace of mind, and alleviate former anxieties.

5. When the links between teaching and meaning are grasped, together with the importance of the background to all human activities, the place of scepticism and doubt can be properly understood. Doubt has to be learned, and it presupposes belief in what is not to be doubted. Beliefs and methods are learned as systems, and our basic convictions are not consciously arrived at. Above all, we are taught what it is reasonable to do, and non-conformists tend to be socially ostracised. Ordinary certainty is so basic as to be 'animal' in nature.

6. In these contexts, Hume clearly differs from Wittgenstein in two major respects. He has no theory of meaning, and thus cannot link the concepts of teaching and meaning. He does not restrict philosophy to a description of the grounds of judgment, although that is a part of his endeavour. On the contrary, Hume is centrally interested in the causes of certain phenomena.

7. For our purposes, however, some of the parallels are more interesting, especially because some readers have sensed a discontinuity between Wittgenstein's thought and that of his predecessors, although there are many precedents even for the tone and style of his presentation. Both Hume and Wittgenstein characterised philosophy in the light of the fundamental fact that man is a social animal, governed by basic

instincts and powerful habits. Even the most commonplace (natural) philosophical problems are un-natural in comparison with our basic instincts and needs, and if we recognise the proper limits and functions of our human capacities, including thought. Not all philosophical problems, of course, have the same source or the same kind of solution, but any reasonings, Hume holds, "lose their force by being carried too far" (G.1.118n): "there is no virtue or moral duty, but what may, with facility, be refined away, if we indulge a false philosophy, in sifting and scrutinizing it, by every captious rule of logic, in every light or position, in which it may be placed" (G.1.456).

In what may have been intended as a preface to the 1741 essays, Hume wrote that learning had been a great loser "by being shut up in Colleges and Cells, and secluded from the World and good Company":

> Philosophy went to Wrack by this moaping recluse Method of Study, and became as chimerical in her Conclusions as she was unintelligible in her Stile and Manner of Delivery. And indeed, what cou'd be expected from Men who never consulted Experience in any of their Reasonings. (G.11.368)

In the first volume of the essays Hume contrasted the philosopher, whose "general abstract view of the objects leaves the mind so cold and un-moved", and the man of "business", who "has his judgment warped on every occasion by the violence of his passion", with the historian: "history keeps in a just medium betwixt these extremes, and places the objects in their true point of view" (G.11.391). It is no accident that Hume associates historical investigation with one kind of justification (G.1.464), because all of his writings after Book 1 of the *Treatise* can be seen as a natural progression towards a broader conception of philosophy, in which history is an integral element. For Hume, an understanding of social phenomena requires an understanding of the causal factors involved; in this book we have seen his own attempts to pursue such enquiries in con-nection with religious phenomena on the one hand, and artistic pheno-mena on the other. And his own solution to the dilemmas posed by scepticism is achieved by placing even the philosopher and his abstract speculations in social contexts where all men must live. In contrast to Wittgenstein's claim that extreme scepticism is logically incoherent, however, it might be urged that Hume is able to dismiss it only on prag-matic grounds, having failed to defeat the excesses of reasoning by further reasoning. Although Hume does cite pragmatic objections, the criticism overlooks Hume's basic contention that the criteria of formal logic are in-adequate for assessing the complex modes of man's natural and social prac-tices. Excessive scepticism is not logically self-contradictory; but Hume regards it as unjustifiable according to the only relevant criteria for judging man in his threefold aspect as a reasonable, social and active being.

With his Ciceronian insistence on making abstract philosophy subservient to practical life, it is not surprising that, after the *Treatise*, he never returns to his early speculations on space and time, or even personal identity; such speculations can be justified, if at all, only on aesthetic grounds, because they give pleasure to those whose constitution fits them for such endeavours. Even to these people, of course, a surfeit is likely to be displeasing. Philosophy in a narrow sense can be pursued for its own sake, then, but for both Cicero and Hume it is a moral tenet that reflection pursued for some social end is more valuable. There is a further moral tenet that philosophers should regard themselves as guardians of the traditions which secure the intelligibility and stability of social transactions; here again history must combine with analysis to achieve and disseminate understanding. Neither of these tenets is evident in the first book of the *Treatise*, although Hume does there insist that the source of, and check to, philosophy must be the common opinions embodied in the traditions we inherit through education. Few of Hume's contemporary critics extended their attention beyond Book I, and their horror at its anti-theological implications blinded them to the virtues of his secular theses, and coloured any interpretation they might venture of Books II and III. In writing the essays, and undertaking the historical research necessary for his work on religion, politics, economics, and then the history of the nation, Hume became clearer in his own mind about the nature and proper methods of philosophy. By the time of the two *Enquiries* its Ciceronian aspect should have been clear to all readers.

Our understanding of Hume is increased if we discern the ways in which he interacted with his predecessors and contemporaries. As an historical prelude to analysis of Hume's arguments, which must be undertaken elsewhere, this book has shown how his overall attitudes and some of his particular claims can be appreciated better in the light of their sources. The discussion, however, has implications for the interpretation of all of Hume's views, as most readers will have realised. Here, we have seen that in Hume, as in Wittgenstein and Cicero, we find an attempt to reconcile us to practices which our theory fails to justify, unless we radically alter our notions of justification;[22] in Hume, as in Cicero, we find that man's natural resistance to unbridled scepticism is strengthened by his social nature, and the public judgments it generates; and that those very same judgments ensure that discussions of value, in art as in morals, satisfy all man's needs for objectivity and rationality, without *a priori* thought on the one hand, and without having to concede a place to religious claims and practices on the other. Hume's own elaboration of the claim that man is governed not by reason but by his passions, considerably weakened its first dramatic impact: man is influenced primarily by inductive reasoning, which is more like feeling than it is like *a priori* thought, by his passions, which can be modified by inductive reasoning, and by certain basic responses which seem to be independent of any thought; the domain and practical influence of *a priori* thought and deductive reasoning from necessary premises are very slight.

Hume was not, of course, asking twentieth-century questions, did not have twentieth-century ideas of philosophy, and did not express himself in twentieth-century English. In discussing his thought it would be immoderate merely to substitute one label for another. But if Hume intended to incorporate Ciceronian elements within his philosophy, or if, as a separate point, much of his work can be illuminated by reading it as Ciceronian, we do well to establish the detail and significance of those perspectives. A balanced interpretation of Hume's thought requires a careful assessment of the extent to which his ends were in his beginnings, and his beginnings in his ends.

Notes

INTRODUCTION

1. John Laird, *Hume's Philosophy of Human Nature*, London, 1932.

2. Norman Kemp Smith, *The Philosophy of David Hume*, London, 1941. R. H. Popkin, 'David Hume: His Pyrrhonism and his Critique of Pyrrhonism', *Philosophical Quarterly*, Vol.1, 1951; see also his *The History of Scepticism from Erasmus to Descartes*, New York, 1964; and entries in the invaluable bibliographical guide to Hume studies: R. Hall, *Fifty Years of Hume Scholarship*, Edinburgh, 1978. Reference should also be made to T. E. Jessop, *A Bibliography of David Hume and of Scottish Philosophy*, London, 1938. John Passmore, *Hume's Intentions*, Cambridge, 1952, refers only briefly to Hume's debts.

3. Draft letter from William Cullen to William Hunter on the death of David Hume; Glasgow University Library, Thomson-Cullen Papers, 161.

4. John Leland, *A View of the Principal Deistical Writers*, 5th edn, London, 1766, I.360, 362.

5. See opening statement of Appendix I to the second *Enquiry*: "examine how far either *reason* or *sentiment* enters into all decisions of praise or censure" (M.104).

6. Hall, *Fifty Years*, p.14; P. M. S. Hacker, *Insight and Illusion*, Oxford, 1972, p.218n.

7. J. Harrison & P. Laslett, *The Library of John Locke*, Oxford, 1965; cp. J. Lough, 'Locke's Reading during his stay in France, 1675-79', *The Library*, Vol.8, 1958; J. Bonar, *A Catalogue of the Library of Adam Smith*, London, 1894.

8. P. Bayle, *Dictionaire Historique et Critique*, 3rd edn, Rotterdam, 1720, III.2143; *A General Dictionary, Historical and Critical*, London, 1734-41, VIII.100.

9. P. Bayle, *Pensées Diverses*, §§136, 138, in *Oeuvres Diverses*, La Haye, 1727-31, III.88, 89.

10. 'Sceptical doubts concerning the operations of the Understanding'; 'Sceptical solution of these doubts'.

11. John Gregory, *A Comparative View of the State and Faculties of Man with those of the Animal World* (1765), 4th edn, Dublin, 1768, pp.15, 83-4. Gregory (1724-73) was Professor of Philosophy, and then of Medicine at Aberdeen, before moving

to Edinburgh as Professor of Physic. His book, published anonymously, ran to at least nine editions by the end of the century.

CHAPTER ONE

1. Valuable background studies include: L. I. Bredvold, *The Intellectual Milieu of John Dryden*, Ann Arbor, 1934; G. Bryson, *Man and Society: The Scottish inquiry of the eighteenth century*, Princeton, 1945; M. S. Kuypers, *Studies in the Eighteenth Century Background of Hume's Empiricism*, Minneapolis, 1930; R. E. Schofield, *Mechanism and Materialism*, Princeton, 1970. See also note 44 below, and Chapter 2, note 1. I have already indicated the importance of the commentaries by Laird, Smith and Passmore; three recent books which offer different interpretations from mine are: N. Capaldi, *David Hume: The Newtonian Philosopher*, Boston, 1975; R. H. Hurlbutt, *Hume, Newton and the Design Argument*, Lincoln, 1965; J. Noxon, *Hume's Philosophical Development*, Oxford, 1973.

2. See E. Section 1 and L.1.16.

3. The 1737 letter was published in *Archiwum Historii Filozofii i Myśli Spolecznej*, 9, 1963, 127-41. It is unclear why Hume thought Descartes's work would be difficult to find, since most scholars had copies; Locke, for example, possessed all of Descartes's available works.

4. Hume incorporates the remark at M.135n.

5. F. Bacon, *The Philosophical Works of F. Bacon*, ed. J. M. Robertson, London, 1905; T. Hobbes, *Leviathan*, intro. W. G. Pogson Smith, Oxford, 1909, p.555.

6. A. Arnauld & P. Nicole, *La Logique ou l'art de penser*, ed. P. Clair & F. Girbal, Paris, 1965; N. Malebranche, *De la Recherche de la Vérité*, ed. G. Rodis-Lewis, Paris, 1962, Book II, Part II, Chs.6-8; Book IV, Chs.3, 7, 8; Book V, Chs.7, 11. Hereafter references to Malebranche will be to volume and page of this edition.

7. Not *a priori* reason, of course. Note the derision of authorities in D.142.

8. L.1.284; cp. L.1.189, where Sir Henry Erskine made the same complaint.

9. Sir A. Grant, *Story of the University of Edinburgh*, London, 1884, I.80ff.

10. I am most grateful to my colleague Eric G. Forbes for allowing me to study his transcript of Colin Maclaurin's student notebooks. The notebooks, which are in private hands, have been translated for later publication by Eric G. Forbes and Christine M. King. There are two sets of notes on ethics, and one on metaphysics, the latter probably dictated in Gershom Carmichael's class at the University of Glasgow, 1713. In the ethics notes there is extended discussion of natural law, with

references to Grotius and Pufendorf. See also, E. Gibbon, *Memoirs of My Life*, ed. G. A. Bonnard, London, 1966, Ch.3.

11. C. Maclaurin, *An Account of Sir Isaac Newton's Philosophical Discoveries*, London, 1748, p.v.

12. A. Carlyle, *The Autobiography of Dr Alexander Carlyle*, ed. J. H. Burton, Edinburgh, 1910, pp.36, 52, 57.

13. W-J. s'Gravesande, *Mathematical Elements of Natural Philosophy*, English trans., London, 1720; H. Pemberton, *A View of Sir Isaac Newton's Philosophy*, London, 1728. I. B. Cohen, in his Preface to Sir Isaac Newton, *Opticks* (4th edn, 1730), Dover Publications, 1952, holds that most readers of the time had insufficient mathematics to manage anything other than parts of the *Opticks*. See Schofield for an account of how Newton was understood in the first part of the eighteenth century.

14. Voltaire (F. Arouet), *Lettres Philosophiques*, ed. G. Lanson, Paris, 1909, 11.5. Voltaire's *Elemens de la philosophie de Neuton* appeared in 1738. The English translation of Fontenelle's *Elogium of Sir Isaac Newton* is contained in *Isaac Newton's Papers and Letters on Natural Philosophy*, ed. I. B. Cohen & R. E. Schofield, Cambridge, 1958. For the scientific and deistic interests of Voltaire, see C. Kiernan, 'The Enlightenment and Science in Eighteenth-century France', *Studies on Voltaire and the Eighteenth Century*, Vol.59A, Banbury, 1973. Kiernan also discusses the relations between science and atheism among the *philosophes*, especially Diderot, and devotes a chapter to the influence of Buffon. Kiernan argues for important differences between the upholders of the physical and life sciences, not least in their emphasis on reason and feeling; the names of Descartes and Newton were often used as slogans in the battle between proponents of mechanism and those of organicism, and it is misleading to take the conflict as one of rationalism versus empiricism.

15. John Harris, *Lexicon Technicum: or an Universal English Dictionary of Arts and Sciences*, London, 5th edn 1736; E. Chambers, *Cyclopaedia: or an Universal Dictionary of Arts and Sciences*, London, 1727. Chambers's work, of course, was the initial inspiration of the *Encyclopédie*, 1751, and a source of some of the entries in it.

16. Sir Isaac Newton, *Mathematical Principles of Natural Philosophy*, trans. Motte, intro. F. Cajori, Berkeley, 1966, Vol.1, p.xviii.

17. Ibid., p.6.

18. Ibid., 11.398.

19. T.173. R. Kuhns, 'Hume's Republic and the Universe of Newton', in *Eighteenth Century Studies presented to A. M. Wilson*, ed. P. Gay, Hanover, N.H., 1972, discusses Hume's dissatisfaction with a Newtonian mechanical account.

20.   Newton, *Principia*, 11.631. Scotland was well in advance of
        England in Newtonian studies; Cajori states that Rohault's
        text was still standard in Cambridge as late as 1730.

21.   See P. Brunet, *L'Introduction des théories de Newton en France
        aux XVIIIe siècle, Avant 1738*, Paris, 1931. Maupertuis,
        Discours sur les différentes figures des Astres, 1732, was
        acknowledged by d'Alembert as the first French scholar to
        declare himself openly as Newtonian: see J. le R. d'Alembert,
        Discours préliminaire de l'encyclopédie, ed. F. Picavet, Paris,
        1894, p.109.

22.   See H. Guerlac, in *Aspects of the Eighteenth Century*, ed. E. R.
        Wasserman, London, 1965.

23.   Newton, *Principia*, I.xxvii.

24.   Newton, *Opticks*, p.401.

25.   Ibid., p.404.

26.   I. B. Cohen, *Franklin and Newton*, Philadelphia, 1968, pp.138,
        575. The senses of 'hypothesis' are: a system of the world; a
        mathematical premise; an unproved general mathematical
        proposition; a premise in a physical proposition; propositions
        Newton was unable to prove; counter-factual conditions;
        mechanisms supposed in order to explain laws or phenomena;
        'philosophical romance'; axioms or postulates. See also N. R.
        Hanson in *The Methodological Heritage of Newton*, ed. R. E.
        Butts & J. E. Davis, Toronto, 1970.

27.   Pemberton, *Newton's Philosophy*, p.14; Maclaurin, *Newton's
        Philosophical Discoveries*, pp.3, 90.

28.   Pemberton, *Newton's Philosophy*, pp.16, 58.

29.   Ibid., p.23.

30.   Ibid., pp.25-6, 184; 24, 254. Hume may also have been
        interested in another remark on p.254: "we can only say that
        the neighbourhood of a loadstone and a piece of iron is attended
        with a power, whereby the loadstone and the iron are drawn
        toward each other".

31.   Ibid., pp.406-7.

32.   Hurlbutt, *Hume, Newton and the Design Argument*.

33.   Maclaurin, *Newton's Philosophical Discoveries*, pp.98, 225n.

34.   Ibid., p.14.

35.   Ibid., pp.22, 381ff.

36.   Ibid., pp.97-8.

37.   Ibid., pp.109, 94.

38.   Ibid., p.8.

39.   Ibid., p.85.

40.   E.84n.

41.   An early accusation of Locke occurred in John Edwards, *The
        Socinian Creed*, London, 1697; Stillingfleet also accused Locke
        and Toland of being Socinians. For Newton, see B. J. T.
        Dobbs, *The Foundations of Newton's Alchemy*, Cambridge,
        1975.

42.   T.61. J. H. Burton, *Life and Correspondence of David Hume*,
        Edinburgh, 1846. References to 'animal spirits' are part of the
        legacy of the mechanistic natural science of his predecessors:
        see E. J. Dijksterhuis, *The Mechanization of the World Picture*,
        Oxford, 1961. For characteristic scientific analyses, see
        T.443-4.

43.   See B. le B. de Fontenelle, *Entretiens sur la pluralité des mondes*,
        ed. R. Shackleton, Oxford, 1955.

44.   Valuable background studies include: E.Cassirer, *The Philo-
        sophy of the Enlightenment*, English trans., Princeton, 1951;
        L. G. Crocker, *An Age of Crisis: Man and World in Eighteenth
        Century French Thought*, Baltimore, 1959; G. L. Davies, *The
        Earth in Decay*, New York, 1969; C. Frankel, *The Faith of
        Reason*, New York, 1948; C. J. Glacken, *Traces on the Rhodian
        Shore*, Berkeley, 1967; J. C. Greene, *The Death of Adam*, New
        York, 1961; E. Guyénot, *Les Sciences de la vie aux XVIIe et
        XVIIIe siècles: l'idée d'évolution*, Paris, 1941; A. Wolf, *A
        History of Science, Technology and Philosophy in the 18th
        Century*, London, 1938.
           For La Mettrie, see: *L' Homme Machine*, ed. A. Vartanian,
        Princeton, 1960; L. C. Rosenfield, *From Beast-Machine to
        Man-Machine*, New York, 1968; A. Vartanian, *Diderot and
        Descartes: A Study of Scientific Naturalism in the Enlighten-
        ment*, Princeton, 1953. It is a remarkable coincidence that La
        Mettrie was studying medicine in Rheims at the same time
        Hume was working there on the *Treatise*, in 1734. There is no
        evidence that they met. See also, F. A. Lange, *The History of
        Materialism* (1865), London, 1925.
           For Buffon, see: *Oeuvres Philosophiques de Buffon*, ed. J.
        Piveteau, Paris, 1954; *Buffon. Les Epoques de la Nature*, ed. J.
        Roger, in *Mémoires du Muséum National d'Histoire Naturelle*,
        Series C, Vol.10, Paris, 1962; A. O. Lovejoy, 'Buffon and the
        Problem of Species', in *Forerunners of Darwin: 1745-1859*,
        ed. B. Glass, Baltimore, 1959.
           For Hutton, see: *James Hutton's System of the Earth, Theory
        of the Earth, Observations on Granite*, ed. G. W. White, New
        York, 1973; *James Hutton's Theory of the Earth: The Lost
        Drawings*, ed. G. Y. Craig, D. B. McIntyre & C. D. Waterston,
        Edinburgh, 1978. I shall discuss the relations between Hume
        and Hutton elsewhere.

45.   L.1.40.

46.   J. P. Pittion, 'Hume's Reading of Bayle: an enquiry into the
        source and role of the *Memoranda*', *Journal of the History of
        Philosophy*, Vol.15, 1977.

47.   Laird, *Hume's Philosophy*, and J. Passmore, *Hume's Intentions*,
        Cambridge, 1952.

48.   Arnauld & Nicole, *La Logique*, p.300n acknowledges the debt,
        but not the extent of it. For a survey of French reactions to

Cartesianism see, J. S. Spink, *French Free-Thought from Gassendi to Voltaire*, London, 1960. Spink shows the extent to which Pascal had fallen into obscurity by the end of the seventeenth century.

49. Arnauld & Nicole, *La Logique*, 30. I modify the translation of T. S. Baynes, Edinburgh, 1857.

50. Ibid., pp.30, 39.

51. Ibid., p.41. Cp. Descartes's definition of *idée* in *Méditations* III, in *Oeuvres Philosophiques*, ed. F. Alquié, Paris, 1967, II.434ff.; also in the letter of July 1641 to Mersenne, ibid., p.345: "j'appelle généralement du nom d'idée tout ce qui est dans notre esprit, lorsque nous concevons une chose, de quelque manière que nous la concevions".

52. Arnauld & Nicole, *La Logique*, p.41.

53. Ibid., p.38.

54. Ibid., pp.88, 87, 164, 165.

55. Ibid., pp.43, 83.

56. Ibid., pp.94. Cp. Descartes's views on language in his letters to Mersenne.

57. Ibid., p.94.

58. Ibid., p.94. For the unoriginality of the Port-Royal *Grammar*, and the elements incorporated from it into the *Logic*, recognised by only a few contemporaries, see G. A. Padley, *Grammatical Theory in Western Europe, 1500-1700*, Cambridge, 1976, pp.249ff.

59. Arnauld & Nicole, *La Logique*, pp.23, 26. Bayle constantly endorses their rebuke.

60. Ibid., pp.39, 44, 184, 316.

61. Ibid., p.84.

62. Ibid., p.306.

63. J-P. de Crousaz, *A New Treatise of the Art of Thinking*, English trans., London, 1724, Vol.I, p.298.

64. Ibid., pp.7-8.

65. Ibid., p.32: following J. Locke, *An Essay concerning Human Understanding*, III.xi.24.

66. Crousaz, *A New Treatise*, I.305-7; II.32-3, 43, 46, 37.

67. Ibid., II.51, 349.

68. Ibid., II.340.

69. Ibid., II.387.

70. See Monte Cook, 'Arnauld's Alleged Representationalism', *Journal of the History of Philosophy*, Vol.12, 1974; R. A. Watson, *The Downfall of Cartesianism, 1673-1712*, The Hague, 1960.

71. In the Rodis-Lewis edition all the marked passages occur between pp.11-57, apart from one mark on p.373. In spite of his article, 'Malebranche's Theory of the Perception of Distance and Magnitude', *British Journal of Psychology*, Vol.I, 1904-5, N. K. Smith makes no reference to Male-

branche's natural judgments when discussing Hume's natural
beliefs in 'The Naturalism of Hume', *Mind*, Vol.14, 1905.
Only Laird, and R. W. Church, in 'Malebranche and Hume'
Revue Internationale de Philosophie, Vol.1, 1938-9, begin to
appreciate the significance of the parallels they quote.

72.   D.142 refers to Malebranche, *De la Recherche*, 1.473. The
other references are at: E.17, 84n; M.27.

73.   Malebranche, *De la Recherche*, 11.313.

74.   Ibid., 111.205.

75.   Ibid., 11.314-16.

76.   Ibid., 111.205, 207.

77.   Ibid., 11.313.

78.   Ibid., 111.208.

79.   Ibid., 11.420.

80.   Ibid., 1.42, 414.

81.   Ibid., 1.86, 121, 423.

82.   Ibid., 1.192.

83.   Ibid., 1.425.

84.   Ibid., 1.66.

85.   Ibid., 1.194.

86.   Ibid., 11.52.

87.   Ibid., 1.63.

88.   Ibid., 1.97.

89.   Ibid., 1.119. Malebranche follows Descartes, Meditation VI,
Oeuvres, 11.497.

90.   Malebranche, *De la Recherche*, 1.191n, 130, 158. Cp. Descartes,
Meditation 111, *Oeuvres* 11, 435, 437: "une certaine
inclination"; "une aveugle et téméraire impulsion".

91.   Ibid., 1.130n.

92.   Ibid., 1.120.

93.   Ibid., 1.166.

94.   Ibid., 1.77.

95.   Arnauld & Nicole, *La Logique*, p.261.

96.   Malebranche, *De la Recherche*, 1.463, 426; 11.316. Cp. also
Eclaircissement xv. Ibid., 111.203ff.

97.   Ibid., 1.149; 11.302.

98.   Ibid., 1.321.

99.   Ibid., 11.242.

100. D. Bouhours, *Les Entretiens d'Ariste et d'Eugène*, Paris, 1671,
Entretien v.

101. Malebranche, *De la Recherche*, 11.365.

102. Ibid., 1.145, 472. Cp. Arnauld & Nicole, *La Logique*, p.43.

103. Malebranche, De la *Recherche*, 1.148.

104. Ibid., 1.219.

105. Ibid., 1.319.

106. Ibid., 1.415.

107. Ibid., 111.164, 168.

108. Ibid., 1.230, 270; 11.128. Cp. Hume, T.60, 230, 372.

109.   Malebranche, *De la Recherche*, III.185.

110.   Ibid., III.345.

111.   Montaigne at M.86; Pascal at E.135n, M.158. Malebranche's
        discussion of Pascal was based on the misleading Port-Royal
        edition. Laird, *Hume's Philosophy* (p.71) suggested Claude
        Buffier as a possible source of some of Hume's views; although
        there is no direct discussion of Hume, evidence for the influence
        can be found in K. S. Wilkins, 'A Study of the works of
        Claude Buffier', *Studies on Voltaire*, Vol. 66, 1969. Buffier
        (1661-1737) was an early French follower of Locke, and
        exercised some influence over Scottish common-sense
        philosophers, such as Reid.

112.   B. le B. de Fontenelle, *Oeuvres de M. de Fontenelle*, Paris, 1752
        (10 vols.). See L. M. Marsak, 'B. de Fontenelle: The Idea of
        Science in the French Enlightenment', *Transactions of the
        American Philosophical Society*, Vol. 49, 1959; J-R. Carré, *La
        Philosophie de Fontenelle ou le sourire de la raison*, Paris, 1932.

113.   Fontenelle, *Entretiens*, ve Soir, p.132.

114.   Ibid., Ie Soir, p.68.

115.   Ibid., Ie Soir, p.71; IIIe Soir, p.107; VIe Soir, p.146. Cyrano
        de Bergerac, *Etats et Empires de la lune*, Paris, 1657, speculates
        on the possibility of inhabitants on the moon and the animate
        nature of the universe. See Spink, *French Free-Thought*.

116.   See P. Gay, *The Enlightenment*, London, 1967; W. S. Howell,
        Eighteenth Century British Logic and Rhetoric, Princeton, 1971.
        1971.

117.   John Pringle, Lectures from Cicero, Edinburgh University
        Library, MS Collection, Gen.74. D.

118.   H. A. K. Hunt, *The Humanism of Cicero*, Melbourne, 1954.
        Cicero's works are all cited in the variously translated Loeb
        series; I have occasionally modified the translations.

119.   Anthony, Earl of Shaftesbury, *Characteristics*, ed. J. M.
        Robertson, Indianapolis, 1964, II.67: also F. de S. de la
        M. Fénelon, *Démonstration de l'existence de Dieu*, Amsterdam,
        1713, from which Hume quoted in the *Memoranda*.

120.   J. Butler, *The Analogy of Religion and Two Brief Dissertations*,
        Oxford, 1874, p.330.

121.   Hume contrasts the transience of abstract theories with the
        absolute nature of true values; it is unclear whether he thinks
        that the abstract theories tackle genuinely perennial problems:
        "Theories of abstract philosophy, systems of profound theology,
        have prevailed during one age: In a successive period, these
        have been universally exploded: Their absurdity has been
        detected: Other theories and systems have supplied their
        place, which again gave place to their successors: And nothing
        has been experienced more liable to the revolutions of chance
        and fashion than these pretended decisions of science. The
        case is not the same with the beauties of eloquence and poetry"

(G.I.279).

122. Cicero, *Academica*, x.31.
123. Cicero, *Tusc.* II.ii.5.

CHAPTER TWO

1. Valuable studies, all of which have important bibliographies, include: D. C. Allen, *The Legend of Noah*, Urbana, 1949; H. G. van Leeuwen, *The Problem of Certainty in English Thought, 1630-1690*, The Hague, 1963; F. E. Manuel, *The Eighteenth Century Confronts the Gods*, Cambridge, Mass., 1959; R. H. Popkin, *The History of Scepticism from Erasmus to Descartes*, New York, 1964; L. Stephen, *History of English Thought in the Eighteenth Century* (1876), 3rd edn, London, 1902; N. L. Torrey, *Voltaire and the English Deists*, New Haven, 1930; H. Vyverberg, *Historical Pessimism in the French Enlightenment*, Cambridge, Mass., 1958.

2. R. Simon, *Histoire critique du Vieux Testament*, Paris, 1678; English trans., 1682. Collins refers to Simon in 'A Discourse of Free-Thinking', 1713, in '*A Collection of Tracts Written by Mr. . . .*', London, 1717. Hume refers to Huet (L G,21, D.138n), who discussed Simon; and Bayle, of course, cites Simon. Locke possessed his own copy of the French edition of 1685 of Simon: see G. Bonno, *Les relations intellectuelles de Locke avec la France*, Berkeley, 1955. For Simon, see also R. H. Popkin, in *Problems in the Philosophy of Science*, ed. I. Lakatos & A. Musgrave, Amsterdam, 1968.

3. Bacon, *Novum Organum*, II.xxvii; I.iii, xxxixff.
4. Burton, *Life and Correspondence*, I.84, drew attention to Glanvill's Humean account of cause.
5. G.I.118, L G.21, L.I.151.
6. J. Tillotson, *The Rule of Faith*, in *The Works*, Vol.I, 9th edn, London, 1728, p.559. Collins disingenuously quoted Tillotson in 'A Discourse of Free-Thinking'. Hume was probably adopting the same tactics as the Deists.
7. Tillotson, *The Works*, I.16.
8. Hobbes, *Leviathan*, p.84. Cp. Leland, *A View*, I.31.
9. Ibid., pp.83, 84, 283.
10. Ibid., pp.338-9.
11. Ibid., p.345.
12. Ibid., p.341; see also pp.297-301.
13. M. de Montaigne, *Essais*, ed. Thibaudet, Paris, 1939, III.xi, 'Des boiteux'.
14. Pascal was an intimate friend of Arnauld and Nicole, and in his own incomplete apology for Christianity, *Pensées* (ed. L. Brunschvicg, Paris, 1909), discusses miracles and revelation (see e.g. Section XIII), and deplores the insidious speculations of Montaigne. Before the nineteenth century, readers of Pascal had access only to the misleading and inaccurate Port-Royal

edition: see M. Vamos in *Studies on Voltaire and the Eighteenth
Century*, Vol.97, 1972. Hume's passing references to Pascal
(see e.g. M.157-8) imply agreement with Voltaire's influential
verdict in *Lettres Philosophiques*.

15.   It is worth comparing some of the proposed definitions.
Hobbes, *Leviathan*, p.341: "A *Miracle*, is a work of God,
(besides his operation by the way of Nature, ordained in the
Creation,) done, for the making manifest to his elect, the
mission of an extraordinary Minister for their salvation".
Locke, 'Discourse of Miracles', *Works*, IX.256: "a sensible
operation, which, being above the comprehension of the
spectator, and in his opinion contrary to the established course
of nature, is taken by him to be divine". J. Toland, *Christianity
not Mysterious . . .*, London, 1696, p.150: "A Miracle then is
some Action exceeding all human Power, and which the Laws
of Nature cannot perform by their ordinary Operations".
S. Clarke, *A Demonstration of the Being and Attributes of God*,
4th edn, London, 1716, II.311: "a work effected in a manner
unusual, or different from the common and regular Method of
Providence, by the interposition either of God himself, or of
some Intelligent Agent superior to Man, for the Proof or
Evidence of some particular Doctrine, or in attestation to the
Authority of some particular Person". See also, P. Helm,
'Locke on Faith and Knowledge', *Philosophical Quarterly*,
Vol.23, 1973.

16.   Toland, *Christianity not Mysterious*, pp.41, 150. Cp. Tillotson,
The Works, I.17.

17.   Leland, *A View*, I.59.

18.   Collins, 'A Discourse of Free-Thinking'; in *An Essay Concerning the Use of Reason in Propositions*, 2nd edn, London,
1709, he writes: "Testimony is of itself not sufficient to
procure Faith or Assent, unless accompanied with these two
Circumstances, credibility of Persons, and credibility of Things
related".

19.   G. Berkeley, *Alciphron, or the Minute Philosopher*, in *The Works
of George Berkeley*, ed. A. A. Luce & T. E. Jessop, Edinburgh,
1950, Vol.3. The title, borrowed from Cicero (*minuti philosophi –
De Senectute*, xxiii.85; cp. *De Divinatione* I.xxx.62), denotes
the free-thinkers who belittle what is generally esteemed,
including the nature of man himself. Berkeley's dialogue form
certainly interested Hume, who refers to the work at G.1.253,
but it is surprising that Hume took no apparent notice of the
speculations on language, or of the objections raised against
scepticism in natural religion.

20.   For *notions*, see *Principles* 27, 142, in *Works* II; for *gravity*, see
De Motu, in *Works* IV. 17: "*Force, gravity, attraction* and
terms of this sort are useful for reasonings and reckonings
about motion and bodies in motion, but not for understanding

the simple nature of motion itself or for indicating so many
distinct qualities. As for attraction, it was certainly introduced
by Newton, not as a true, physical quality, but only as a
mathematical hypothesis."

21. See D. C. Stove, *Probability and Hume's Inductive Scepticism*,
Oxford, 1973. On testimony, see D. F. Norton in *David Hume:
Philosophical Historian*, ed. D. F. Norton & R. H. Popkin,
Indianapolis, 1965, pp.xl-l.

22. In the middle of his discussion of historical evidence occurs a
paragraph in which Hume refers to "a very celebrated argument against the *Christian Religion*", according to which "each
link of the chain in human testimony" goes not "beyond
probability" and is "liable to a degree of doubt and uncertainty"
(T.145). Hume remarks that according to the argument
"(which however is not a true one) there is no history or
tradition, but what must in the end lose all its force and
evidence". Green and Grose suggested that reference is to
J. Craig, *Theologiae Christianae Principia Mathematica*,
London, 1699, which argues that the evidence for the truth of
the Gospels gradually reduces to zero, by passing through
successive hands. Hume could have heard of this work from
Bayle, who quoted Craig's distinction between faith and knowledge: "what is faith but that persuasion of the mind, whereby,
by reasons drawn from probability, we believe certain propositions to be true . . . for as probability begets faith, so it
destroys knowledge, and, on the contrary, certainty begets
knowledge and destroys faith": 'Eclaircissement sur les
Pyrrhoniens', *Dictionaire*, IV.3006. Shaftesbury and Berkeley
both used Craig's argument about diminishing probability,
e.g. *Alciphron*, VI.222. The argument was also widely
publicised in the article on 'Certitude' in Chambers's
Cyclopaedia, and was cited by many later writers, including
the Encyclopédistes who relied on Chambers for several
entries: see J. E. Barker, *Diderot's Treatment of the Christian
Religion in 'The Encyclopédie'*, New York, 1941.

23. Burton, *Life and Correspondence*, 1.285. In the first sentence of
the chapter on miracles, Hume refers to Tillotson's 'Discourse
against Transubstantiation'. Tillotson argues: "For if a Miracle
were wrought for the Proof of it, the very same Assurance
which any Man hath of the Truth of the Miracle, he hath of
the Falsehood of the Doctrine, that is the clear Evidence of his
Senses. For that there is a Miracle wrought to prove *that what
he sees in the Sacrament is not Bread but the Body of Christ*,
there is only the Evidence of Sense; and there is the very same
Evidence to prove, *that what he sees in the Sacrament is not the
Body of Christ but Bread*": *The Works*, 1.244. For discussion
of Hume's Sections X and XI, and of miracles in particular,
see A. Flew, *Hume's Philosophy of Belief*, London, 1961.

24.   Collins, for example, specifically attacked the plausibility of the
        Pentateuch. But Hume may have had in mind the numerous
        attempts to answer Woolston's attacks on miracles: for a partial
        list of combatants, see Leland, I.109-11.

25.   For Bayle, see especially the article 'Rorarius' in *Dictionaire*,
        which lists other authors who discuss the problem; and the
        article 'Simonides'.

26.   Leland, *A View*, I.287-8.

27.   See e.g. *Continuation* §16, *Oeuvres Diverses*, III.208; cp.
        III.692.

28.   See *Early Memoranda*, p.502, entry 34. Leland is an example
        of a contemporary of Hume's who misses the crucial points
        about the analysis of causation, and consequently fails to ask
        himself what Hume must be trying to do (see e.g. I.292ff.;
        343n); nevertheless, he pinpoints several problems in Hume's
        discussion.

29.   Cp. Leland, *A View*, I.274-5, 277.

30.   See Pittion.

31.   See e.g. the article 'Pyrrho'. See Popkin's note in his *Bayle . . .
        Selections*, Indianapolis, 1965, p.199.

32.   The clergy had attempted to prevent the study of Locke's
        Essay at Oxford: see J. W. Yolton, *John Locke and the Way of
        Ideas*, Oxford, 1956.

33.   Bayle constantly made the same point. One of Hume's targets
        was W. Warburton, *The Divine Legation of Moses*, London,
        1738.

34.   In 1746, Hume wrote: "As to the Idea of Substance, I must
        own, that as it has no Access to the Mind by any of our Senses
        or Feelings, it has always appeared to me to be nothing but an
        imaginary Center of Union amongst the different and variable
        Qualities that are to be found in every Piece of Matter"
        (NL.20).

35.   Shaftesbury, *Characteristics*, II.50.

36.   Toland, *Christianity not Mysterious*, p.38.

37.   B. le B. de Fontenelle, *Histoire des Oracles*, ed. L. Maigron,
        Paris, 1934: Bayle praised this work in *Continuation* §47,
        Oeuvres Diverses, III.252. See also Fontenelle, *De l'origine des
        Fables*, in *Oeuvres*, III.270ff., where he argues that the first idea
        of some superior being must have been derived from extra-
        ordinary events, not from "l'ordre réglé de l'univers", which
        early men could neither recognise nor admire (ibid., p.277).

38.   It is interesting that Hume cites Fontenelle as an example,
        because it was Fontenelle himself who originally made the
        point; Bayle drew attention to the claim in *Continuation* §21,
        Oeuvres Diverses, III.215.

39.   Shaftesbury, *Characteristics*, I.5ff.; II.173ff.

40.   Burton, *Life and Correspondence*, II.11-13; E. C. Mossner,
        The Life of David Hume, Edinburgh, 1954, pp.306-7.

41.   *Early Memoranda*, p.502, entry 28.

42.   Shaftesbury, *Characteristics*, II.226, 232.

43.   Ibid., II.91.

44.   Burton, *Life and Correspondence*, II.11-13; Mossner, *Life of Hume*, 306-7.

45.   Toland, *Letters to Serena*, London, 1704, especially Letter III, 'The Origin of Idolatry'. See also F. E. Manuel, and for a modern view W. McKane, *Patriarchal Narratives*, Edinburgh, 1977.

46.   Bayle, *Continuation* §106, *Oeuvres Diverses*, III.333.

47.   Cp. Shaftesbury, *Characteristics*, I.238: "If we are told a man is religious, we still ask 'What are his morals?'" and Hume: "when we have to do with a man, who makes a great profession of religion and devotion; has this any other effect upon several, who pass for prudent, than to put them on their guard, lest they be cheated and deceived by him?" (D.221).

48.   Shaftesbury, *Characteristics*, I.241; Fontenelle, *De l'origine des Fables*, *Oeuvres*, III.276.

49.   For the first, see D.143, 144, 146, 154, 163; for the second, D.145, 183, 184.

50.   See e.g. Diderot, *Pensées Philosophiques* XXI, in *Oeuvres Philosophiques*, ed. P. Vernière, Paris, 1964.

51.   Bayle, *Continuation* §17, *Oeuvres Diverses*, III.209; cp. 713.

52.   In *Eclaircissements* II and III to the *Dictionaire*, Bayle asserts that the mysteries of the Gospel were not made to be tested by philosophy; it is almost as impossible to join faith and philosophical enquiry, as to join the properties of a square and a circle.

53.   See e.g. Rem. M to 'Spinoza' in *Dictionaire*, II.2637; Rem. F to 'Simonides', ibid. II.2588.

54.   Writers such as Leland precisely objected to the Deists' disregard for the roles of metaphor and allegory in the Scriptures: Leland, *A View*, I.54, 93-4.

55.   Since this chapter was completed there has appeared the first book devoted wholly to Hume's views on religion: J. C. A. Gaskin, *Hume's Philosophy of Religion*, London, 1978.

CHAPTER THREE

1.   I have discussed various aspects of Hume's views on aesthetics in *Philosophical Quarterly*, Vol.20, 1970; Vol.26, 1976; *Philosophical Studies*, Vol.33, 1978; *Hume: A Re-evaluation*, ed. D. W. Livingston & J. T. King, New York, 1976; *McGill Hume Studies*, ed. D. F. Norton, N. Capaldi & W. L. Robison, San Diego, 1979. I am grateful to the editors of these publications for permission to include in this chapter extracts from my previous discussions. General studies of Hume's views include: T. Brunius, *David Hume on Criticism*, Stockholm, 1952; W. J. Hipple, Jr, *The Beautiful, The Sublime, and The*

Picturesque in Eighteenth-Century British Aesthetic Theory, Carbondale, 1957.

2. See James Harris, *Three Treatises . . . concerning Music, Painting and Poetry*, London, 1744, p.5: "I called upon my Friend to give me his Opinion of the Word ART: A word it was (I told him) in the Mouth of every one; but for all that, as to its precise and definite Idea, this might still be a Secret; that so it was in fact with a thousand Words beside, all no less common, and equally familiar, and yet all of them equally vague and undetermined". His own definition of *art* as "an *intentional cause founded in Habit*" was meant to capture the Aristotelian position he espoused.

3. J-B. Dubos, *Réflexions critiques sur la poésie et sur la peinture*, Paris, 1719; English trans. T. Nugent, London, 1748. See also: A. Lombard, *La querelle des Anciens et des Modernes: l'abbé du Bos*, Neuchatel, 1908; B. Munteano, *Revue de litérature comparée*, Vol.30, 1956, who discusses the rhetorical dimension of form and content in Dubos; E. Caramaschi, 'Du Bos et Voltaire', *Studies on Voltaire and the Eighteenth Century*, Vol.10, 1959; C. Hogsett, 'J. B. Dubos on Art as Illusion', *Studies on Voltaire and the Eighteenth Century*, Vol.73, 1970, who discusses Dubos's need for limited illusion in relation to taste. An important background article is: P. O. Kristeller, 'The Modern System of the Arts', *Journal of the History of Ideas*, Vols.12, 13, 1951, 1952.

4. See H. Rigault, *Histoire de la querelle des anciens et des modernes*, Paris, 1856; R. F. Jones, *Ancients and Moderns*, 2nd edn, St Louis, 1961; R. G. Saisselin, *The Rule of Reason and the Ruses of the Heart*, Cleveland, 1970; I. O. Wade, *The Intellectual Origins of the French Enlightenment*, Princeton, 1971. T. Blackwell, *An Enquiry into the Life and Writings of Homer*, London, 1735, p.279, claims that consideration of climate, manners of his country, language and religion suffices to demonstrate "Homer's advantages from Nature and Education" above all others.

5. C. Perrault, *Parallèle des anciens et des modernes*, Paris, 1688-97; Fontenelle, 'Digression sur les Anciens et les Modernes', Paris, 1688, in *Entretiens*, ed. Shackleton. Hume discounts "any influence of the soil and climate" (T.317). On the relative superficiality of discussion, and the reluctance of both sides to press the enquiry, see M. Cardy, 'Discussion of the theory of climate in the *querelle des anciens et des modernes*', *Studies on Voltaire and the Eighteenth Century*, Vol.163, 1976. See also C. J. Glacken, *Traces on the Rhodian Shore*, Berkeley, 1967, especially Part IV; one aspect of the debate concerned the relation of man to the earth, and led to speculation on population and perfectibility.

6. Sprat, Temple and Wotton in J. E. Spingarn, ed., *Critical*

Essays of the Seventeenth Century, Oxford, 1908, II.112ff.; III.32ff., 202ff. Hume refers to Temple on the final page of his *History of England*, Ch.71.

7. Malebranche himself had speculated on moral and physical causes, including the influence of air. For Hume's views on the influence of the will over the blood, see G.I.198, and for a reference to Dubos on climatic influence G.I.439n (1752). Dubos remarks, in one place (*Réflexions*, II.xiii), that everyone knows the North has been capable of producing nothing but wild poets, coarse versifiers, and frigid colourists.

8. Fontenelle, 'Digression', in *Entretiens*, ed. Shackleton, p.162.

9. Shaftesbury, *Characteristics*, I.149.

10. See, e.g. Shaftesbury, *Characteristics*, I.30, 67, 69, 80, 97, 146, 184, 231, 232, 252; II.55, 201, 293, 305. Hutcheson frequently uses the term, but Hume uses it less often: e.g. T.361, 519, 522; G.I.120, 155, 210, 222; it becomes more prominent in his work by the time of the second *Enquiry*.

11. Especially Cicero, *De Oratore* III.l.195: "everybody is able to discriminate between what is right and what is wrong in matters of art and proportion by a sort of subconscious instinct (*tacito quodam sensu*), without having any theory of art or proportion of their own; and while they can do this in the case of pictures and other works to understand which nature has given them less equipment, at the same time they display this much more in judging the rhythms and pronunciations of words, because these are rooted deep in the general sensibility (*in communibus infixa sensibus*), and nature has decreed that nobody shall be entirely devoid of these faculties". Dubos quoted the passage (*Réflexions*, II.xxii), and Gerard uses the passage as an epigraph on his title page. Fontenelle's reference to the sixth sense is in *Entretiens*, p.108; cp. Locke, *Essay*, IV.xviii.3.

12. Locke criticised Malebranche for his ambiguous use of 'senti-ment', Locke, *Works*, IX, pp.237, 249. J. Wilkins, *An Essay towards a Real Character*, 1668, associates 'sentiment' with 'understanding, common sense, apprehension, opinion'. Shaftesbury refers to "sentiment or judgment" (*Characteristics*, I.253), and later T. Reid, 'Essays on the Active Powers', V.vii, insists on a judgmental element. G. Girard, *Synonymes François* (1736), new edn, augmented M. Beauzée, Paris, 1769, associates 'sentiment' with the heart and with taste. J. le R. d'Alembert, *Discours préliminaire*, p.57 defines 'le goût' as 'le sentiment qui juge'.

13. Dubos also adopted Perrault's views that progress requires prosperity, peace and political calm, and that there are historical cycles. Hutcheson adopted the distinction between real and comparative merit, without acknowledgement, *An Inquiry Concerning Beauty, Order, Harmony, Design* (1725),

ed. P. Kivy, The Hague, 1973, 1.16, 11.3. Other references will
be to: *An Essay on the Nature and Conduct of the Passions and
Affections*, London, 1728; and *An Inquiry concerning Moral
Good and Evil* (1725), in *British Moralists*, ed. L. A. Selby-
Bigge, Indianapolis, 1964.

14. Descartes' *bon sens* is closely related to *sens commun* of later writers
such as Buffier. The latter notion appeared in all the major
dictionaries of the time, e.g. A Furetière, *Dictionnaire Universel*,
La Haye, 1701, P. Richelet, *Nouveau Dictionnaire français*,
Genève, 1710. The article in Diderot & d'Alembert's
Encyclopédie on *sens commun* is derived from Buffier. Girard
defines *bon sens* in terms of both judgment and taste, and quotes
La Bruyère: "entre le *bon sens* et le *bon goût*, il y a la différence
de la cause à son effet". Shaftesbury often uses the English
phrase, see e.g. *Characteristics*, 1.170, 214; 11.158; and Hume
also uses it, see e.g. G.1.171n, T.608, M.85, 133. Much French
critical work was available in English translation before 1700,
and subsequent English thought was greatly influenced by
French concepts and vocabulary, although not always by the
theories that lay behind them. The popularity of the expression
was recorded in book titles such as J-B. d'Argens, *La Philosophie
du bon sens*, London, 1737; (P. H. Thiry) Baron d'Holbach,
Le Bon Sens, ou Idées naturelles opposées aux idées surnaturelles,
London, 1772.

15. B. Pascal, *Pensées*, ed. L. Brunschvicg, Section 1.§3, p.321:
"les autres, au contraire, qui sont accoutumés à raisonner par
principes, ne comprennent rien aux choses de sentiment,
y cherchant des principes et ne pouvant voir d'une vue".
Brunschvicg remarks that 'sentiment' here refers not to an
irrational faculty, but to Descartes's "intuition ou évidence,
la vue immédiate qui saisit l'unité et l'intégralité d'un objet".
Pascal's claim, however, was not published in editions available
to Hume: see Vamos.

16. Hutcheson, *Beauty, Order*, Treatise 1, Section 1, §16: "beauty,
like other names of sensible ideas, properly denotes the
perception of some mind; so *cold, heat, sweet, bitter*, denote the
sensations in our minds, to which perhaps there is no
resemblance in the objects which excite these ideas in us".
Like Hutcheson, Hume sometimes seems uncertain whether
beauty is a primary or secondary quality, or whether it is an
objective or subjective property; we shall see that, generally,
he treats it as an objective 'power' in objects, detectable only
by minds under certain conditions. Hutcheson's remark that
"our inquiry is only about the qualities which are beautiful
to *men*" (Treatise 1, Section 11, §1) and his references to man's
"fear of contempt", pretending and prejudice, all echo Dubos.

17. Everyone referred to Addison at some stage; Hume quotes
from *Spectator*, Number 412 at T.284. Hutcheson frequently

used Addison's expression "pleasures of the imagination";
see e.g. *Passions and Affections*, pp.112, 156, 171, 174, 185.
George Cheyne, *Philosophical Principles*, London, 1705,
Ch.2, §24, argues that "had the world lasted from all Eternity,
Arts and Sciences, and particularly Mathematics had arrived
at a greater degree of Perfection than they have attained".

18. Also Wotton, in Spingarn, *Critical Essays*, III.211, and
Shaftesbury, *Characteristics*, I.155.

19. Cp. Shaftesbury, *Characteristics*, II.139, and Hume L G.20.

20. In 1754 Hume proposed the topic for discussion at a meeting
of the Select Society, in Edinburgh. For general background
to the society, see R. L. Emerson, 'The Social Composition of
Enlightened Scotland: the Select Society of Edinburgh, 1754-
1764', *Studies on Voltaire and the Eighteenth Century*, Vol.114,
1973.

21. Gerard, *Essay on Taste*.

22. Shaftesbury, *Characteristics*, II.139. Addison, *Spectator*,
No.409 on taste, and No.416 on diverse responses, had discussed the issue. In the former paper he tried to "lay down
rules how we may know whether we are possessed of" "mental
taste".

23. Hutcheson, *Passions and Affections*, p.128.

24. Gerard, *Essay on Taste*, p.117n.

25. Shaftesbury, *Characteristics*, I.208.

26. D. Diderot, in his important article 'Beau' in Vol.2 (1752) of
the *Encyclopédie* (also in Diderot, *Oeuvres Esthétiques*, ed. P.
Vernière, Paris, 1968) listed twelve sources of diversity in
critical judgments. Diderot does not mention Dubos, but
Shaftesbury was an influence on him, of course. See D. Funt,
Diderot Studies, Vol.11, Genève, 1968.

27. Shaftesbury, *Characteristics*, II.257, during his own discussion
of taste, which influenced Addison, argues for "use, practice,
and culture"; "a legitimate and just taste can neither be
begotten, made, conceived, or produced, without the antecedent
labour and pains of criticism".

28. Ibid., II.130.

29. Ibid., I.217. In D.167 Hume implies that we need to learn how
to assess the *Aeneid*.

30. M. de Cervantes Saavedra, *Don Quixote*, trans. P. Motteux,
London, 1909, Vol.2, Part 11, Ch.13: one of Sancho's relations
"tried it with the tip of his tongue, the other only smelled it".
Hume is wrong that the taste of one of them proved to be "dull
and languid" (G.1.273).

31. Hutcheson, *Passions and Affections*, p.226 had argued that the
notion of justifying reasons presupposes a 'moral sense'.

32. Bayle, *Oeuvres Diverses*, III.692; *Dictionaire*, IV.2998,
'Eclaircissement sur les Manichéens'.

33. Malebranche, *De la Recherche*, I.400; II.65ff., 72, 233:

Shaftesbury, *Characteristics*, I.125, 156: Dubos, *Réflexions*,
II.xxiv, xxxiv: Hutcheson, *Beauty, Order*, p.87, *Passions and
Affections*, p.112.

34.   Cp. Hutcheson, in *British Moralists*, ed. Selby-Bigge, p.70.

35.   Shaftesbury, *Characteristics*, I.57; adapted by Hume, T.293.

36.   Cp. Butler, *Analogy of Religion*, pp.186, 268.

37.   Published in *Forum for Modern Language Studies*, Vol.6, 1970.

38.   Cp. M.89 (which parallels T.612): "there is a *manner*, a grace,
        an ease, a genteelness, an I-know-not-what, which some men
        possess above others, which is very different from external
        beauty and comeliness, and which, however, catches our
        affection almost as suddenly and powerfully. . . . This class of
        accomplishments, therefore, must be trusted entirely to the
        blind but sure testimony of taste and sentiment, and must be
        considered as a part of ethics left by nature to baffle all the
        pride of philosophy". Robert Wallace, 'A Treatise on Taste',
        Edinburgh University Library Ms. Dc.1.55, written about
        1765, frequently refers to Kames and Hume, and defines
        'taste' thus: "a faculty of forming just opinions, and of having
        a proper relish of the merit or beauties and defects, of its
        objects"; "a good taste and a good judgment are intimately
        connected" (pp.6, 167).

39.   Cp. Butler, *Analogy of Religion*, p.269 who argues that the
        apparent completion of prophecy must be allowed as explaining
        scriptural meaning.

40.   Shaftesbury, *Characteristics*, I.94: "all beauty is truth. True
        features make the beauty of a face; and true proportions the
        beauty of architecture; as true measures that of harmony and
        music". See P. Nicole, *An Essay on True and Apparent Beauty*
        (1659), London, 1683, pp.3, 12: "That is truly beautiful which
        agrees both with the nature of things themselves and with the
        inclinations of our senses and our soul"; "truth is the source
        of beauty". It is thought that Locke translated Nicole's work
        into English.

41.   Hutcheson in *British Moralists*, ed. Selby-Bigge, I.175.

42.   J-P. de Crousaz, *Traité du Beau* (1715), new edn., Amsterdam,
        1724, p.6. Diderot, in his *Encyclopédie* article 'Beau' (Vol.2,
        1752), criticised Crousaz's definition of beauty on the grounds
        that it concerned only the effect of beauty, not the nature of
        beauty itself.

43.   Crousaz, *Traité du Beau*, pp.11, 302.

44.   Ibid., p.195.

45.   Diderot, *Oeuvres Esthétiques*, p.399.

46.   Hutcheson in *British Moralists*, ed. Selby-Bigge, p.121; *Beauty,
        Order*, III.v. Cp. Shaftesbury, *Characteristics*, II.137. One of
        Hume's alternative phrases may also be noted: "the pleasing
        sensation arising from beauty" (T.394).

47.   Shaftesbury, *Characteristics*, II.136, 138.

48. Ibid., 11.137: "there is in certain figures a natural beauty, which the eye finds as soon as the object is presented to it. . . . No sooner the eye opens upon figures, the ear to sounds, than straight the beautiful results and grace and harmony are known and acknowledged".

49. I. Kant, *The Critique of Judgment*, trans. J. C. Meredith, Oxford, 1952, pp.154-5.

50. See e.g. Shaftesbury, *Characteristics*, 11.127: Hutcheson, *Passions and Affections*, p.102; cp. pp.28, 156, 171, 185: also, Hume, T.440: Kant, *Critique*, pp.48-9.

51. Berkeley, *Alciphron*, 1.124.

52. Cp. Cicero, *De Officiis*, 1.xxviii.

53. Cp. Hutcheson in *British Moralists*, ed. Selby-Bigge, p.148.

54. The example of the diamond appears in the Port-Royal *Logic*, I.xv.

55. Hutcheson, in *British Moralists*. Hume, T.279 uses the expression "consider as . . .".

56. Cp. Hutcheson in *British Moralists*, ed. Selby-Bigge, p.115. Diderot makes the point also, *Oeuvres Esthétiques*, p.400.

CHAPTER FOUR

1. Valuable studies in this context include: H. Aarsleff, *The Study of Language in England 1780-1860*, Princeton, 1971. P. France, *Rhetoric and Truth in France*, Oxford, 1972; G. Harnois, *Les Théories des Langage en France de 1660 à 1821*, Paris, 1929; P. Juliard, *Philosophies of Language in Eighteenth Century France*, The Hague, 1970. See also: Howell, *Eighteenth Century British Logic*, and Padley, *Grammatical Theory*. For Diderot and d'Alembert, see: H. Josephs, *Diderot's Dialogue of Language and Gesture*, Columbus, Ohio, 1969; D. F. Essar, 'The Language Theory, Epistemology, and Aesthetics of Jean L. d'Alembert', *Studies on Voltaire and the Eighteenth Century*, Vol.159, 1976.

2. Claude Favre de Vaugelas, *Remarques sur la Langue Françoise*, Paris, 1647, facsimile ed. J. Streicher, Paris, 1934.

3. Ibid., pp.60, 226.

4. Ibid., pp.503-8.

5. Adam Smith, *Lectures on Rhetoric and Belles Lettres*, ed. J. M. Lothian, Edinburgh, 1963, p.2.

6. Vaugelas, *Remarques*, Preface x.

7. Cp. L.1.243.

8. C. Lancelot & A. Arnauld, *Grammaire Generale et Raisonée*, Paris, 1660, facsimile edn, Menston, 1969, p.5.

9. Arnauld & Nicole, *La Logique*, p.37; cp. Lancelot & Arnauld, *Grammaire*, pp.27-8. Hume objected to these claims T.96n.

10. Arnauld & Nicole, *La Logique*, pp.41, 38.

11. Ibid., pp.94, 87, 164.

12. Lancelot & Arnauld, *Grammaire*, p.27.
13. Arnauld & Nicole, *La Logique*, p.94.
14. Ibid.
15. Crousaz, *A New Treatise*, pp.7-8.
16. Ibid., 1.305, 307.
17. Ibid., 11.32.
18. Samuel Pufendorf, *Of the Law of Nature and Nations* (1672), trans. B. Kennett with Barbeyrac's notes, London, 1728, Book IV, Ch.I, §v.
19. Samuel Pufendorf, *The Whole Duty of Man according to the Law of Nature* (1675), 3rd edn English trans., London, 1705, p.132.
20. Ibid.
21. Hutcheson, *Passions and Affections*, p.257. Hutcheson's own remarks on intentions, signs and signification are important.
22. Because of his references to other aspects of Tillotson's discussion, it is possible that Hume had in mind Tillotson's remarks in his 'Discourse against Transubstantiation': see *The Works*, 1.243.
23. B. Lamy, *L'Art de Parler*, Paris, 1675, Part II, Ch.I, §1; Ch.II, §2; Part IV, Ch.V, §4; Part I, Ch.IV, §2.
24. J. F. du Tremblay, *A Treatise of Language* (1700), English trans. M.H., London, 1725, Ch.3.
25. Ibid., Ch.4, Ch.14; du Tremblay also holds that although speech, in great measure, answers internal representation, our thoughts, which are spiritual, suffer diminution in the signs that represent them – a view that became sacred to romantic poets a century later.
26. C. C. du Marsais, *Des Tropes ou des Diférens Sens*, Paris, 1730, Part I, Article vii; Part III, Article xi.
27. Ibid. Part III, Articles ix, xi.
28. Smith owned a copy of the 1748 edition. See J. Bonar, *A Catalogue*; A. Smith, *Lectures on Rhetoric*, p.7.
29. See e.g. L.1.208.
30. See e.g. Cicero, *De Natura Deorum*, 11.lix.148, as quoted in Chapter 1.
31. See e.g. F. Zabeeh, *Hume, Precursor of Modern Empiricism*, 2nd edn, The Hague, 1973; J. F. Bennett, *Locke, Berkeley, Hume: Central Themes*, Oxford, 1971. But see Passmore, *Hume's Intentions*, and also Burton, *Life and Correspondence*, p.70.
32. Locke, *Essay*, III.iv.6.
33. Ibid., III.xi.14.
34. Ibid., III.xi.8; x.20; xi.11.
35. Ibid., III.x.23.
36. See H. Aarsleff, 'Leibniz on Locke on Language', *American Philosophical Quarterly*, Vol.1, 1964; N. Kretzmann, 'The Main Thesis of Locke's Semantic Theory', *Philosophical Review*,

Vol.77, 1968.

37. Wotton, in J. E. Spingarn ed., *Critical Essays*, III.226. John Horne Tooke, *Diversions of Purley* (1786), enlarged edn, London, 1805, Ch.2, p.30.

38. Several writers of the time insisted that, in Wollaston's words, "there can be no images" of "grammatical inflexions, particles, and other additions necessary to modify and connect the ideas": William Wollaston, *The Religion of Nature Delineated*, London, 1726, p.122.

39. Ibid., p.123: "if any one observes himself well, he will find, that he *thinks*, as well as *speaks* in some language, and that in thinking he supposes and runs over silently and habitually those sounds, which in speaking he actually makes".

40. I agree with Páll S. Árdal that, for Hume, meanings are not mental images. See his 'Convention and Value', in *David Hume. Bicentenary Papers*, ed. G. P. Morice, Edinburgh, 1977; also L. J. Cohen, *The Diversity of Meaning*, London, 1962; I. Hacking, *Why Does Language Matter to Philosophy?* Cambridge, 1975.

CHAPTER FIVE

1. I am grateful to the editors concerned for permission to include in this chapter material from my previous discussions of these topics in: *Hume: A Re-evaluation*, ed. Livingston & King; *McGill Hume Studies*, ed. D. F. Norton, N. Capaldi & W. L. Robison, San Diego, 1979. For discussion of notions of nature, see especially: J. Ehrard, *L'Idée de Nature en France dans la première moitié du XVIIIe siècle*, Paris, 1963; Glacken, *Traces on the Rhodian Shore*; and essays by A. O. Lovejoy, some of which are collected in, Lovejoy, *Essays in the History of Ideas*, New York, 1960. For Hume's naturalism, the fundamental reference is N. K. Smith, 'The Naturalism of Hume', *Mind*, Vol.14, 1905. Recent discussions of Hume's attitude towards scepticism occur in: T. Penelhum, *Hume*, London, 1975; B. Stroud, *Hume*, London, 1977.

2. The influence of Aristotle on both Cicero and Hume is here likely.

3. Descartes, *Oeuvres Philosophiques*, II.495.

4. Bayle, *Continuation* §149, *Oeuvres Diverses*, III.400.

5. Berkeley, *Alciphron*, I.55. Bayle made the same complaint, and listed Taylor's different senses, *Oeuvres Diverses*, I.705. William Wollaston, *Religion of Nature Delineated*, p.86, lists six senses of 'nature', including the intrinsic manner of existing, the idea of a thing, the world, the laws of nature, habit, God. Hume was familiar with Wollaston's work (see e.g. M.20n).

6. Bayle, *Oeuvres Diverses*, III.713.

7. Aristotle, *Ethica Nicomachea*, trans. W. D. Ross, Oxford, 1925, Book II; cp. G.I.431. In his earliest extant essay, possibly

written in 1725, Hume refers approvingly to "the just mean".
See E. C. Mossner, 'David Hume's "An Historical Essay on
Chivalry and Modern Honour"', *Modern Philology*, Vol.45,
1947. Cp. Wollaston's discussion, *Religion of Nature
Delineated*, pp.24-5.

8.   Hume was attracted to the recently introduced phrases 'balance
of trade', and 'balance of power' (G.I.112, 122, 160, 330, 348)
to denote appropriately moderate notions (cp. G.II.368).

9.   Shaftesbury, *Characteristics*, I.98.

10.   Descartes, *Oeuvres Philosophiques*, III.

11.   L. Wittgenstein, *On Certainty*, Oxford, 1969; abbreviated as
O C in later references, together with paragraph number.

12.   Pufendorf, *The Whole Duty*, p.39.

13.   Butler, *Analogy of Religion*, p.91.

14.   Leland, *A View*, I.286, objected to the cant term 'experience'
in Hume's arguments.

15.   Cp. Wollaston, *Religion of Nature Delineated*, p.58, who argues
that the force of probability "results from observation and
reason together. For here the one is not sufficient without the
other. Reason without *observation* wants matter to work on:
and observations are neither to be made justly by our selves,
nor to be rightly chosen out of those made by others, nor to be
aptly applied, without the assistance of *reason*. Both together
may support opinion and practice in the absence of knowledge
and certainty".

16.   Cp. Shaftesbury, *Characteristics*, II.78-83. Even orthodox
theologians held such views: cp. Wollaston, *Religion of Nature
Delineated*, p.145.

17.   L. Wittgenstein, *Zettel*, Oxford, 1967; abbreviated as Z in
later references, together with paragraph number.

18.   L. Wittgenstein, *Philosophical Investigations*, Oxford, 1953;
abbreviated as P I in later references, together with paragraph
number.

19.   Montesquieu (C. L. de Secondat), *Lettres Persanes*, ed. P.
Vernière, Paris, 1967, p.72. It has been overlooked that the
principal correspondent, Usbek, re-appears in Hume's
'A Dialogue'.

20.   Voltaire, *Lettres Philosophiques*, II.205.

21.   Hume specifically refers to the central Ciceronian notions in
Appendix IV of the second *Enquiry*, and in an additional
footnote of 1770 (M.134, 135n).

22.   In his view of how to subject reason, Hume closely follows
Bayle, 'Eclaircissement sur les Pyrrhoniens', *Dictionaire*,
IV.3006: "le vrai moien de la dompter est de connoître que si
elle est capable d'inventer des objections, elle est incapable d'en
trouver le dénoûment".

Bibliography

Only the books and articles referred to in the notes to each chapter are listed. The editions of Hume that have been used are listed under Abbreviations on page viii.

Aarsleff, H. *The Study of Language in England 1780-1860*, Princeton, 1971.
—— 'Leibniz on Locke on Language', *American Philosophical Quarterly*, Vol.1, 1964.
Addison, J. *The Spectator*, London, 1711-14.
d'Alembert, J. le R. *Discours préliminaire de l'encyclopédie*, ed. F. Picavet, Paris, 1894.
Allen, D. C. *The Legend of Noah*, Urbana, 1949.
Árdal, P. S. 'Convention and Value', in *David Hume. Bicentenary Papers*, ed. G. P. Morice, Edinburgh, 1977.
d'Argens, J-B. *La Philosophie du bon sens*, London, 1737.
Aristotle, *Ethica Nicomachea*, in *The Works*, trans. W. D. Ross, Oxford, 1925.
Arnauld, A. & Nicole, P. *La Logique ou l'art de penser*, ed. P. Clair & F. Girbal, Paris, 1965.
Bacon, F. *The Philosophical Works*, ed. J. M. Robertson, London, 1905.
Barker, J. E. *Diderot's Treatment of the Christian Religion in 'The Encyclopédie'*, New York, 1941.
Bayle, P. *Dictionaire Historique et Critique*, 3rd edn, Rotterdam, 1720.
—— *A General Dictionary, Historical and Critical*, London, 1734-41.
—— *Oeuvres Diverses*, La Haye, 1727-31.
—— *Historical and Critical Dictionary: Selections*, ed. R. H. Popkin, Indianapolis, 1965.
Bennett, J. F. *Locke, Berkeley, Hume: Central Themes*, Oxford, 1971.
Bergerac, Cyrano de. *Etats et empires de la lune*, Paris, 1657.
Berkeley, G. *The Works*, ed. A. A. Luce & T. E. Jessop, Edinburgh, 1949-57.
Blackwell, T. *An Enquiry into the Life and Writings of Homer*, London, 1735.
Bonar, J. *A Catalogue of the Library of Adam Smith*, London, 1894.
Bonno, G. *Les relations intellectuelles de Locke avec la France*, Berkeley, 1955.
Bouhours, D. *Les Entretiens d'Ariste et d'Eugène*, Paris, 1671.
Bredvold, L. I. *The Intellectual Milieu of John Dryden*, Ann Arbor, 1934.

Brunet, P. *L'Introduction des théories de Newton en France aux XVIIIe siècle, Avant 1738*, Paris, 1931.

Brunius, T. *David Hume on Criticism*, Stockholm, 1952.

Bryson, G. *Man and Society: The Scottish Inquiry of the Eighteenth Century*, Princeton, 1945.

Buffon, J.-L. Leclerc, Comte de. *Oeuvres Philosophiques de Buffon*, ed. J. Piveteau, Paris, 1954.

—— *Buffon. Les Époques de la Nature*, ed. J. Roger, in *Mémoires du Muséum National d'Histoire Naturelle*, Series C, Vol.10, Paris, 1962.

Burton, J. H. *Life and Correspondence of David Hume*, Edinburgh, 1846.

Butler, J. *The Analogy of Religion and Two Brief Dissertations*, Oxford, 1874.

Capaldi, N. *David Hume: The Newtonian Philosopher*, Boston, 1975.

Caramaschi, E. 'Du Bos et Voltaire', *Studies on Voltaire and the Eighteenth Century*, Vol.10, 1959.

Cardy, M. 'Discussion of the Theory of Climate in the *querelle des anciens et des modernes*', *Studies on Voltaire and the Eighteenth Century*, Vol.163, 1976.

Carlyle, A. *The Autobiography of Dr Alexander Carlyle*, ed. J. H. Burton, Edinburgh, 1910.

Carré, J-R. *La Philosophie de Fontenelle ou le sourire de la raison*, Paris, 1932.

Cassirer, E. *The Philosophy of the Enlightenment*, English trans., Princeton, 1951.

Cervantes, M. de. *Don Quixote*, trans. P. Motteux, London, 1909.

Chambers, E. *Cyclopaedia: or an Universal dictionary of arts and sciences*, London, 1727.

Cheyne, G. *Philosophical Principles of Natural Religion*, London, 1705.

Church, R. W. 'Malebranche and Hume', *Revue Internationale de Philosophie*, Vol.1, 1938.

Cicero, M-T. *De Finibus, Tusculan Disputations, De Natura Deorum, Academica, De Divinatione, De Fato, De Officiis, De Oratore, De Partitione Oratoria*, Loeb Classical Library, Vols.3, 4, 16-21, London, 1913-33.

Clarke, S. *A Demonstration of the Being and Attributes of God* (Boyle Lecture, 1704), 4th edn., London, 1716.

Cohen, I. B. *Franklin and Newton*, Philadelphia, 1968.

—— Preface to Newton, I. *Opticks* (4th edn., 1730), Dover Publications, 1952.

Cohen, L. J. *The Diversity of Meaning*, London, 1962.

Collins, A. *An Essay Concerning the Use of Reason in Propositions*, 2nd edn., London, 1709.

—— *A Collection of Tracts Written by Mr . . .*, London, 1717.

Cook, M. 'Arnauld's Alleged Representationalism', *Journal of the History of Philosophy*, Vol.12, 1974.

Craig, J. *Theologiae Christianae Principia Mathematica*, London, 1699.

Crocker, L. G. *An Age of Crisis: Man and World in Eighteenth Century*

French Thought, Baltimore, 1959.

Crousaz, J-P. de, *La Logique, ou système de réflexions qui peuvent contribuer à la netteté et à l'étendue de nos connaissances*, Amsterdam, 1712.

—— *Traité du Beau* (1715), new edn., Amsterdam, 1724.

Davies, G. L. *The Earth in Decay*, New York, 1969.

Descartes, R. *Oeuvres Philosophiques*, ed. F. Alquié, Paris, 1967.

Diderot, D. & d'Alembert, J. le R. *Encyclopédie ou Dictionnaire Raisonné des sciences, des arts et des métiers*, Paris, 1751-80.

Diderot, D. *Oeuvres Esthétiques*, ed. P. Vernière, Paris, 1968.

—— *Oeuvres Philosophiques*, ed. P. Vernière, Paris, 1964.

Dijksterhuis, E. J. *The Mechanization of the World Picture*, Oxford, 1961.

Dobbs, B. J. T. *The Foundations of Newton's Alchemy*, Cambridge, 1975.

Dubos, J-B. *Réflexions critiques sur la poésie et sur la peinture*, Paris, 1719. English trans. T. Nugent, London, 1748.

Edwards, J. *The Socinian Creed*, London, 1697.

Ehrard, J. *L'Idée de nature en France dans la première moitié du XVIIIe siècle*, Paris, 1963.

Emerson, R. L. 'The Social Composition of Enlightened Scotland: the Select Society of Edinburgh, 1754-1764', *Studies on Voltaire and the Eighteenth Century*, Vol.114, 1973.

Essar, D. F. 'The Language Theory, Epistemology, and Aesthetics of Jean L. d'Alembert', *Studies on Voltaire and the Eighteenth Century*, Vol. 159, 1976.

Fénelon, F. de S. de la M. *Démonstration de l'existence de Dieu*, Amsterdam, 1713.

Flew, A. *Hume's Philosophy of Belief*, London, 1961.

Fontenelle, B. le B. de. *Entretiens sur la pluralité des mondes*, ed. R. Shackleton, Oxford, 1955.

—— *Histoire des Oracles*, ed. L. Maigron, Paris, 1934.

—— *Oeuvres de M. de Fontenelle*, Paris, 1752.

Frankel, C. *The Faith of Reason*, New York, 1948.

France, P. *Rhetoric and Truth in France*, Oxford, 1972.

Funt, D. *Diderot Studies*, Vol.11, Genève, 1968.

Furetière, A. *Dictionnaire Universel*, La Haye, 1701.

Gaskin, J. C. A. *Hume's Philosophy of Religion*, London, 1978.

Gay, P. *The Enlightenment*, London, 1967.

Gerard, A. *An Essay on Taste*, London, 1759.

Gibbon, E. *Memoirs of My Life*, ed. G. A. Bonnard, London, 1966.

Girard, G. *Synonymes François* (1736), new edn., augmented M. Beauzée, Paris, 1769.

Glacken, C. J. *Traces on the Rhodian Shore*, Berkeley, 1967.

Grant, Sir A. *Story of the University of Edinburgh*, London, 1884.

s'Gravesande, W-J. *Mathematical Elements of Natural Philosophy*, English trans., London, 1720.

Greene, J. C. *The Death of Adam*, New York, 1961.

Gregory, J. *A Comparative View of the State and Faculties of Man with those of the Animal World* (1765), 4th edn., Dublin, 1768.

Guerlac, H. 'Where the Statue Stood: Divergent Loyalties to Newton in the Eighteenth Century', in *Aspects of the Eighteenth Century*, ed. E. R. Wasserman, London, 1965.

Guyénot, E. *Les Sciences de la vie aux XVIIe et XVIIIe siècles: l'idée d'évolution*, Paris, 1941.

Hacker, P. M. S. *Insight and Illusion*, Oxford, 1972.

Hacking, I. *Why Does Language Matter to Philosophy ?*, Cambridge, 1975.

Hall, R. *Fifty Years of Hume Scholarship*, Edinburgh, 1978.

Hanson, N. R. 'Hypotheses Fingo', in *The Methodological Heritage of Newton*, ed. R. E. Butts & J. W. Davis, Toronto, 1970.

Harnois, G. *Les théories des langage en France de 1660 à 1821*, Paris, 1929.

Harris, James. *Three Treatises . . . concerning Music, Painting and Poetry*, London, 1744.

Harris, John. *Lexicon Technicum: or an Universal English Dictionary of Arts and Sciences*, London, 1704, 1710, 5th edn., 1736.

Harrison, J. & Laslett, P. *The Library of John Locke*, Oxford, 1965.

Helm, P. 'Locke on Faith and Knowledge', *Philosophical Quarterly*, Vol.23, 1973.

Hipple, W. J. Jr. *The Beautiful, The Sublime, and the Picturesque in Eighteenth-Century British Aesthetic Theory*, Carbondale, 1957.

Hobbes, T. *Leviathan*, intro. W. G. Pogson Smith, Oxford, 1909.

Hogsett, C. 'J. B. Dubos on Art as Illusion', *Studies on Voltaire and the Eighteenth Century*, Vol.73, 1970.

d'Holbach, Baron (P. H. Thiry). *Le Bon Sens, ou Idées naturelles opposées aux idées surnaturelles*, London, 1772.

Howell, W. S. *Eighteenth Century British Logic and Rhetoric*, Princeton, 1971.

Hunt, H. A. K. *The Humanism of Cicero*, Melbourne, 1954.

Hurlbutt, R. H. *Hume, Newton and the Design Argument*, Lincoln, 1965.

Hutcheson, F. *An Essay on the Nature and Conduct of the Passions and Affections*, London, 1728.

—— *An Inquiry Concerning Beauty, Order, Harmony, Design*, (1725), ed. P. Kivy, The Hague, 1973.

—— *An Inquiry concerning Moral Good and Evil*, (1725), in *British Moralists*, ed. L. A. Selby-Bigge, Indianapolis, 1964.

Hutton, J. *James Hutton's System of the Earth, Theory of the Earth, Observations on Granite*, ed. G. W. White, New York, 1973.

—— *James Hutton's Theory of the Earth: The Lost Drawings*, ed. G. Y. Craig, D. B. McIntyre & C. D. Waterston, Edinburgh, 1978.

Jessop, T. E. *A Bibliography of David Hume and of Scottish Philosophy*, London, 1938.

Jones, P. 'Hume's Two Concepts of God', *Philosophy*, Vol.47, 1972.

—— 'Cause, Reason, and Objectivity in Hume's Aesthetics', in *Hume: A Re-evaluation*, ed. D. W. Livingston & J. T. King, New York, 1976.

—— 'Strains in Hume and Wittgenstein', in *Hume: A Re-evaluation*, ed. D. W. Livingston & J. T. King, New York, 1976.

—— 'Hume's Aesthetics reassessed', *Philosophical Quarterly*,

Vol.26, 1976.

—— 'Hume on Art, Criticism, and Language: Debts and Premises', *Philosophical Studies*, Vol.33, 1978.

—— '"Art" and "Moderation" in Hume's *Essays*', in *McGill Hume Studies*, ed. D. F. Norton, N. Capaldi & W. L. Robison, San Diego, 1979.

Jones, R. F. *Ancients and Moderns*, 2nd edn., St Louis, 1961.

Josephs, H. *Diderot's Dialogue of Language and Gesture*, Columbus, Ohio, 1969.

Juliard, P. *Philosophies of Language in Eighteenth Century France*, The Hague, 1970.

Kant, I. *The Critique of Judgment*, trans. J. C. Meredith, Oxford, 1952.

Kiernan, C. 'The Enlightenment and Science in Eighteenth-Century France', *Studies on Voltaire and the Eighteenth Century*, Vol.59A, Banbury, 1973.

Kretzmann, N. 'The Main Thesis of Locke's Semantic Theory', *Philosophical Review*, Vol.77, 1968.

Kristeller, P. O. 'The Modern System of the Arts', *Journal of the History of Ideas*, Vols.12, 13, 1951, 1952.

Kuhns, R. 'Hume's Republic and the Universe of Newton', in *Eighteenth Century Studies presented to A. M. Wilson*, ed. P. Gay, Hanover, 1972.

Kuypers, M. S. *Studies in the Eighteenth Century Background of Hume's Empiricism*, Minneapolis, 1930.

Laird, J. *Hume's Philosophy of Human Nature*, London, 1932.

Lamy, B. *L'Art de Parler*, Paris, 1675.

Lancelot, C. & Arnauld, A. *Grammaire Generale et Raisonée*, Paris, 1660; facsimile edn, Menston, 1969.

Lange, F. A. *The History of Materialism* (1865), London, 1925.

van Leeuwen, H. G. *The Problem of Certainty in English Thought, 1630-1690*, The Hague, 1963.

Leland, J. *A View of the Principal Deistical Writers*, 5th edn, London, 1766.

Livingston, D. W. & King, J. T. *Hume: A Re-evaluation*, New York, 1976.

Locke, J. *The Works*, 10th edn, London, 1801.

Lombard, A. *La querelle des Anciens et des Modernes: l'abbé du Bos*, Neuchatel, 1908.

Lough, J. 'Locke's Reading During his Stay in France 1675-79', *The Library*, Vol.8, 1958.

Lovejoy, A. O. 'Buffon and the Problem of Species', in *Forerunners of Darwin: 1745-1859*, ed. B. Glass, Baltimore, 1959.

—— *Essays in the History of Ideas*, New York, 1960.

Maclaurin, C. *An Account of Sir Isaac Newton's Philosophical Discoveries*, London, 1748.

Malebranche, N. *De la Recherche de la Vérité*, ed. G. Rodis-Lewis, Paris, 1962.

Manuel, F. E. *The Eighteenth Century Confronts the Gods*, Cambridge, Mass., 1959.

du Marsais, C. C. *Des Tropes ou des Diférens Sens*, Paris, 1730.

Marsak, L. M. 'B. de Fontenelle: The Idea of Science in the French Enlightenment', *Transactions of the American Philosophical Society*, Vol.49, 1959.

Maupertuis, P-L. M. de. *Discours sur les différentes figures des astres*, Paris, 1732.

McKane, W. *Patriarchal Narratives*, Edinburgh, 1977.

Mettrie, J. O. de la. *L'Homme Machine*, ed. A. Vartanian, Princeton, 1960.

Montaigne, M. de. *Essais*, ed. Thibaudet, Paris, 1939.

Montesquieu (C. L. de Secondat), *Lettres Persanes*, ed. P. Vernière, Paris, 1967.

Mossner, E. C. *The Life of David Hume*, Edinburgh, 1954.

—— 'David Hume's "An Historical Essay on Chivalry and Modern Honour"', *Modern Philology*, Vol.45, 1947.

Munteano, B. 'Survivances Antiques: L'Abbé Du Bos', *Revue de Litérature comparée*, Vol.30, 1956.

Newton, I. *Mathematical Principles of Natural Philosophy*, trans. Motte, intro. F. Cajori, Berkeley, 1966.

—— *Opticks*, (4th edn, 1730), Dover Publications, 1952.

—— *Isaac Newton's Papers and Letters on Natural Philosophy*, ed. I. B. Cohen & R. E. Schofield, Cambridge, 1958.

Nicole, P. *An Essay on True and Apparent Beauty* (1659), London, 1683.

Norton, D. F. 'History and Philosophy in Hume's Thought', in *David Hume: Philosophical Historian*, ed. D. F. Norton & R. H. Popkin, Indianapolis, 1965.

Norton, D. F., Capaldi, N. & Robison, W. L., eds *McGill Hume Studies*, San Diego, 1979.

Noxon, J. *Hume's Philosophical Development*, Oxford, 1973.

Padley, G. A. *Grammatical Theory in Western Europe, 1500-1700*, Cambridge, 1976.

Pascal, B. *Pensées*, ed. L. Brunschvicg, Paris, 1909.

Passmore, J. *Hume's Intentions*, Cambridge, 1952.

Pemberton, H. *A View of Sir Isaac Newton's Philosophy*, London, 1728.

Penelhum, T. *Hume*, London, 1975.

Perrault, C. *Parallèle des anciens et des modernes*, Paris, 1688-97.

Pittion, J. P. 'Hume's Reading of Bayle: an enquiry into the source and role of the *Memoranda*', *Journal of the History of Philosophy*, Vol.15, 1977.

Popkin, R. H. *The History of Scepticism from Erasmus to Descartes*, New York, 1964.

—— 'David Hume: His Pyrrhonism and his Critique of Pyrrhonism', *Philosophical Quarterly*, Vol.1, 1951.

—— 'Scepticism, Theology and the Scientific Revolution in the Seventeenth Century', in *Problems in the Philosophy of Science*, ed. I. Lakatos & A. Musgrave, Amsterdam, 1968.

Popkin, R. H. ed. *Bayle . . . Selections*, Indianapolis, 1965.

[Port-Royal] *The Port-Royal Logic*, English trans. T. S. Baynes, 2nd edn,

Edinburgh, 1851.

Pringle, J. 'Lectures from Cicero', E U L. Ms. Gen. 74. D.

Pufendorf, S. *Of the Law of Nature and Nations* (1672), trans. B.
    Kennett, with Barbeyrac's notes, London, 1728.

—— *The Whole Duty of Man according to the Law of Nature*, (1675),
    3rd edn, English trans., London, 1705.

Reid, T. 'Essays on the Active Powers', in *The Works*, ed. W. Hamilton,
    Edinburgh, 1852.

Richelet, P. *Nouveau Dictionnaire français*, Genève, 1710.

Rigault, H. *Histoire de la querelle des anciens et des modernes*, Paris, 1856.

Rosenfield, L. C. *From Beast-Machine to Man-Machine*, New
    York, 1968.

Saisselin, R. G. *The Rule of Reason and the Ruses of the Heart*,
    Cleveland, 1970.

Schofield, R. E. *Mechanism and Materialism*, Princeton, 1970.

Shaftesbury, A. Earl of. *Characteristics*, ed. J. M. Robertson,
    Indianapolis, 1964.

Simon, R. *Histoire critique du Vieux Testament*, Paris, 1678; English
    trans., 1682.

Smith, A. *Lectures on Rhetoric and Belles Lettres*, ed. J. M. Lothian,
    Edinburgh, 1963.

Smith, N. K. *The Philosophy of David Hume*, London, 1941.

—— 'Malebranche's Theory of the Perception of Distance and
    Magnitude', *British Journal of Psychology*, Vol.1, 1904.

—— 'The Naturalism of Hume', *Mind*, Vol.14, 1905.

Spingarn, J. E. ed. *Critical Essays of the Seventeenth Century*,
    Oxford, 1908.

Spink, J. S. *French Free-Thought from Gassendi to Voltaire*,
    London, 1960.

Stephen, L. *History of English Thought in the Eighteenth Century*
    (1876), 3rd edn, London, 1902.

Stove, D. C. *Probability and Hume's Inductive Scepticism*, Oxford, 1973.

Stroud, B. *Hume*, London, 1977.

Taylor, J. *The Liberty of Prophesying*, London, 1648.

Tillotson, J. *The Works*, Vols.1 (9th edn), 11, 111 (4th edn), London, 1728.

Toland, J. *Letters to Serena*, London, 1704.

—— *Christianity not Mysterious . . .*, London, 1696.

Tooke, J. H. *Diversions of Purley* (1786), enlarged edn, London, 1805.

Torrey, N. L. *Voltaire and the English Deists*, New Haven, 1930.

du Tremblay, J. F. *A Treatise of Language* (1700), English trans. M.H.,
    London, 1725.

Vamos, M. 'Pascal's *pensées* and the Enlightenment: the roots of a
    Misunderstanding', *Studies on Voltaire and the Eighteenth
    Century*, Vol.97, 1972.

Vartanian, A. *Diderot and Descartes: A Study of Scientific Naturalism in
    the Enlightenment*, Princeton, 1953.

Vaugelas, C. F. de. *Remarques sur la Langue Françoise*, Paris 1647;
    facsimile edn J. Streicher, Paris, 1934.

Voltaire (F. Arouet), *Lettres Philosophiques*, ed. G. Lanson, Paris, 1909.
—— *Élémens de la philosophie de Neuton*, Amsterdam, 1738.
Vyverberg, H. *Historical Pessimism in the French Enlightenment*,
       Cambridge, Mass., 1958.
Wade, I. O. *The Intellectual Origins of the French Enlightenment*,
       Princeton, 1971.
Wallace, R. 'A Treatise on Taste', EUL. Ms. Dc. 1.55.
Warburton, W. *The Divine Legation of Moses*, London, 1738.
Watson, R. A. *The Downfall of Cartesianism, 1673-1712*, The Hague, 1960.
Wilkins, J. *An Essay towards a Real Character*, London, 1668.
Wilkins, K. S. 'A Study of the works of Claude Buffier', *Studies on
       Voltaire and the Eighteenth Century*, Vol.66, 1969.
Wittgenstein, L. *On Certainty*, Oxford, 1969. (Abbreviated to OC in
       text references.)
—— *Philosophical Investigations*, Oxford, 1953. (Abbreviated to PI in
       text references.)
Wolf, A. *A History of Science, Technology and Philosophy in the 18th
       Century*, London, 1938.
Wollaston, W. *The Religion of Nature Delineated*, London, 1726.
Yolton, J. W. *John Locke and the Way of Ideas*, Oxford, 1956.
Zabeeh, F. *Hume, Precursor of Modern Empiricism*, 2nd edn,
       The Hague, 1973.

Index